D0038528

"THIS BOOK IS WISE AND WONDERFUL!
Lawrence Cohen illuminates play. . . . He speaks to our questions and hesitations as parents, and offers a bounty of ideas and anecdotes that convey his generous spirit and deep understanding of both parents and children. He offers simple things to try, and shows what a difference play can make. . . . A lot of hope for parents springs from these pages."
—PATRICIA WIPFLER
Director, Parents Leadership Institute

"Too many conscientious mothers and fathers think parenting is all about homework, car pools, and town soccer and are not experiencing much joy with their families. Larry Cohen . . . encourages parents to 'lose their dignity' in order 'to find their child,' and then he demonstrates exactly how that can be done. . . . You will find that you can be closer to your children and can enjoy them more. When I finished the book I immediately wanted to go wrestle with my kids—no tickling—and let them win!"
—MICHAEL THOMPSON, Ph.D.
Coauthor of *Raising Cain*

"According to Cohen, children of all ages have an ongoing need for connectedness, security, and attachment; playful interaction with parents is an important way to develop such bonds. . . . The book explores play with compassion, but is often so funny that parents will find themselves chortling out loud with recognition and anticipation."
—*Publishers Weekly* (starred review)

*Please turn the page to hear what parents have to say
about* Playful Parenting. . . .

PARENT TESTIMONIALS
FOR *PLAYFUL PARENTING*

"Your ideas are so creative and fun and just generally terrific. . . . It's one thing to read about how important it is to have a sense of fun as a parent, it's another thing entirely to have it modeled, and in a way that I can try out immediately. Instead of feeling like I am not being a good enough parent, it makes me think, Oh, I could do this!"

—ANNE STRAINCHAMPS

"I *love* your book. It is so gentle and kind—a great antidote to our stressed out lives and a prescription for making them less so. It is insightful, accessible, and educational without being pedantic."

—PAUL HOLLINGS

"I thank you for helping me find new ways to communicate with my little girl—this was so much more fun than yelling at her!"

—DIANA PARTINGTON

"Your book has had an immediate effect on me and my playing with [my son]. I am discovering a whole new dimension to being a parent, which is making me thrive as a mother. And amazingly I can see the difference on my boy as well. At the risk of sounding overly dramatic, this has been a truly ground-breaking book for me."

—PIA LOFDAHL

Playful Parenting

An exciting new approach
to raising children that will help you:

- Nurture Close Connections
- Solve Behavior Problems
- Encourage Confidence

Lawrence J. Cohen, Ph.D.

A LIVING PLANET BOOK

BALLANTINE BOOKS

NEW YORK

Most of the personal stories presented in this book are either composite portraits or identifying characteristics have been changed or eliminated in order to protect the privacy of individuals. Any resemblance to living persons is unintended and coincidental.

A Ballantine Book
Published by The Random House Publishing Group

Copyright © 2001 by Lawrence J. Cohen, Ph.D.

All rights reserved.

Published in the United States by Ballantine Books, an imprint of The Random House Publishing Group, a division of Random House, Inc., New York, and simultaneously in Canada by Random House of Canada Limited, Toronto.

Ballantine and colophon are registered trademarks of Random House, Inc.

www.ballantinebooks.com

Library of Congress Catalog Card Number: 2002090324

ISBN 0-345-44286-5

Cover design by Julie Metz
Cover photo © Sean Justice Productions/Image Bank

Manufactured in the United States of America

First Hardcover Edition: June 2001

First Trade Paperback Edition: May 2002

12 14 16 18 19 17 15 13 11

CONTENTS

ACKNOWLEDGMENTS

Like most psychologists—and most parents—I have learned most of what I know about children from getting down on the floor and playing with them. My warmest thanks to all those children, and to their parents, especially Eileen Ryan and her family. Your names are all changed in this book, but I hope I have been true to all that you have taught me. Thanks also to my teachers, especially Holly Jorgenson and Patty Wipfler.

It has been a privilege to be involved in various writing, teaching, and consulting projects with two gifted child psychologists, Sam Roth and Michael Thompson. Listening to them and talking with them about children and childhood has shaped my thinking more than I could possibly convey through a footnote.

I want to thank Anne Strainchamps for saying, "You should write a book"; my agent, Josh Horwitz, for saying, "You can sell this book," and for showing me how; and my editors, Elizabeth Zack, Ginny Faber, and Joanne Wyckoff, for making it a reality. I would never have had the nerve to write a book at all if it weren't for Kathryn Deputat's writing classes and seminars, and I could not have written this book without the emotional and intellectual support of the Re-evaluation Counseling Communities. Thanks also to Kate Bowditch, for careful and thoughtful reading of earlier drafts.

My deepest appreciation goes to my parents and my sisters for a lifetime of loving support, and to my wife, Anne Fabiny, who encouraged me every step of the way. This book is dedicated to our daughter, Emma, who graciously let me take time away from playing with her to write about play.

PREFACE

When I began working as a therapist, my clients were primarily adults. We spent hour after hour talking about their childhoods, and I saw how important it was for a child to have a good connection with a parent or another adult. Naturally, when I had my own child, I was determined to establish and maintain a strong emotional bond with her. I quickly came to appreciate how challenging this can be. Attachment between parents and babies is virtually instinctual, but it gets complicated as soon as the child becomes more active and verbal.

Regardless of whether I was having a good day or a bad day, was in the mood or not, my daughter, Emma, wanted to play. She wanted to interact with me when I didn't feel like interacting with anybody; she wanted my complete attention when I had other things to attend to; she wanted me to be on call, even if she was playing alone. I was surprised at the intensity of mixed emotions this aroused in me. More often than I'd like to admit, I'd find myself wanting to do anything else rather than get down on the floor and engage Emma's seemingly bottomless need for attention and play. Or I'd get on the floor and promptly fall asleep—and not just from being a tired parent. After all, I had already given so much of myself, and now she wanted me to *play*.

As time went on, my practice began to shift toward play therapy with children and support for their parents. While adult therapy tends to cast parents as the villains, I started to see what a powerful positive force they can be in their children's lives. And the single most important skill parents could acquire, it seemed to me, was playing. Fortunately, unlike many personality changes we might like to make, better playing skills can be learned pretty easily.

We all know we are supposed to turn off the TV and spend more time together. But then what? *Playful Parenting* is a guide to having more fun with young people of all ages as they tackle new accomplishments, recover from being hurt, or are simply bursting with youthful exuberance. Through the practice of Playful Parenting—joining children in their world, focusing on connection and confidence, giggling and roughhousing, reversing the roles and following your child's lead—you will learn how to help them work through their emotional blocks and how to handle their strong emotions (and your own). You will also learn how to deal effectively with sibling rivalry and other tricky problems, and how to rethink your ideas about discipline and punishment.

Finally, in order to be fountains of hopefulness and enthusiasm for children, we must find ways to replenish ourselves. *Playful Parenting* offers practical help in becoming the best parents, and the most playful parents, we can be. Parents can learn to balance the serious business of heartfelt connections with the silliness of wild play. *Playful Parenting* can help solve a variety of family difficulties, but it is also for families where everything is going fine. It helps every child have more fun, and it's great for grown-ups. After all, we need to play, too.

CHAPTER 1

THE VALUE OF BEING A PLAYFUL PARENT

Play is the essence of life.[1]

Think about the loving gaze of an infant, the no-holds-barred embrace of a toddler, the intimacy of a shared bedtime story, or a silent hand-in-hand walk. These moments of heartfelt connection with our children are part of the great payoff for the hard work of parenting. Yet this connection all too often eludes us. We find ourselves locked in battle instead of joined in partnership. We all know the rest: the inconsolable baby, the toddler in the throes of a tantrum, the third-grader in a huff over bedtimes, the twelve-year-old sulking in her room.

Children's natural exuberance and exploration often gives way to what I call "fighting and biting." Or they hide themselves behind a Gameboy or a locked door. Meanwhile, our profound feeling of parental love is replaced by resentment and aggravation, even rage. We nag or punish, or we say, "Fine, stay in your room." We yell when we reach the end of our rope, or just out of habit. All because we feel helpless, rejected, and cut off. We want to reconnect, as much as our children do, but we don't know how. We still love them, but we barely remember those melting eye gazes of babyhood. If we do remember, it is a bittersweet memory, as if that closeness were lost forever.

Play—together with Playful Parenting—can be the long-sought bridge back to that deep emotional bond between parent and child. Play, with all its exuberance and delighted togetherness, can ease the stress of parenting. Playful Parenting is a way to enter a child's world, on the child's terms, in order to foster closeness, confidence, and connection. When all is well in their world, play is an expansive vista where children are joyful, engaged, cooperative, and creative. Play is also the way that children make the world their own, exploring, making sense of all their new experiences, and recovering from life's upsets. But play is not always easy for adults, because we have forgotten so much. Indeed, children and adults often seem to reside in radically different worlds, even within the same household. We find each other's favorite activities boring or strange: How can she spend all afternoon dressing up Barbies? How can they sit around all evening just talking?

Parenting and playfulness can seem like contradictions, but sometimes we just need a little push to find one another and have fun together. I was at an outdoor concert, dancing off on the side with my nine-year-old daughter, when a mother and son came over to the dance area. She started dancing a little, but he just stood with his arms folded, a little too shy to dance now that he was there. He was about six or seven. His mother said, starting to get angry, "You dragged me up here, and now you're not going to dance?" He folded his arms tighter and literally dug his heels in. I thought, We can all see where this is going. I said, "Oh no, he's doing a new dance," and I folded my arms just like his and gave him a big smile. He smiled back and moved his hands to a different position, which I copied. His mom caught on right away and started copying him, too. We all laughed. He started moving his shoulders up and down to the music, and his mother said, "You're dancing!" Then he started to dance, and he had a great time. We all did (including my daughter, who waited patiently while I did "the Playful Parenting thing," and then wanted my complete attention again). A little playfulness turned the tide.

This small episode demonstrates that Playful Parenting can happen anywhere and anytime, not just during designated playtimes. Playful Parenting begins with play, but it includes much more—from comforting a crying baby to hanging out at the mall; from waging pillow fights to taking the training wheels off the bicycle; from negotiating rules to dealing with the emotional fallout of a playground injury; from getting ready for school to listening to a child's fears and dreams before bed. Sadly, these simple interactions can seem out of reach sometimes, or full of complications and hard feelings.

The fact is, we adults don't have much room in our lives for fun and games. Our days are filled with stress, obligations, and hard work. We may be stiff, tired, and easily bored when we try to get on the floor and play with children—especially when it means switching gears from a stressful day of work or household chores. We might be willing to do what they want—like the mom at the outdoor concert—but then we get annoyed when they don't play the way we expect or when they demand too much from us.

Others of us may be unable to put aside our competitiveness or our need to be in control. We get bored, cranky, and frustrated; we're sore losers; we worry about teaching how to throw the ball correctly when our child just wants to play catch. We complain about *children's* short attention spans, but how long can *we* sit and play marbles or Barbies or Monopoly or fantasy games before we get bored and distracted, or pulled away by the feeling that getting work done or cooking dinner is more important?

When my daughter was in preschool, she made up a great game that helped me be playful instead of shouting at her to hurry up and get ready. One morning she came downstairs, hid behind the doorway, and whispered to me, "Pretend that I'm still upstairs and that we're really gonna be late and you're really mad." So I shouted upstairs, "We're late, and I am *really mad*!" and I started storming around and stamping my foot. Meanwhile, she was behind the door giggling, her hand over her mouth. I said, "You better get down here, or I'm leaving without you. I'm going to go *by myself* to Big Oak Preschool!" She started laughing out loud, so I pretended I couldn't hear her. While letting her sneak out ahead of me, I made a big show of leaving the house without her, supposedly not noticing she was there. She got in the car and I pretended I was talking to myself out loud, saying, "I am so mad. The teachers are going to say, 'Where is Emma?' And I'm going to say, 'She wasn't ready, so I just left without her.' " She was giggling and giggling and trying not to let on that she was really there. She was making getting ready for preschool fun for *me*!

Pretending to be mad helped me not to be really mad, and playing instead of shouting helped her get ready faster!

—WHY CHILDREN PLAY—

Some children are leaders and some are followers; some prefer fantasy dress up while others are drawn to ball games. But virtually every child has an instinct for play that buds immediately after birth and is in full bloom by the age of two or three. Play is possible anywhere and anytime, a parallel universe of fantasy and imagination that children enter at will. For adults, play means leisure, but for children, play is more like their job. Unlike many of us adults, they usually love their work and seldom want a day off. Play is also children's main way of communicating, of experimenting, and of learning.

A child who won't or can't play is instantly recognizable as being in significant emotional distress, like an adult who can't work or won't talk. Severely abused and neglected children often have to be taught how to play before they can benefit from play therapy. Why do we consider child labor such an abomination? Because it means children grow up without having a childhood, without play. It's even worse when their labor is exploited so that adults can have more leisure, as depicted in this nineteenth-century poem by Sarah Norcliffe Cleghorn:

The Golf Links Lie So Near the Mill

The golf links lie so near the mill
That almost every day
The laboring children can look out
And watch the men at play.

Many experts describe play as a place—a place of magic and imagination, a place where a child can be fully one's self. As psychologist Virginia Axline wrote about children in preschool: "They can build themselves a mountain and climb safely to the top and cry out for all the world to hear, 'I can build me a mountain, or I can flatten it out. In here, I am big!' "[2] I had a great reminder of the basic nature of play at my daughter's third birthday party. I had organized all kinds of games to play in the park across the street from our house, and, of course, being a psychologist, I explained all of these complicated games to the children, who stood around looking at me as if I were from outer space. I wasn't sure what to do. The children were too revved up to go back inside, but they weren't going for my games. My wife interrupted and said, "Okay, everybody, run to the other side of the park and back!" They all ran happily across the park, shrieking and laughing, then ran back and flopped on the ground, giggling and panting for breath. They looked at me, and one boy asked, "That was fun, can we do that again?" I got the point.

Nevertheless, I can't quite stop talking about the serious side of play. Play is fun, but it is also meaningful and complex. The more intelligent the animal, the more it plays. Unlike slugs or trees, every human learns new things about the world, and themselves, through discovery and practice. Some of this learning just happens automatically, by virtue of being alive, but much of it happens through play. Human childhood has gotten longer and longer, which means an increasing amount of time available for play. Play is important, not just because children do so much of it, but because there are layers and layers of meaning to even the most casual play.

Take an apparently simple game like catch—a child and a parent tossing a baseball back and forth. Much like observing pond water under a microscope, close observation of a game of catch reveals a great deal going on right under our noses. The child is developing hand-eye coordination and gross motor skills; the pair are enjoying their special time together; the child practices a new skill until it is mastered, and then joyfully shows it off; the rhythm of the ball flying back and forth is a bridge, reestablishing a deep connection between adult and child; and comments like "good try" and "nice catch" build confidence and trust.

But this straightforward game can also contain strong undercurrents of feeling. A father I was seeing in therapy described a game of catch during which his son threw him one zinger after another. He could see how angry and frustrated his son was by how hard he was throwing the ball. Together we figured out that perhaps his son was really asking him, "Can you catch what I throw at you? Are my feelings too much for you? Am I safe from my own impulses, my own anger?" Another father's son loved to play catch, but whenever he missed the ball, the boy would dissolve into tears and tantrums and say, "I told you to throw it lower—you never listen to me!" In this case, the child seemed to be using the game as a way to release a pile of hurt feelings that had nothing to do with baseball.

Not every game of catch, or every playtime with a child, contains all of these multiple levels of meaning. But all play is more profoundly meaningful than we usually think. First, play is a way to try on adult roles and skills, just as lion cubs do when they wrestle with one another. Human children roughhouse, and they play house. As children discover the world, and discover what they are able to do in the world, they develop confidence and mastery.

Play is also a way to be close and, even more important, a way to reconnect after closeness has been severed. Chimpanzees like to tickle one another's palms, especially after they have had a fight. Thus, the second purpose of play serves our incredible—almost bottomless—need for attachment and affection and closeness.

The third purpose of play for children, and perhaps the one that is most uniquely human, is to recover from emotional distress. Imagine children who have had a hard day at school. They come home and one way or another show you that they're hurting. They talk about it, or they are irritable and obnoxious. They lock themselves in their room, or they insist on extra attention. But most often, they spontaneously use play to feel better. Perhaps they play school, only this time *they* are the teacher. Maybe they play a video game and blow up alien enemies for a while. Or they call a friend and talk about it, which is what older children and adults often do instead of play. By pretending, or by retelling the story, the scene can be re-created. This time, the child is in charge. Through playing it out, emotional healing takes place. Escaping into a book or playing a hard game of tennis can also be helpful after a bad day.

One child I knew, who had lots of reading difficulties, would always come home from school and do something she was really good at, which was drawing. Before dinner she would show her parents what she had drawn. In one sweet moment, she was reconnecting with them, restoring her sense of competence, and recovering from the frustration and humiliation of feeling like a failure at school.

Before going into greater detail about these deep meanings of play, let me repeat that play is *fun*. Spending time with children is supposed to be joyful. My daughter's preschool teacher told me that preschoolers laugh an average of three hundred times a day. What would happen if we all did that? Let's have more fun: sing goofy songs, fall over, exaggerate, have pillow fights, tell jokes. If you are frustrated because you have to re-mind your child for the twelfth time to pack her lunch or take out the garbage, next time try singing the request in a fake-opera voice instead of using the usual nagging tones. At the very least it will get her attention.

As we shall see, however, Playful Parenting is more than just play. We can interact playfully, or on a deep emotional level, no matter what we are doing: working on chores, playing sports, completing homework, hang-ing out, watching television, cuddling, even imposing discipline.

—FOSTERING CLOSENESS INSTEAD OF ISOLATION—

From the time babies and parents begin to gaze lovingly at each other, they are starting to use play as a way to connect. Any game that people en-joy playing together can bring them closer, but some games are actually *about* connection. Games like peekaboo, hide-and-seek, and tag all play with the idea of closeness and distance. I consulted with a family whose son invented a great connection game. He would have his parents sit on the couch; then he'd run toward them, landing right between them. They would then fight over who could grab him first, and it usually turned into a giggly human tug-of-war. Play is one of the best things ever invented to build closeness. I think that must be why school-age children, when asked to define play, focus on the human connectedness of play: Play is what you do with your friends.[3]

My daughter, when she was around five and loved fantasy play, would sometimes say to me, if I was getting frustrated with her: "Let's pretend you're the dad and I'm the daughter and you're mad at me." Well, that won't be hard to pretend, I would think, but soon we would be laughing instead of arguing. I thought it was very clever of her to trans-form, through play, disconnection into connection. Then I read about the way chimpanzees use fantasy play, and I was even more impressed.[4]

Chimpanzees, especially the adult males, fight each other a lot, but they are also experts at reconciliation. They love to make up. When two chimps are having trouble making up after a fight, sometimes one of them will pretend to find something interesting in the grass. He'll hoot and holler and all of the other chimps will come over to check out what he found. Since there's nothing really there, one by one they wander off. All except the other one who was in the fight. The two ex-rivals will continue to excitedly jump up and down over the imaginary something in the grass. Finally, they settle down and begin grooming each other, the sign among chimpanzees of friendship restored.

If chimpanzees and five-year-olds do it, then I think we can agree that using play to reconnect is a pretty basic idea. But sometimes children do not connect or reconnect so easily. They may feel so isolated that they retreat into a corner, or come out aggressively with both arms swinging. They may be annoying, obnoxious, or downright infuriating as they try desperately to signal us that they need more connection. These situations call for creating more playtime, not doling out punishment or leaving the lonely child all alone.

When children feel isolated, they can look withdrawn and depressed. Or they might look hyperactive instead, unable to pay attention, sit still, or calm down. Either way, the world is *not* their oyster, as it is for children who are able to reconnect.

- A lonesome child says, "I'm bored."
- A twelve-year-old sobs, "Nobody likes me."
- A parent says, "I don't know what my three-year-old is thinking; she looks so sad sometimes, but won't tell me what's the matter."
- You try to get your daughter to call a friend, and she screams, "I can't call her; what if she's not home?"
- An eight-year-old child is always on the edge of the playground, even after he knows the other children well. He says, "I just don't like to play soccer."

The most common response by parents to children's isolation is aggravation or worry. We may focus on the annoying behavior, not seeing the pain underneath, or we see the pain all too clearly and feel helpless to fix it. These are difficult moments for any parent. What we need are keys to unlock the door to that fortress of isolation and help the child out again into the fields of play. Playful Parenting provides those keys.

While I was writing this chapter, a mother I'd worked with called to tell me how she'd used the principles of Playful Parenting to reconnect with her son. Her three-year-old, David, had been out of sorts ever since his mother and father had returned from a long-weekend vacation they had taken without him.

"David has been really clingy and whiny," she said. "Every time I try to leave the house, or even the room, he grabs on to me for dear life. Yesterday I had my weekly tennis game with a friend. It's my only exercise, and my most precious personal time of the week. As soon as David saw me heading out the door with my tennis racquet, he grabbed hold of my leg and started crying for me not to go. I tried to explain that this was 'Mommy's play date,' but he clung only tighter. I could tell this was going to escalate into a major power struggle, and I didn't have the heart to peel him off me and hand him over to his baby-sitter.

"Then I remembered what you and I had talked about. Instead of pulling away from David, I lifted him up and carried him to the couch. 'Okay,' I told him happily, 'I won't play tennis. I'll stay here with you and take a nap. I'm soooo tired. What a comfy pillow.' I yawned and lay down on top of him and pretended to snore loudly. He began laughing and putting his hand over my mouth to quiet me. I pretended to wake up and look around, saying, 'Where's David? This sure is a lumpy pillow, and squiggly, too!' Then I pretended to go back to sleep, using him as a pillow and snoring some more.

"After a few minutes' more giggling, David pushed me off him and said, 'Go, go—late for your play date.' We had a really sweet hug good-bye at the door, and he had a fine time without me. When I came home, he had drawn a picture of me playing tennis with an enormous racquet."

—FOSTERING CONFIDENCE INSTEAD OF POWERLESSNESS—

What do you think of when you hear the phrase "playing doctor"? Most people's first association to this phrase involves children's secret sexual explorations: "You show me yours, and I'll show you mine." That type of playing doctor illustrates the way children use play to explore their own bodies. Though playing doctor and other forms of sexual exploration are often difficult for adults to handle, it is really just a special case of "playing house." After all, there are many rooms in the house, and most children have a great interest in what goes on in each of them. Through play, they practice cooking, cleaning, going to work, fighting, taking care of the baby—every adult activity they see around them. This kind of playful practice, performed over and over, makes them more confident.

Young children also play to learn about the world. Why aren't we amused when our toddler drops her food off the high chair for the hundredth time? Because we know about gravity (and we have to clean it up). She, however, is extremely amused, because everything about the universe is new and interesting and open to playful discovery. Including the funny faces and noises we make trying to get her to stop.

I mentioned before that older children define play as whatever you do with your friends. However, toddlers and preschoolers define play as doing whatever you choose.[5] This self-determination is part of the power aspect of play. My niece Bailey, when she was about six months old, had a rattle shaped like a bunch of grapes. She loved to make that thing shake. Her parents called her the boss of the grapes. When you can choose what to do, you are more likely to throw yourself into it.

My daughter and I had a period during her kindergarten year when she didn't want to get dressed by herself. She thought I was being mean because I didn't come dress her or keep her company the way I used to do in preschool. Meanwhile, I thought she was being difficult and uncooperative, since I knew she could do it herself. Instead of saying she was lonely, she would insist that she *couldn't* get dressed on her own. I was frustrated at this helpless attitude, this powerlessness. I was also frustrated because I had better things to do in the morning.

It took me way too long to figure out that nagging wasn't ever going to help. Finally, out of desperation more than cleverness, I picked up two of her dolls and I made one of them say (in a nasty voice), "Oh, *she* can't get dressed by herself; *she* doesn't know how to get dressed by herself." Then I made the other one say (in a cheerfully encouraging voice), "She can so; she really can do it." And then the first one would say, "Oh no,

that's ridiculous; she's just five years old, she can't get dressed by herself."
The nasty doll would always somehow happen not to be watching as
Emma dressed herself. This doll would say, "You see, she didn't get
dressed by herself," and the other one would yell back, "She did so! You
weren't paying attention!" Meanwhile, she was not only getting dressed by
herself, she was laughing instead of whining. I was laughing instead of
fussing or tapping my foot impatiently for her to hurry.

After just a few times playing this game, getting dressed on her own
became a habit, and I didn't have to spend every morning making up doll
dialogue. Once in a while after that, instead of being pokey and driving
me nuts, she would say, "Come in and be those people saying I can't get
dressed." Playfulness turned a time that used to be full of frustration
for both of us into something fun, enjoyable, and confidence-building.
Emma got over her loneliness and reluctance and got used to a new path.
Of course, to get to that point, I had to put in some time up front. As
every parent knows, that time may be hard to find, but it paid off in a very
short while. If I take into account the time I used to spend nagging, fussing, and supervising, then I really come out ahead.

Children who are frustrated too much, or are unable to use play to
master their world, retreat into what I call the tower of powerlessness.
The meadows and fields are inviting, but confidence is required in order
to play out there. Locked inside this tower, unable to play freely, they may
appear weak and helpless. Or they may bounce off the tower walls, looking wild and reckless, even aggressive, but feeling powerless underneath.
If children are too afraid of getting hurt, or expect to be rejected, or can't
believe the world is theirs to explore, then they retreat: "I don't want
to. . . ." "I can't. . . ." "I'm no good at that. . . ." "Timmy's hitting me!"

Yet powerlessness sometimes expresses itself in confusing ways. As
one worried mother put it, "You say my child feels powerless, so how
come he's getting sent home from school for hitting? How come the
teachers are afraid of him?" Powerlessness is a well-defended fortress,
perfect for hiding out, but it is also good for preemptive strikes: "I hate
you. Take that (with a kick or a shove or a bite)!" "You're stupid." "I'm
only playing if I get to be the captain."

Just as Playful Parenting provides the key for helping children unlock the tower of isolation, engaging playfully with children also helps them build the confidence it takes to step out of the tower of powerlessness.

—FOSTERING EMOTIONAL RECOVERY INSTEAD OF EMOTIONAL DISTRESS—

Children don't just play doctor as a cover to make their sexual explorations more respectable. Sometimes when children play doctor they are actually pretending that someone is sick or injured. This type of playing doctor is an example of the way children use play to recover from a traumatic incident, large or small.[6] A three-year-old gets a shot at the doctor's office. She comes home, and what game does she want to play? Doctor, of course. And who does she want to be? The doctor or nurse, the giver of the shot—definitely *not* the patient. And who does she want to give it to? Well, her first choice is a parent or another adult. If no one is available, she might use a stuffed animal or doll. And how does she want the game to go? She wants you to pretend to howl and say, "No, no, no, *please* don't give me a shot. I hate shots! No, no, no," and act as if you are in an agony of pain and terror.

This response lets the child be in the more powerful position. It is a simple game of role reversal (the one who got the shot is now the one who gives the shot), but it is very satisfactory. Getting the shot made her feel powerless and reminded her of all the little frustrations that she's had, all the times when she hasn't been able to choose what to do or what to eat or what to wear—you know, the millions of things that children don't get to decide in their lives. It certainly wasn't *her* idea to go get a shot that day. Playing doctor this way lets her recover because she gets to see *you* as helpless and powerless and undignified, while *she* gets to be the powerful one.

The play shot might be pretend, but the need for emotional recovery is real. The child chooses this fantasy game because she wants a hand with her genuine feelings about the actual shot. This isn't just play for fun (though the child may have lots of fun with it); it is play with a purpose. The purpose is to go through the incident again, but this time letting the scary feelings out—usually through giggles. That's why a child likes to play this kind of game over and over and over.

We are all familiar with the comic-book sequence: the boss yells at the dad, the dad yells at the mom, the mom yells at the kid, the kid shoves the little brother, the little brother kicks the dog, the dog pees on the rug. (I call this emotional hot potato.) The way out of this cycle is for *adults* actively to help children recover. Unlike the child's younger sibling, we can tolerate the pretend needle without saying, "Why do you always get to be the doctor?" or without yelling, "Mom, Ronnie's poking me!" Unfortunately, being civilized adults, we are more likely to say, "Go away, I'm busy" or "Get away from me, I hate needles," instead of playing this game with them. Sometimes, of course, the child does not need a playful approach; he just needs a lap to crawl into so he can cry about how much the shot hurt.

When children are discouraged or punished for attempting to recover emotionally in this playful way, they retreat into themselves. They may try to feel better in less playful ways, like finding a real needle and then jabbing baby brother or the cat with it. Or they may bury the feelings temporarily, at least until they have to go back to the doctor, where they then have a major screaming fit. When we see a child who is fearful, or violent, or out of control, we usually don't stop to put the pieces together. We don't think to ask ourselves if she had enough chance to play it through or talk it through. Usually we just see the problem behavior, which angers or worries us so much that we don't think about using play to help solve it.

A friend of mine, Lori, was at a playground, chatting with a woman she had just met and playing with the woman's two young children, a three-year-old girl and her little brother. Lori is very tolerant of wrestling and boisterous play, and soon the children were climbing all over her. Their mother thought the children should settle down. Before Lori could say anything, the mom whacked the older one, hard. My friend was torn—she's strongly against hitting children and wanted to tell the mother it was wrong—but she knew that the mother was in no shape to listen to her right then. Everyone was upset and angry. So Lori decided to keep an eye on the child who had been spanked. The little girl immediately picked up a stick and went after her little brother. Just in time, Lori grabbed her gently, pulled her aside, took the stick away, and said, in a playful voice, "Ohhhhh no you don't!" The girl laughed and laughed and wanted to play that game over and over. All thoughts of *really* whacking her brother were forgotten (for the time being, at least). The mother, who was able to see that my friend had defused a potentially dangerous situation, without yelling or hitting, watched them play with great interest.

It is not hard to imagine the punishment this young girl would have received if she had succeeded in clobbering the baby. The mother then may have felt totally justified in punishing her severely, forgetting that the aggression started with her own unnecessary spanking of her daughter. Instead, the whole situation was handled playfully. The girl's *ineffective* attempt to deal with being hit, by passing the hit on to someone smaller, was transformed into *effective* recovery, where no one got hurt. And my friend didn't even have to do much; she just stayed close to the child, made sure nobody got whacked, and used a relaxed and playful tone of voice. The little girl did the rest, deciding to *play* "try to hit the baby" instead of *actually* hitting him.

A shot at the doctor's office or a spanking from Mom or Dad are only two of the thousands of childhood injuries and insults that need emotional healing. None of us gets all of our needs perfectly met; none of us escapes childhood without insult or injury. And that's not all. Besides the big traumas and little upsets, children also need to process the new information they receive every day. Just think how many billions of bits of data that is for a child. So much is new to them, and it all has to be sifted through and sorted out. Play is their favorite way to do this. Luckily, play is one of the best ways available to heal from those hurts and to process that new information.

One father who called me for help said that his daughter had several classmates who were just beginning to learn English. This was fascinating to her, and for weeks, walking home from school, she would say, "Let's pretend we speak a different language." She and her father would speak gibberish to each other, pretending it was the language of some other country. The father was a little worried that someone would hear them and think they were being insensitive, making fun of the children from Russia and Japan. I reassured him that, in fact, his daughter was practicing being empathic. She was dealing with something brand new in the only way she knew how: by playing.

Happy play can spontaneously heal minor upsets, but when children are stuck inside their emotional distress, they have trouble playing happily. Once again, they are locked in the towers of isolation and powerlessness. It may be hard to tell which one your child is holed up in. Your daughter says, "I don't want to go to soccer, I stink at it," and you wonder whether she is embarrassed because the other girls are better soccer players, or if she is having trouble making friends on the team. A first-grade bully hits someone every time the teacher's back is turned. Is he feeling isolated from his peers, not realizing that his behavior will only get him excluded more? Or is he testing his power, seeing what he can get away with, seeing how people will react?

Some children—those who are really hurting badly—spend most of their time feeling isolated and powerless, and little or no time playing freely. But even the healthiest, best-loved children will retreat into these two fortresses when they feel scared, overwhelmed, or abandoned. Think about when children are having a bad day. Do they seem unable to play happily, and instead resort to hiding or attacking or annoying you? Are they just going through the motions of life, without any real joy or spark? Maybe they're stuck, repeating the same words or games over and over without any fresh ideas and without having much fun. Perhaps their play is wilder than usual, or more reckless. These are signs of isolation and powerlessness.

If they are unable to recover by using play, children may be flooded with emotions (such as tantrums). They might lash out at others, storm around, or burst into tears at the slightest upset. Others may withdraw to their room, or shut all their feelings down (such as by staring blankly at the TV, compulsively flipping through channels). They seem lifeless and listless. Often adults overlook this second set of problems. Emotional shutdown, because it is quiet, can be confused with being "good." But it doesn't feel good.

When children lock themselves away in one of the towers and pull up the drawbridge behind them, parents wonder how to help them. We may feel helpless and rejected ourselves. We may even go so far as to retreat into our own fortresses of powerlessness and isolation, which makes us even less effective in dealing with our children.

- "He's a spoiled brat."
- "I don't know what to do with her."
- "I hate myself when I yell at them, but the next time I just yell again."
- "Suddenly she's afraid of the water, but I paid for a whole year of swimming lessons, so she's going to swim or else."
- "Go away, I'm busy."

Play is one of the best ways to engage with children, pulling them out of emotional shutdown or misbehavior, to a place of connection and confidence.

—BECOMING A PLAYFUL PARENT—

When I talk to parents about playfulness, someone always says, "I don't really play much with my children; that's more my husband's job." Another frequent comment is, "My children play great on their own. They don't need me to be involved." I appreciate these responses, because they challenge me to explain why play is so important to children, why participating in play is so important for adults, and why being more playful is possible for any parent who is willing to give it a try.

I hope the next fourteen chapters provide clear guidance on how to break through the walls that divide children from adults, to discover ways to meet heart to heart. Playful Parenting helps with the toughest aspects of parenting: tantruming toddlers, biting preschoolers, anxious third-graders, out-of-control preteens. Playfulness resolves our battles over getting dressed and ready in the morning, soothes our frazzled nerves at the end of a long day, and restores family harmony. Playful Parenting offers a hand even when playfulness seems a dream that's out of reach or a joke in poor taste. When we are exhausted or when we are at the end of our rope, we tend to think that play will be just more of an energy drain. But when we engage playfully with our children, we find that suddenly we *do* have energy, both for fun and for finding creative solutions to thorny problems.

Many parents tell me, "I could never be as goofy as you." I am not sure whether to take this as a compliment or an insult, but either way, it just takes practice. Contrary to what my daughter might tell you, I had to train myself to be as goofy as I am today. I had to get over my shyness and embarrassment about playing on the climbing structure with her when she asked me to, instead of sitting on the bench with the other parents. As long as we are grown up enough to handle things like keeping them safe and getting dinner on the table, our children want us and need us to loosen up. I don't think it makes sense to leave the playing for others, who are "better at it." Why should they have all the fun?

And if we don't play, we miss out on more than fun. Play is where children show us the inner feelings and experiences that they can't or won't talk about. We need to hear what they have to say, and they need to share it. That's why we have to join children where *they* live, on *their* terms. Children don't say, "I had a hard day at school today; can I talk to you about it?" They say, "Will you play with me?" If we say yes, they play out what happened in the best way they know how. Or they don't say anything, needing us to take the initiative. By the end of the game, we may have helped them boost their confidence and their inner feeling of being loved—just what they need to go back to school and solve the problem themselves. If they don't think we will play, they may not even ask. They just go about their business, and we go about ours, and we all miss chance after chance to reconnect.

I spend a lot of my time at work reintroducing play and playfulness into families that are quite normal and average but that have lost a bit of that zestfulness and joy. For example, I was a few minutes late when I knocked on the door of my friend Connie's apartment to play with her and her son Brian. They had been having some minor troubles—nothing serious, just typical stuff between a nine-year-old boy and his mother: not wanting her to hug and kiss him; being sarcastic; talking back; living and breathing sports; dismissing his mother and everything else female. Brian and I had played together once before. That time, Connie and Brian came over and we swapped kids—I did the rough-and-tumble thing with Brian while she played Barbies with my daughter. This was lots of fun and a big relief for all of us: finally an adult who knows how to really play; finally a child who wants to play something I'm good at.

This time, as I knocked on the door, I wasn't sure what to expect. As Connie shouted, "Come in!" Brian yelled out, "You're late, you idiot!" We were off and running. I came in and said playfully, "What did you call me?" I chased him into the other room, where he collapsed onto the couch. I buried him in pillows. He leaped up and we started a pillow fight. Connie was sitting next to me, chuckling. She loved seeing his nastiness aimed at someone else for a change; he loved that he could get away with it without getting a lecture or a punishment or an end to playtime. I loved it because Brian was showing us what he was feeling inside. Not directly, but by calling me an idiot and whacking me with a pillow, he was revealing what I call the hard spots, places where he felt pounded or stupid himself.

I whacked Connie with a pillow to get her into the action. It was *their* relationship with each other that was important, not mine with Brian. "Oh, ho ho," Connie said to me. "So you want me to play, too?" "Yes!" answered Brian, and we had a great three-way pillow fight. A couple of weeks later, I talked to Connie about what this playtime was like for her. She felt that it had greatly improved her relationship with her son, by helping her notice that he really did still want to play with her and be close to her, even though he often seemed to push her away. She also realized that she had been feeling drained from all her caretaking duties—cooking, driving, helping with homework, chauffering to sports—and she had little or no energy for play. Getting in some good playtime, though, not only helped her see how much her son wanted it and needed it, but also how revitalizing this kind of play can be. Since then they have played much more, and from Connie's reports, I am not sure who has enjoyed it more.

CHAPTER 2

JOIN CHILDREN IN THEIR WORLD

When you are dealing with a child, keep all
your wits about you, and sit on the floor.
—AUSTIN O'MALLEY, 1915

I learned a great game from Jimmy, my eight-year-old neighbor. Jimmy's little cousin would come visit, and he would take her to the swings across the street. He would stand in front of her and give her a push. When she came back toward him, he would stand so that her feet just barely touched him on the chest. Then he would make a big show of falling over and pretending to be mad at her. He would get up and say, "You better not do that again!" She would laugh with delight and he would patiently play this game with her again and again.

Why is this such a great game? It manages to cover all of the deep purposes of play, as well as just plain being fun. The contact, or near miss, is a great way to play with connection. Having the younger child be the more powerful one builds confidence. Besides, why are toddlers called toddlers? Because they fall down a lot. Having someone else fall down, in a funny way, lets the toddler release—in waves of giggles—all her frustration about walking. Much better than finding another toddler and pushing him over, or whining to be carried because walking is so difficult.

I often use Jimmy as my model when I think of ways to help children out of their twin towers of isolation and powerlessness and into the open vistas of delighted, exuberant play. First and foremost, what Jimmy did at the swing set was join the younger child *in her world*. He went to her level and played in a way that was most fun for her. Playful Parenting begins with an eagerness to connect with children in the way Jimmy connected with his cousin, and a willingness to provide children with unlimited refills of love, encouragement, and enthusiasm. Loosening up—literally and figuratively—also helps, as most of us adults are rather stiff when we try to get down on the floor and play. Since fun and laughs are the currency of children's play, we may need some work on lightening up a bit. When we get disconnected from children—and we do, again and again—play is our best bridge back to deep connection with them. We have to be ready.

—REENTERING A WORLD WE ONCE KNEW—

Many adults feel like outsiders to this world of play that children inhabit, a world we once knew but seem to have forgotten. We may look at this world wistfully, wishing we could still play the way we used to. Or we might be glad to finally be an adult, with the children off playing on their own in the next room, or outside. One of my friends says to his kids, only half jokingly, "Call me only if someone's bleeding." Many adults, especially busy parents, are resistant to the idea of joining children in their world. They will say to me, "Kids like being on the floor; I don't. If I was meant to be on the floor, my knees wouldn't be so creaky and I wouldn't mind getting dirty. Can't children just play on their own, or with a friend, or outside with the neighborhood kids?" Of course children can and should play by themselves or with friends part of the time. Leaving children to their own devices is useful for fostering independence, and *very* useful for giving parents a break so they can rest or finish their work or cook dinner. Leaving a pair or group of children alone lets them work things out on their own as they play freely, without worrying about adult intervention. Children benefit from and need this time away from adults. We don't need to *move into* their world.

But to fulfill the promise of play, children need adults to play with them *some* of the time. This kind of play can be hard, at first, for adults, but it is a skill that anyone can develop with practice and commitment. It is also fun. A great deal has been written in the last ten or twenty years about the power of parents and other adults to harm children. But adults also have the power to *help* children. Not just to get out of their way, or to keep them safe from harm, but to actively help them develop, heal from being hurt, and maintain close human connections. Since children already use play to connect, to heal, and to develop confidence, it is a logical next step for adults to play with them to offer the additional helping hand they need.

—PROVIDING A HELPING HAND—

Play is children's main way of communicating. To stop a child from playing is like stopping an adult from talking and thinking. To control every minute of their play is like controlling every word someone says. But to leave children all alone in their play is like spending the day with other adults and never talking with them.

The adult role in play can be quite minimal—just making sure of basic safety and being there if needed. Some of our most important parenting happens when we are in a different room, while our children play happily, knowing we will come when they call. Maybe they just need an audience for their skits and magic tricks, or just need someone to fill the tub and get the funnels out, or drive them to a friend's house. At these times we may feel more like a servant than a parent. Anybody can do this, why does it have to be me? But it does make a difference if it is you—children need the adults with whom they are closest to be nearby some of the time, even when they don't need much from us.

Brian and Shirley Sutton-Smith wrote a wonderful book in the 1970s about playing with children. They have a lovely example of what I call the light touch in participating in play. They call it a play interlude.

> In the middle of your vacuuming your little child will suddenly appear with a suitcase and, going to the door, will wave good-bye. "I'm going to the hospital. Good-bye. Good-bye." This small act of leaving may be repeated twenty times. Your role is to enter into the play just a little but not too much. Wave good-bye but go on vacuuming. Wave good-bye and make a mock crying face but then go on with your vacuuming. Finally go to him and

ask, "Have you come home now?" "Yes," he replies. Then hug
him to pieces, exclaiming how happy you are.[1]

A play interlude is not always enough, of course. The deeply meaningful aspects of play may happen so easily and spontaneously that no
one is even aware of them (except nosy psychologists like me). Parents
and children use play for these emotionally important purposes all the
time, without even thinking much about it. Just as we can breathe and
walk without giving it any thought, children and adults use play naturally
to connect, to build confidence, and to heal from emotional distress. But
meaningful play may need more effort and more awareness on the part of
adults. Children have a special need of more active participation from
grown-ups:

- when they are having a difficult time connecting with peers
  or adults;
- when they seem unable to play freely and spontaneously;
- when things are changing in their life (the start of
  kindergarten, the birth of a new sibling, a death or divorce
  in the family);
- when they are in danger.

Now let's look at how play can satisfy each of these needs.

—WHEN CHILDREN ARE HAVING A DIFFICULT TIME CONNECTING WITH PEERS OR ADULTS—

Austin was a ten-year-old boy who had difficulty playing happily and
freely. He had trouble with friendships, and it was no wonder; the only
game he ever wanted to play was a rough version of soccer, which involved lots of tackling and punching. He was quickly running out of anyone who would play this with him, and he would sulk whenever other
children wanted to play something different. In consultation with his parents, we decided to set aside special playtimes with each parent that involved a great deal of playful physical contact. They would wrestle, have
pillow fights, and have piggyback rides around the house, as well as more
hugs and more cuddle time. If Austin started to get aggressive, they took a
break, and then went back to playing. These small changes made a huge
difference in his ability to play well with his peers.

Sitting off alone—unhappily—is another clear sign that a child is having trouble connecting with others. These children need adults to make an extra effort at playfulness, designed to lure them out of their isolation and into contact. They may need practice in playing so that they know how to interact with their peers. This infusion of love, affection, and attention will help them enter into peer play with confidence and playfulness. Or they may just need a parent to patiently pay attention to them as they make their way out of their bored, listless hole and figure out something fun to do. Instead, children are often punished or ignored when they are already feeling excluded and lonely. Sitting alone in one's room is not the best way to develop better ways to play with friends.

—WHEN CHILDREN SEEM UNABLE TO PLAY FREELY AND SPONTANEOUSLY—

My colleague Sam Roth and I taught a class together for teachers in after-school programs. We tried to draw a distinction between two types of play, which require two different levels of adult involvement. We asked the teachers to describe "good" play, and they listed these adjectives: fluid, creative, imaginative, fun, adaptive, inclusive of others, and cooperative. We asked them what children need from adults to continue this kind of play. They listed safety, a nurturing environment, a home base where they can check in, play and art materials, and backup conflict resolution if things get out of hand. Then we asked for a description of play that was a problem for them, and their list included these words: repetitive, stuck, aggressive, destructive, boring, or exclusive of others. With that kind of play, they said, children need adults to provide more structure, information, redirection, enthusiasm, fresh ideas, calming, extra attention, guidelines and limits, and help in verbalizing their behaviors and feelings ("say it in words").

To put it another way, some children seem to know all they need to know about play, while others need specific lessons in rules, skills, or sportsmanship. Teaching these lessons is another obvious role for adults. I am amazed at how often I see children who want to play but don't know the rules, have never practiced the skills, and can't bear to lose. That makes it hard for children to play freely and spontaneously. It usually takes a little adult intervention for the child who is always stuck in left field, because he doesn't play as well as the others, to get some extra catching practice. The child who disputes every call, and makes his friends angry with him every time they play, may need some special playtime focused on sportsmanship.

—WHEN THINGS ARE CHANGING IN CHILDREN'S LIVES—

My friend Linda provides a wonderful example of parents' need to participate more in their childrens' play when things change at home. She had just had a third child: the older ones now were clinging to her and demanding her attention because they felt as if the new baby was taking away from their time with her. Linda made up a game that they called fill-up. She would take each child on her lap and say that she was going to fill them up with Mommy love. She would start at their toes, work her way up, and end with a kiss on top of their heads. Then she added another element—the love egg. Do you know that trick where you pretend to crack an egg over someone's head by gently tapping them on the head and then spreading your fingers down their hair? She would call this the love egg and crack it over them, spreading more love. Both older kids loved this and wanted to do it every day. This five-minute game helped them to be able to play on their own and with each other while their mom was busy with the baby; it also helped them to be loving and warm toward the baby instead of resentful and aggressive.

—WHEN CHILDREN ARE IN DANGER—

When children are in danger, especially from each other, we can see the need for adult participation clearly. There are times when it is dangerous to let children work things out on their own. I've done a lot of work with adults who were sexually abused as children, and Jack's story was pretty typical. When he was five, he was assaulted by two older boys who lived next door to him. They had a "game" they played, which they probably thought was fun. I'll spare you the details. From Jack's point of view it was traumatic and abusive. Looking back, Jack realized that his tormentors were trying to deal with their own misery by passing it on to him. Maybe someone was brutal to them, or just ignored them when they needed help. They must have had a pile of bad feelings and nowhere to go with them—except to act them out on someone younger and smaller.

The problem was, Jack was in no position to help them with their anger and aggression. He was only five. Apparently the parents next door wanted no part of their boys' aggressive impulses either; they told the boys to get lost. Well, the boys did indeed "get lost." They got lost in their painful feelings—until they found Jack to unleash them on. Unable or unwilling to intervene directly with the boys, the adults were equally unavailable to intervene in the "play."

The abusive boys needed play experiences that would have interrupted and rechanneled their aggressive impulses. Jack needed help with play also. He didn't need the same kind of help the older boys did, since he responded to their violence by being timid and fearful. He needed play that would have helped him to be more assertive and to trust the world enough to come out of his towers of isolation and powerlessness. Jack had to wait until he was an adult before he could recover, and then he used therapy, rather than play, to aid in the process.

Luckily, most examples of adults helping children through play are not quite so dramatic, but they do point to the same basic principle: *Children's difficulties do not always sort themselves out if the children are left alone,* as much as busy parents and teachers wish they would.

—THE IMPORTANCE OF GETTING DOWN ON THE FLOOR—

In Playful Parenting, "getting on the floor" may mean literally getting down on the floor, right where children like to play. Other times we get on the floor metaphorically, by meeting children on their home ground, doing what they like to do. For young children this means being at their level, eye to eye. For older children, it means hanging out on their turf, whether that's the mall, the ball field, or plopped in front of the TV or computer.

Getting on the floor also means joining in with play that we would rather ignore or eliminate. One mother, a parent at a preschool where I gave a talk on aggressive play, was shocked and horrified at my answer when she asked for advice about her son. Instead of offering ideas to get him to stop his awful testosterone-driven mayhem (chopping the heads off action figures and hurling them down the stairs was his favorite game), I suggested that she join in the play. Enthusiastically. Repetitive play does not change as long as it is played in isolation, and the mom's disapproval just made him feel even more isolated. Children need our approval and enthusiasm first, before they can get out of a rut. So even if the goal is to have him stop that violent play, the only effective way is to play it with him for a while, which gives him the elbow room to try out new ideas and new ways of dealing with his aggressive impulses.

A. S. Neill, headmaster of the experimental Summerhill school in England, when faced with a student who was sneaking out of the dorm to cause mischief of one kind or another, was known to wake the child up in the middle of the night while dressed in some ridiculous outlaw outfit, and ask if he could come along on the next outing. The child would always say no and give the headmaster a lecture on proper behavior, and the mischief would stop.

I think what Neill provided for his students, as they were teetering on the edge between acting responsibly and getting in trouble, was a special kind of play. By showing up in the night looking silly, he helped the child think the whole thing through for himself. When we constantly tell children what they should or shouldn't do, they have no room to think for themselves and are forced to choose between resentful obedience or defiant rebellion. Playfulness helps them think for themselves, even about serious topics.

There are many resources that parents give their children as they get on the floor and join in the play. Some are material things, like good toys and a comfortable room and healthy snacks. Some are intangible, like introducing a new idea into the game. One of my favorites is when two children are pounding on each other, and I say, "Pick on someone your own size!" and put up my hands to fight, with a goofy expression on my face. They both turn on me and I run away in mock fright, a little twist that changes the whole nature of the game.

One of my favorite ideas for thinking about different ways of joining children in their play comes from the work of Leston Havens, a psychiatrist at Cambridge Hospital in Massachusetts. He writes about therapy with adults, and one of his most useful and playful concepts has to do with seating arrangements in the therapy session.[2] He uses seating arrangements as a way to understand different types of therapy. The first psychiatrists sat across a desk from their patients, creating a formal distance. Sigmund Freud invented the idea of sitting on a chair out of sight of the patient, so the patient has to imagine what the therapist is thinking and feeling. Carl Rogers sat face-to-face, knee-to-knee, which fits with his goal of warm, genuine communication. Harry Stack Sullivan often sat side-by-side, shoulder-to-shoulder with his patients, so the two of them could be partners in facing the scary world outside.

In his own work, Leston Havens takes these models a step further, thinking about each individual patient and how to sit with them. For some he wants to be out of kicking range; for others he wants to be close enough to reach out and touch their arm or knee. I often think about these seating arrangement ideas when I am deciding how best to join the world of a child through play. For example, sometimes Playful Parenting involves very close physical contact, such as wrestling or cuddling. Sometimes the degree of contact varies during the play, as in chase or tag. Other times the adult and the child sit across from each other over a board game. The best example of Sullivan's side-by-side seating arrangement is the way that nontalkative boys are known for doing their best talking in the car, staring straight ahead, while their mom or dad watches the road and listens.

Playing catch usually involves a considerable distance, but the ball serves as a bridge between the two players. Finally, as we'll see in the story of the boy behind the locked door in the next chapter, there may be a unique seating arrangement. It's important to find the approach your child will most respond to—and you can find this only if you're trying to interact with your child on their level.

There will always be room for children to play on their own or with peers. In fact, when young people have had effective adult participation in play, they can then get even more enjoyment from playing on their own. But for the times when they need more from us than just a warm body to give them juice or make sure they don't burn the house down, we need to understand why it is often hard for us to play.

—WHY IT'S HARD FOR ADULTS TO PLAY—

When we were children, the current generation of parents did not play with adults very much. We spent our toddlerhoods in playpens, our elementary-school years in front of the TV, our teen years hanging out. Not that earlier generations had much playtime with adults either, or much time to play, period. It is only recently that children have had much chance to play at all. Experts in early childhood development all agree that this increased playtime has been a great benefit for children. But sometime in adolescence or early in adulthood we pretty much stop playing, and we may even forget how. We may replace play with competitive sports, or with leisure, but these are not as free or spontaneous or imaginative as children's play. We have lost much of our ability to play— through lack of practice, and through adult preoccupations and worries—and this loss gets in our way of being with children.

Nowhere is this loss more painful or poignant for parents than when we have trouble connecting through play with our children. Too often we hit a wall, and on the other side of that wall sit our children, waiting for us to reconnect with them on their turf, and on their terms. We have to take the initiative in reconnecting, instead of waiting for them or giving up. Since we don't usually play as much or as spontaneously as children, we have to *choose* to play, even if we don't really feel like it.

Unfortunately, if you look back at the list of times children's play requires more adult involvement (see p. 22), they tend to be the very same times when we have the most difficulties in playing with our children:

- When children are not connecting well with us or their peers, we usually feel disconnected as well (which may make us sad, mad, bored, or irritable, rather than playful).
- When children's play is repetitive, aggressive, or inhibited, we usually want to punish them, ignore them, or get away from them—anything but join in.
- Transitions are hard for adults, too. We have even less time and attention for children when we are preoccupied with big changes in our lives.
- When our children are in danger, we may be too worried to

be playful (they might be in danger because we were not

paying enough attention to them in the first place).

Maybe we swore we would never be harsh with our children the way others were harsh with us. Then, just when they need us most—when they act up and misbehave and call us names and so on—we get angry and punish them, or feel hurt and block them out. We momentarily forget how fragile our little ones are, just as they forget about cooperation or sharing or calming down or following the rules. When things are in upheaval, such as during the arrival of a new sibling, a move, or a divorce, we are preoccupied with our own feelings and all the things we have to do, so we tend to give children even less attention right when they need extra. And so they act up and we have still less attention for them, the break in the connection grows wider, and so on. No wonder parenting is often hard!

Plus, we adults have unhealed hurts from our own childhoods, which sometimes get in the way right when our children need our support. Our own piles of old feelings interfere with parenting playfully. In turn, that makes it hard to help children with their emotional difficulties. One mother I worked with could talk clearly about her daughter's problems (at age five, she seemed depressed and withdrawn), but she seemed at a loss as to where these problems came from. After playing with the girl I could see how much trouble she had in maintaining a connection. Our play revolved around variations of my coaxing her out of corners, where she would hide like a scared kitten. When I had finally managed to establish a fairly good connection with the daughter, I invited the mother to join the game. She was very stiff and awkward, but both mother and daughter clearly enjoyed the coaching on how to have fun together.

As I eased myself out of the play, however, the mother was frozen. She sat in a chair almost paralyzed, unable to play. Confronted with this obvious emotional block, the mother was able to see how her own difficulties in connecting had affected her daughter. Before, she had successfully avoided facing these feelings by simply saying she was too busy or too tired to play. The whole dynamic in the family changed as the mother took the initiative to work through her own obstacles to closeness and connection.

By avoiding playing, this mom had avoided feeling bad, but with serious consequences for the whole family. It is no wonder that we try to avoid these feelings, though; they are extremely uncomfortable. What else besides painful emotion could keep us from playing with children whom we love? Sometimes parents have to spend some time on the floor actually playing games their children want to play in order even to recognize the deep feelings inside that get in the way. As one parent told me, "Playing with my kids isn't always fun, but I do it anyway because I know in the end we are all happier. Also, the more I choose to play with them their way, the more likely they will go along with some of the things I want to do."

When we play with our children, there's often more that we feel than simply being bored by the game, or too tired even to play at all. Some parents get angry, responding to children's play with rigid rules, harsh discipline, and violent outbursts. Some adults are fine until a child starts to cry or makes a mess—which, of course, is bound to happen eventually—then they explode. Others feel competitive, having to build a higher tower or a better Lego structure than their child. Others feel helpless, afraid to wrestle, for example, for fear of getting hurt, or feeling awkward, as if their playing muscles had gotten flabby from lack of use. Children need us to make a big effort to overcome all of these feelings and play the games they want to play, the way *they* want to play them. If there are adults who can play with children all day without having any of these feelings, I haven't met them yet.

Chapter fifteen will go into detail about releasing these feelings, and other chapters will show how to play well in the meantime, but the brief solution is this: Talk with other parents honestly about these feelings. Talk about what your childhood was like, when you were the age your child is now. Take time for yourself to get recharged as a parent so you can have energy to play with your children without your own emotions getting in the way. And last, give yourself some credit: This is hard work and we *all* get bored, exasperated, and angry at times.

Before leaving the topic of adults and play, let's take a closer look at two groups that tend to be shoved off to the side when it comes to children's growth and development: fathers and nonparents.

—I CALL IT FATHERING—

In the words of John Updike, who often writes about the alienation of husbands and fathers, "If men do not keep on speaking terms with children, they cease to be men, and become merely machines for eating and for earning money." Obviously Updike was making an understatement; fathering takes more than just being on speaking terms with our children. But he captures the way our society pulls fathers away from the center of their families. And for what? To be cogs in the economic machine. The nurturing abilities of fathers are seldom acknowledged, and even more rarely encouraged.

Fathers often feel marginalized within families—pushed out of the middle of family life and over to the fringes—assigned by themselves or others to a narrow range of roles that may or may not include playing. The title of this section, "I Call It Fathering," comes from a conversation I had with my mother when my daughter was a newborn. My wife was out and I was home alone with Emma when my mother called. She said, "Oh, so you're baby-sitting?" As politely as I could manage, I answered, "I call it fathering." She realized immediately what she had said and apologized. I realized that when she was a child, and again as a mother of young children, fathers' active involvement with their infants was so minimal that it could fairly be called baby-sitting. Given this history, it is no wonder that many fathers feel as if they are sitting out the game on the sidelines. Many books on parenting reinforce this separation of the father from the family, saying, for example, that the most important thing a father can do for his child is to love and support the mother.

Fathers are parents and they are men; unfortunately, they get much more training in being a man than in being a parent. Some of that masculinity training actually gets in the way of fatherhood, especially with connecting playfully or on a deep emotional level. Untrained in nurturing, men feel helpless. And most men hate to feel helpless.

Once, when my daughter was a baby and my parents came to visit, my father was holding her when she started to cry. She had just eaten and wasn't wet, so when he started to give her back to me, I said, "There's nothing I would do that you aren't doing." He was amazed. He had always thought there was some mysterious thing you do when a baby cries, something he didn't know how to do. My father is not alone in believing there's a mystery to parenthood; even men of my generation are confused about their role. One of the best developments of the last ten years or so is the greater participation of fathers in the nuts and bolts of child care. When my daughter was in kindergarten, there were three of us in one classroom who were at-home dads.[3] Many of the other fathers in the class were very involved in school and at home. Still, all working parents, but especially fathers, have trouble reconnecting with the world of the family after work. Feminist authors have decried "the second shift,"[4] the way working mothers come home to do the housework and child care, even in most two-parent, two-income homes. They are right: this is an unfair burden on women, but it is also a disaster for *men*, to be left out of the loop of day-to-day parenting.

My friend Michael and I started a fathers' group when our children were a few months old. At first we would hang out with our babies and talk, then we started chasing after our toddlers, and then we watched our preschoolers play while we once again got a chance to talk. I recommend a group like this to every father. When the children were infants, many of the fathers would leap up to race home with the babies as soon as they started to cry. They thought they had to get them to their mothers to nurse. I had to wean the fathers off this, if you will excuse the pun, and explain that babies cry for many other reasons besides hunger (most of these babies had nursed right before the group anyway). And, even more important, the fathers were missing out on a great joy of fathering: holding a crying baby as he or she releases all those feelings—the only way a baby knows how to talk—and then settles down in our arms. These men had all held their babies more in the first few months than their own fathers had held them their whole lives, but they still couldn't stand to hold a crying baby.

At the other extreme, some fathers completely disconnect from their families, perhaps breaking off contact and never realizing the hole they left behind. They may stay, but remain emotionally distant, not playing unless they feel like it, not really connecting. Real fathering takes a commitment to the everydayness of parenting. Ironically, some men experience this everydayness only after a divorce. They become part-time fathers, but for the first time they must do every aspect of parenting on the days when they actually have their children. Men tend not to believe that they are loved or valued; we are prone to feeling replaceable, interchangeable. I have listened with sadness to so many men who are shocked when they discover, years later, that their families really wanted and needed them. The children, once grown, are themselves shocked to realize that their fathers would have loved to have been close to them, but didn't know how, or didn't feel they had the time or energy.

On the other hand, fathers have always been children's main playmates for rough-and-tumble play. Rough-and-tumble play with Dad has been found over and over to be good for children, as long as it isn't too rough. For example, boys who wrestle around with their dads get along better with other children. Dads are famous for jazzing things up, throwing babies in the air, engaging in special-occasion play. These activities are great, and children need this kind of play. But fathers and children need the ordinary, everyday interactions, too.

Fathers, and men more generally, have the potential to make an enormous, positive difference in the lives of children. Children need the traditional strengths of fathers, namely roughhousing and other forms of physical play. They also need for men to expand their repertoires—to cuddle, comfort, and play dress up. Why is catch the prototype father-son game? I think it's because playing catch is about bridging a distance, and distance is what boys and men struggle against. As more and more men choose closeness over distance, fathering won't have to have a separate section in books about parenting.

—A SPECIAL NOTE ABOUT NONPARENTS—

If fathers are marginalized—outsiders to the world of children's play and development—nonparents are often marginalized even more. Mothers are supposed to do everything and be everything, with little or no support. But nonparents play a unique role in the lives of children. Did you have a favorite uncle, or friend of the family, who would get down on the floor and play Monopoly with you, or show you card tricks? An aunt who took you to tea when you were a preteen and were desperate to be treated like a grown-up?

Many of the examples in this book involve parents with their children, but the principles apply equally well to friends, baby-sitters, grandparents, teachers, play therapists, and so on. In fact, many of these games and activities are especially suited to adults who are not parents. Parents and children often get stuck at an impasse with each other, which makes playtime less than fun. Soon one or both of them avoids playing altogether. Other adults can often intervene in these situations to "unstick" the play and get things going again. One thing I do frequently in my work with families is make a connection with the child through play, and then invite the parents in, coaching them on connecting with their child and making the most of the playtime. I think the key factor in this work is not my special expertise as a psychologist, but my presence as an outside adult who uses play as a bridge to reconnection.

When my daughter was very young, for example, my wife and I were a bit uncomfortable with too much mess. We didn't even realize this until our friend Tina spent some time alone with Emma. We came home to find her delightedly playing in the soup, with a bowl of it dumped over her head and pools of it on the counter. It took someone who was not hung up on mess to offer her this type of play.

Not that playing is always easy for nonparents. For the same reasons that parents have a hard time playing, it can be awfully hard for nonparents, too. Not having children of their own, they may have more energy and more patience for the spots where parents and children butt heads. On the other hand, they may be less used to the daily fact of spending lots of time with children, or they may be confused about their role. As parents, we need to remind these adult friends how special and important they are to our children.

Because our society doesn't take play very seriously, we don't pay our play professionals very well. Day-care providers, camp counselors, after-school program teachers, recreation department workers, and so on are paid absurdly low wages given the important work they do and how well they usually do it. They are often treated more as baby-sitters than as experts on children and play. Some countries have a tradition of "play leaders," well-trained and well-paid adults who supervise adventure playgrounds, modeled after a Danish playground in the 1940s that was basically a junkyard where children could build forts and tree houses, light fires, and cook and play. "Effective play leaders need to possess technical expertise and creative curiosity, knowledge of children, a sense of humor, leadership capability, and community involvement skills. . . . They need to know the basic principle of affirming children's play."[5] Sadly, these types of playgrounds never became popular here, probably because they were considered ugly and unsafe.

One last story about nonparents: I knew a couple who lived on a street with lots of children but who didn't have any themselves. Their porch and yard became a congregating point for the children in the neighborhood, mainly because the husband was so playful. One time the wife asked everyone if they wanted lemonade, and after she went in to make it, one of the children said to her husband, "Your mom is really nice." Nonparents, even if they are recognized as being adults, can be accepted as "one of the gang" in a way that parents generally can't. And children benefit from a thoughtful, respectful adult who can be seen as an ally rather than as the enemy.

—TUNING IN TO YOUR CHILD—

In 1952, a group of researchers was studying primate behavior by closely observing a colony of Japanese macaques. To supplement the monkeys' diet, the scientists tossed sweet potatoes onto the beach. J. Gary Bernhard writes about these monkeys in his book *Primates in the Classroom*.[6] The monkeys loved the sweet potatoes, but they didn't like the sand on them. A young female of the group discovered the idea of washing them in the sea. Since monkeys don't have schools or formal education, the researchers were interested in how this knowledge would spread through the colony. The first to learn was this monkey's mother. Bernhard quotes one of the observers: "This is understandable, since practically the only adult animal to be interested in the behavior of a one-and-one-half-year-old female is her mother."

The breakthrough next passed from the mother to her other offspring, the original monkey's siblings, because these monkeys all paid close attention to their mother. It passed then from these older siblings to their peers. These older juvenile monkeys spent most of their time playing as a group, and part of play is watching your playmates to see what they are doing. The mothers of these playmates learned next, by watching them, and then the playmates' siblings. Out of a large colony, all but thirteen (who were all—surprise!—adult males) eventually learned the sweet-potato-washing trick. Bernhard says, "The adult males were not resistant to the idea on principle; they simply did not notice what was going on in a way that would affect their behavior." They had "more important" things to pay attention to, so they kept on having to eat sandy sweet potatoes. The young monkey who started the trend became known as the Genius Monkey after she also figured out how to separate grain from chaff by tossing it in the water, where the chaff sank and the grain floated. That knowledge spread by the same pattern through the colony.

This story can be read as a fable about the importance of adults "tuning in" to children. We often stop paying close attention to children, especially once they do not require our constant care. After all, like the adult male macaques, we have more important things to think about. Children need time alone and on their own; they need to develop independence. But they also need someone to tune in to their feelings and their discoveries. They probably aren't inventing new ways to wash food, though, so what exactly are we supposed to tune in to?

The first thing to notice is *what children need*. Do they need help figuring something out? Are they too sleepy or hungry to think clearly? Do two children need a break from each other for a while? Do they need to be outside where they can be louder and wilder? Maybe they need more attention. I'm always amazed when adults say that children "just did that to get attention." Naturally children who need attention will do all kinds of things to try to get it. Why not just give it to them?

When human children are overlooked, the consequences are more severe than having to eat sandy sweet potatoes. Being overlooked in this way causes loneliness, and being completely overlooked can cause the most severe forms of mental illness. A strange and wonderful book called *The Singing Creek Where the Willows Grow: The Mystical Nature Diary of Opal Whiteley*[7] is an example. Opal Whiteley was a childhood genius who, at age nine, wrote an amazing diary about her remarkable love for nature.

However, she spent her last forty years in an asylum in England. No one recognized her genius, and indeed, her parents barely acknowledged her existence except to scold her. She tells heartbreaking stories of being ignored, misunderstood, and beaten, all because no one thought to ask her what she was thinking. It turns out that what she was thinking was altogether extraordinary.

My friends Laurie and David, a single mother and her ten-year-old son, have for years been playing what they call the lava game. In the lava game they wrestle on the bed, pretending that the floor is covered with molten lava. The goal of the game is to stay safely on the bed instead of falling into the lava. When Laurie told me about this game, I was struck by one thing she said: "Sometimes we rescue each other and sometimes we push each other in." When I asked her more about it, I could see that they used this game to address important themes in David's life, such as loss, danger, rescue, and aggression. Without thinking much about it, the two of them adjust the game to the prevailing emotions of the moment. That's tuning in.

Remember those science-fiction stories in which there is some device that instantly translates all the languages in the world (or the universe) into English? That's a good metaphor for tuning in to what's really going on with children. I call it the universal translator. You take any troubling or annoying or infuriating message from the child, whether it is in words or behavior, and you translate it in your head into something that you can deal with more effectively. For Playful Parenting purposes, it is especially useful to translate whatever you hear or see into the language of closeness and isolation, confidence and powerlessness. Here are some examples:

The original version: Whenever he walks into the after-school program, a six-year-old boy hits his favorite teacher and then runs under the table.

The translation: "I want to get close to you, but closeness is scary for me. Besides, I'm angry and you probably hate angry kids, so I'll hate you first."

The thoughtful response: "You know, I wonder if you hit me and then run under the table because you kind of want to get close to me, but you're kind of not sure. How about if we shake hands or give each other the high five whenever you come into the room?"

The original version: "This homework is stupid."
The translation: "I'm frustrated because I haven't mastered fractions yet. Can you help me?"
The thoughtful response: "I'd love to help you with fractions."

The original version: "I hate you!"
The translation: "I haven't figured out yet how to be mad at somebody I love; it's confusing."
The thoughtful response: "I love you, and I get confused, too, when I'm mad at somebody I love."

Another time to try to translate in this fashion is when children's behavior just doesn't seem to make sense. In order to find the sense, we have to tune in carefully. In a seminar for after-school teachers, Frank brought up a difficulty he was having. He has an artificial eye, and many of the children ask him about it. He reported that he has no trouble with this, and he gave great examples of talking about it at just the right level for children of different ages, from kindergartners up to fourth-graders. The difficulty was that many of these children would keep asking him about it over and over and over. At first he would go through it again, assuming they had forgotten the details of the story. But after a while it began to feel annoying and intrusive. Besides, he didn't understand why the kids did that, and as a veteran teacher, that was troubling to him. He was reluctant to suggest that the kids were just being obnoxious, but I could sense that he was leaning in that direction. From the way Frank talked about the situation, I guessed that the children experienced a very close, warm bond with him when he told them the story. Later, wanting to experience another shared moment with him, they ask for the same story again. Children rarely say, "Hey, that was great, let's do *something else.*" They almost always say, "Let's do that *again.*" We talked about a few ways to tune in and translate what these children might really be saying. I'll just give a couple of our ideas here:

The original version: "What happened with your eye?" (asked for fourth time)

Translation, version 1: "Hey, Frank, remember that wonderful moment we shared last month when you told me about your eye? I felt so good that you answered me in such a relaxed, honest way instead of telling me it wasn't any of my business, and I felt really close to you. Could we do that again?"

The thoughtful response: "I already told you that story a few times, so let's do something else fun together."

Translation, version 2: "I have all kinds of fears and worries and anxieties about people getting sick or getting hurt, either me or people I care about. It's hard to talk about these things. I don't like to let on that I'm scared, and I don't want anyone to think I'm being silly to worry about it. So instead of bringing up my worries directly, I'm going to ask you about your eye again. You see, when you talked to me about your eye, I could tell that you were someone who is calm and relaxed about this topic."

The thoughtful response: "I see you're real interested in my eye. Since you keep asking me to tell you about it, I'm guessing maybe you have some other questions or thoughts that we haven't ever had a chance to talk about."

Tuning in does *not* mean questioning our children about every little detail of their lives. Instead, tell an interesting story from your day; they might respond with a story of their own. Another mistake we make (I catch myself doing this frequently) is cutting them off when they are talking about "unimportant" things, or when they are chattering away about nothing, or when they are repeating themselves. Then, later, we expect them to tell us what *we* want to hear. That's not fair. We have to listen patiently to their way of telling things, even when it is excruciatingly dull to us, if we want them to get around to telling us the good stuff. Understandably, they want to know that we are really listening and aren't going to interrupt them or scold them, before they are going to share anything important with us.

—

The heartfelt connection we all yearn for is locked away within our everyday routine as parents, teachers, and friends. But human connections are always changing, flowing from connection to disconnection to reconnection. *Playful Parenting* can be a guide through these rapid changes. When we join children in their world of play, we unlock the door to their inner lives and meet them heart to heart.

CHAPTER 3

ESTABLISH A CONNECTION

"Now stop!" Max said and sent the wild things off to bed
without their supper. And Max the king of all wild things was
lonely and wanted to be where someone loved him best of all.

—MAURICE SENDAK,
Where the Wild Things Are

In Maurice Sendak's *Where the Wild Things Are*, young Max's mother sends him to bed without his supper for "making mischief of one kind and another" and behaving like a "wild thing." Max imagines his bedroom as a fantasy land of wild things who make him their king. After a while, though, Max becomes lonely and wants to return to the place "where someone loved him best of all." Sailing home, he finds himself back in his room where a warm supper is waiting for him—the sign that all his mischief is forgiven and the connection with his mother is reestablished.

This story has endured for two generations because children and parents alike are moved by the full circle of human connection: the child violates the parent's rules, is punished, then uses fantasy to play out his feelings—confident in the knowledge that he can return home to his mother's love. In *Where the Wild Things Are*, we don't actually see the reunion of Max and his mother; we just see the warm supper and imagine the rest. That's fine for a children's book, but I think adults need a bit more concrete explanation of how actually to go about this complicated business of connecting and reconnecting.

—CONNECTION, DISCONNECTION, AND RECONNECTION—

The drama of connection, disconnection, and reconnection is repeated constantly throughout infancy and childhood. We spend the first nine months directly connected to our mother, sharing her blood and oxygen supply. Then we have to give up all that warm connection so we can have a life of our own. As soon as we come out into the cold air and bright lights, we immediately try to reconnect with our mother for warmth and touch and food. After that, we're looking around again, checking out what else there is in the world.

Connection is easy to recognize but hard to define—perhaps because we experience it in so many different forms at different stages of our lives. Between infants and their primary attachment figures, this bond is sometimes called eye-love,[1] that deep gaze into each other's eyes, that free flow of emotions, that profound sense of belonging here and belonging together, almost melting into one being. Throughout childhood, adolescence, and adulthood, we are continually connecting, disconnecting, and reconnecting with parents, siblings, friends, and spouses. Later we follow this same pattern with our own children. In between is the famous stage of "leave me alone but first drive me to my friend's house."

If all goes well, the eye-love between infants and parents is replaced by a less blissful, but still solid, connection. You and your child are able to talk or play or hang out easily together, enjoying each other, relatively in tune. These moments can be quiet times, like just before falling asleep, or active playtimes. The next level is a more casual connection, an unspoken bond that may be noticed only when it's gone, replaced by conflict or distance.

At the extreme are the most alienated types of disconnection. Disconnection can be a nightmare of painful isolation, withdrawal, and lashing out. I learned the most about disconnection when I worked with men in and out of prison for violent crimes, but even normal, healthy children have moments when they lose that thread of connection. They retreat into towers of isolation when they feel lonely, afraid, or overwhelmed. We may not even know that they feel disconnected, since children rarely come up to us and say, "I feel isolated." When we ask why they are bouncing off the walls, they don't say, "Because I'm lonely."

When everything is going smoothly, Playful Parenting is about having fun together. The rest of the time, Playful Parenting is all about drawing children out of their isolation. Play is children's natural way of recovering from their daily emotional upheavals, so the more fluent we can become in the language of our child's play, the better we can help them complete the circle of reconnection. Reconnecting can be as simple as a baby and mother looking fondly at each other after an outburst of tears has subsided, or a hug after a long day of school, or shaking hands to seal the deal after tough negotiations over a new bedtime. Reconnection might require a bit of rough and tumble, or getting on the floor at children's level, or spending time doing what they most like to do. In some cases family therapy or play therapy may be needed, if the obstacles to connecting as a family are too big.

—FILLING MY CUP: ATTACHMENT AND THE DRIVE TO RECONNECT—

Child psychologists talk about attachment theory all the time, but it still isn't well understood by parents.[2] To help explain attachment, I like to use the metaphor of filling and refilling a cup. The primary caregiver is a child's reservoir, a place to start from and return to, in between explorations. The child's need for attachment with them is like a cup that is emptied by being hungry, tired, lonely, or hurt. The cup is refilled by being loved, fed, comforted, and nurtured. Besides food, warmth, and loving physical contact, a caregiver's refilling includes soothing when the child is upset, and playing and talking when he or she is happy. Mirroring is a simple game in which the baby's cup is filled by reflecting back his facial expressions, smiles, noises, and feelings. As babies grow, their explorations take them further and further afield, but those whose cups have been consistently filled always carry a strong sense of security within them. They are securely attached.

Children who are not securely attached, on the other hand, tend to be either anxious and clingy, or withdrawn and shut down. They may not feel safe, even with the people closest to them, or they may be unable to venture out confidently. They might *appear* adventurous, but insecurely attached children are more likely to be reckless than truly adventurous. Their cup is empty, or nearly empty.

Between return visits for refills, children with a secure attachment can soothe themselves, can handle their emotions, pay attention, connect well with peers, and feel good about themselves and the world. Parents are often quite confused when their toddler bursts into tears at pick-up time, and the day-care provider says, "She's been great all day; I don't know why she's crying." Yet this behavior is actually a sign of secure attachment. When they are with strangers or day-care providers, securely attached children "save up" their bad feelings for when they reunite with their primary attachment figure. (Gee, thanks!)

The infant whose cup is filled to overflowing with affection, security, and attention is lucky indeed. Little upsets may spill some out, a long hard day may drain the cup nearly empty, but the caregiver is always there for a refill. As children get older, just thinking about the caregiver can refill the cup. In fact, securely attached children can get their cup refilled from friendships, from having fun, or from learning something new and interesting in school.

Of course, no one escapes childhood with a perfect attachment history. We all had moments, or even long periods, of frustration and unmet needs. We sometimes wondered where our next refill might be coming from. Our cups stayed empty, or nearly empty, for too long, and we weren't always sure how to get them filled again.

I find it very helpful to look at children's behavior in terms of how they deal with their cups, especially when they are approaching empty. When children are bouncing off the walls, I think of them as racing around trying desperately to get a refill. Instead, they end up sloshing out the little they have left in their cups. Other children demand constant topping off, coming to adults for the tiniest thing—to repeatedly tattle on their playmates, for example. If their cups aren't totally full, they go into a panic. Occasionally, children will clearly need a refill but won't be able to get it. They lock the cap on their cups so they won't lose the little that is left, but then they can't get a refill very easily. Lacking confidence in the refilling process, they might refuse a hug, or refuse to go to bed, or refuse to sit and eat dinner.

Another group is not able to sit still for a refill; being near empty makes them antsy, but being antsy makes getting a refill even less likely.

One behavior that aggravates adults is when children steal (by force or by wits) from other people's cups. They might do this by actually stealing another child's belongings, by hitting, by bossing others around, or by conning a less-powerful child into letting them have the first turn with the best toy. Lately, I have seen more powerful boys pressure less powerful boys into unfair trades of Pokémon cards, and I think of it as a primitive version of accumulation of wealth. Acting up and getting punished can be a way of getting a bit of a refill when it seems that a free fill-up is unavailable. I think this explains the cliché that *bad attention is better than no attention.* A nasty refill is better than none at all. Unfortunately, the usual response, to ignore these children, makes them only more desperate for a refill.

Children who seem to have *leaky* cups are annoying to adults, especially to teachers, who have twenty or thirty other children to care for. The more you cuddle them, the more they cling to you; the more you give, the more they seem to need. They never get a full refill because their leaky cup can't contain everything they get and store it up for later. The metaphor of the leaky cup also helps explain children who try to punch you when you go to give them a hug. Like drowning swimmers who fight off the lifeguard, they are so disoriented by being left empty that they react aggressively when you try to give them a refill. Meanwhile, children with a secure attachment usually seem to have a full cup. They know how to get a refill, sometimes by simply asking, "Can I have an apple?" or "Can I have a hug?" These children also tend to share freely from their own cups instead of competing for every drop. They take care of younger children and help out their friends.

For infants and their main caregivers, attachment—the original filling of the cup—is created inside the intimate space of gazing into each other's eyes, cradling, rocking to sleep, and bouncing on the knee. Attachment also includes exploring the world, first by looking around, then on hands and knees, then on foot, on a bicycle, in a car. Most of this exploration takes place through play. A scraped knee or an altercation with another child may send a young person to the safety of the parent or teacher, but if they manage to get their cup refilled, they are back at play, often with renewed energy and enthusiasm. If the caregiver is not available, or their own reservoir is empty (or stingily guarded), these children won't get their needed refill. Then they may not feel safe enough to play. Or, burying those scared, insecure feelings inside, they might strike out recklessly or aggressively, becoming the terror of the playground.

Through the daily upsets and frustrations of life, as well as through major illnesses, traumas, and losses, young people's cups get depleted. Their cups empty faster when they are yelled at, hit, neglected, or harshly punished. Children count on us for refills, and they feel hurt and betrayed when we knock their cups over instead. This betrayal is even worse when an adult actually *cracks* a child's cup, through abuse or neglect. A cup with deep cracks in it is hard to ever refill. This child may need a full repair, which takes a concerted effort by parents and/or good therapy. Children whose cups can't hold a refill are so used to being on empty that they actually look empty—that cold hard look of "nobody home," which signals that they may be either deeply depressed or dangerous.

But even the most loved and well-cared-for child, with no major losses or traumas, whose cup is in good shape, seems to have a bottomless need for love. His or her cup may be intact, but it still needs almost constant refilling. Therefore, the most important thing we have to offer to our children is our ability to make them feel loved, respected, wanted, and welcome.

Filling and refilling the child's cup is the basis of heartfelt parent-child connections. It isn't something that happens once, but over and over again, in countless mini-interactions over a span of years. I agree with Stanley Greenspan that attachment isn't just about being connected, it's about getting a big kick out of being alive and out of interacting with other human beings.[3] So a real refill can occur only between humans—not between a child and a television set or computer, no matter how "interactive" it may be. Years of research have shown that the key to secure attachment is responsiveness—a sensitive response to the child's needs by the caregiver. Video screens can offer many useful things: entertainment, information, even distraction from stress. But they can't make goofy faces, give hugs, or provide a deep sense of safety and security.

—PLAYING TOWARD CONNECTION—

Research into primates shows that our closest biological kin play for many of the same reasons we do. Bonobo chimps, for example, tickle and chase one another, tease one another, and have even been seen to play a game that looks exactly like blindman's bluff. Even more significantly, like humans, they play to reconnect after connection has been severed. Some psychologists believe that many expressions of affection evolved from the message "I could hurt you, but I am not." Kissing means "I could be biting you, but I am not"; caressing means "I could be hitting you, but I am not." Waving and shaking hands both say, "Hey, look, I don't have a weapon." In other words, pretend playing at aggression is a very real way to reconnect or show affection.

For very young children, mirroring is a perfect connection game: just do exactly what the baby or toddler does. My favorite way to get a smile from a serious-looking baby is to match their serious expression exactly. One toddler, the baby brother of my daughter's classmate, would sometimes shake his leg as he sat in his stroller outside the classroom. One time I started shaking my leg the same way, and he cracked up. He started going faster, and I went faster. More laughing. After that, every time he saw me he'd start shaking his leg. His mother would say, "Hey, Larry, he's doing that leg thing again," and I'd look over and he'd be shaking his leg like crazy, trying to get my attention. Older kids love this game, too—in the nature of Simon says or follow the leader—as long as you are careful that they don't feel teased. Mirroring can create a fun moment of closeness or a deeply felt connection.

Mirroring does not have to stop when children get older. I will often try to stand or walk exactly like an older child, both as a way to connect with them and as a way to "get into their shoes," especially if they don't talk much. It's important to make sure the child does not feel mocked, but most of the time they are amused or even proud, like the boy at the concert whom I described in the first chapter. He started out too timid to dance, but with a little mirroring ended up leading the dance rather than feeling too shy to jump in.

Even abstract concepts like cause and effect are learned by babies through play and close relationships. There's a game in which the baby gurgles, the parent repeats the noise, and the baby smiles. In the "advanced gurgle" stage, the baby gurgles, the parent gurgles, the baby gurgles, everybody smiles. Before a baby can pull the string on a toy in his crib, he pulls at his mother's and father's heartstrings—the first building block of play.[4]

The ultimate connecting game for babies is peekaboo. Peekaboo not only builds closeness, it plays with the very idea of closeness in a dramatic way—now you see me, now you don't, now I'm back. Peekaboo reflects the delicate balance of connection and loss of connection, presence and absence. If you're old enough to remember the guy with all the spinning plates on *The Ed Sullivan Show*, you know that a precarious balance can be immensely entertaining. It's not quite so much fun for us as for our baby, because *we know* that we are still there, even when we're hiding behind the blanket. But baby is just figuring that out. We know that baby is there even though we ask, over and over again, "Where's baby? Where did baby go?" And we're not really surprised when we exclaim, "There she is! There's baby!" But *baby* is surprised, at least a little, each time. Eventually, the surprise gives way to delighted collusion, like six-year-olds who like to sustain the idea of the tooth fairy even if they know it's their mom or dad fiddling around under the pillow with the loose change.

In peekaboo, the baby can symbolically lose the connection and then quickly regain it. If you experiment with the time it takes to say peekaboo, from half a second, say, to two or three seconds, you can find exactly the length of time that brings the most giggles. Too short and there's no mystery; too long and it's too scary; and there you have the essence of the human romance with connection and disconnection and reconnection.

—THE END OF BLISSFUL EYE GAZING—

Mirroring, cuddling, talking, and singing to babies, showing them the world in child-size pieces—these are the prototypes of play, the forerunners of all the fun times that children and parents will have together, from hide-and-seek to late-night talks to hikes in the woods. Luckily, babies can get us to smile just by lying there. As psychologist John Briere says: "Babies emit cuteness so that adults will emit smoochums." In fact, babies who won't or can't connect on this level are generally identified early, and perhaps diagnosed as having autism or a related disorder.

Sadly, when older children don't connect, it often goes unnoticed. For some reason, after the initial bonding stage between infant and parents, distance and awkwardness set in. Adults seldom play with older children with as much freedom and ease as they did during those early games of peekaboo. Not many parents have experienced that profound bliss of deep, loving eye gazing with a child over age two. Not many even know it's possible to regain. It's as if we don't really expect those close connections to last. When I encourage parents to engage their children age three, or six, or even older, in soulful eye contact, they usually start out quite skeptical, but if they persist through the initial rejections, and get to that deeper level of closeness, they find it to be one of the most rewarding exercises.

Fortunately, when the disconnection is not severe, children give us many opportunities to reestablish the connection. The problem is, we often misread these invitations. I blush to think of all the times I have pushed my daughter away when she wanted to cuddle, because I was busy, or I thought she should be doing her homework, or I felt annoyed by her demands for attention. Then other times I ask her how school is, and it's like pulling teeth. I don't always put two and two together. If I don't connect on her terms, why should she connect on mine?

Sometimes the adult and the child figure out the connection business together, by trial and error. My nine-year-old nephew doesn't talk a lot, especially about what is on his mind or what may be bothering him. I always used to try to cajole him into talking, by begging and pleading or by joking with him about it. That was fun, but it didn't get him to say much. Then one time on a family vacation I just sat with him. It was early in the morning, and we were the only ones up. I held out my arms and he climbed onto my lap and sat there. Neither of us said a word for more than half an hour. I usually hate long silences and hate sitting around "doing nothing," but this wasn't boring. We were truly close. When everyone else came down for breakfast, I said, "Great talking to you." We both laughed, but I meant it. With no pressure to communicate my way— using words—we were able to connect just fine.

—FINDING CONNECTION
EVERYWHERE: THE LOVE GUN—

Once I realized how important connection is, I started seeing it everywhere, even in the most unlikely places, like down the barrel of a squirt gun. One of my daughter's friends came over to play one day. He was six. He quickly found the only gun in the house, a squirt gun, and aimed it at my face. He had "the look," perfected from watching movies and TV, the look that says, "I've got a gun, and you don't."

Fortunately, I knew the squirt gun was empty, so I had a little time to think while he was taking aim and waiting to see what my reaction would be. I remembered all my conversations with parents about how much young boys love to play with guns, and what (if anything) can or should be done about it. One thing I knew was the importance of making a connection with these boys, to insert some connection into the play, no matter how aggressive or solitary the play appears to be, because boys are especially prone to feeling isolated. And, of course, their aggressive play tends to isolate them more.

So, thinking all those things (in the space of about two seconds), I said, "Hey, you found the love gun." He hesitated a little, thrown off by my response. He even looked at the gun in a puzzled way, shocked that this weapon of destruction might have anything to do with *love*. I said, "Oh, yeah, when I get shot with that gun, I just have to *love* the person who shot me." And I opened up my arms wide and took a step toward him with a big, goofy, lovestruck grin on my face.

He fired the gun once, squealed in delight, threw the gun to the floor, and ran out of the room laughing. I chased him and hugged him when I caught him, hamming it up about how much I loved him. He was laughing and laughing. My daughter picked up the gun then and shot me, and I left him to chase after her, putting my hand to my heart and making up bad poetry about my lifelong devotion to her. For at least a half hour, the two of them took turns shooting me, running away, saying, "Yuck, go away, stop loving me," and giggling up a storm.

The next time this boy came to our house a few weeks later, I had forgotten about this episode. He went straight for the gun and aimed it at me. I said, "Don't aim that at me," in that familiar, annoyed, grown-up voice. He said, with that patient voice children use when they realize they are talking to a clueless adult, "But it's the love gun." I remembered, and we played the game again. More giggles.

Since then I have played this game a lot, both with gun-toting boys and when children's play turns to kicking, punching, biting, or spitting. "You got me with a love kick, now I have to hug you." Sometimes they'll say, "No, this is a hate gun." I just say, "Oh, it must be broken because it's making me love you."

Of course, this approach is only for aggressive *play*, not for situations when children want to directly express their feelings of anger or frustration. In these cases, it is very important to hear them out, to allow the feelings to come out, rather than try to cheer them up or cajole them out of feeling bad. This disclaimer is especially true for girls, who are given so many messages not to be angry. I watch carefully to make sure the child is not feeling humiliated by my response to their play. I also make sure that *I* don't get hurt, but I generally do that by holding them close rather than by sending them away. Whether playing or listening or holding, the key is to push for a close and meaningful connection.

The game of love gun has infinite variations: If they barricade themselves in a room, I slip love notes under the door and beg and plead to be allowed in. If they laugh and start sending messages back, I know I'm on the right track. If they come at me with both arms swinging, I say, "Oh, you want to dance, I'd love to dance," and I take both their hands and start dancing and singing. It seems like a cliché to say that all of those behaviors adults find so annoying or threatening are just attempts to make a human connection, but this game shows how true it is.

In fact, I couldn't begin to list all the children's games that are about connection. Chase, tag, follow the leader, and hide-and-seek are obvious examples. Play these games with your child—you'll not only have fun, you'll notice an improvement in your relationship with them. One of my favorites is a game I call *you'll never get away*. I say, "You'll never be able to get away from me, never in a million years!" The child comes over to check this out. I hold on to them, and after a little struggle I let them escape. Very simple. To make it more interesting, I pretend not to notice for a minute that they have escaped: "You see, you'll never get away. . . . Hey, how did you do that?" If they like it (and I have had success with this game with two-year-olds up to eleven-year-olds), I keep it up, saying, "Okay, you think you're so strong. This time I will use the famous Franklinheimer Maneuver; no one has ever gotten out of that," or some-thing equally goofy, and they manage to get out again. With some chil-dren, I gradually increase the resistance so they must increase the effort it takes them to get away—they seem to thrive on the growing challenge. If they don't like to be held, I pretend to hold them with my "psychic powers" and dare them to try to escape.

A mother in a parenting class reported this dialogue she had with her son after a class we had on connecting through play:

"We need to do some connecting. How do you want to connect?"

"What do you mean?"

"Well, we seem to be disconnected. You want to be wild when I want to rest; you want my attention when I have to make dinner; you want to go watch TV when I want to spend time with you. Stuff like that."

"So what are we supposed to do about it?"

"We could have a cuddle, or play a game together, or wrestle, or something. . . ."

"Can I jump on your bed?"

"Sure, let's make it a game."

"Okay, how about if I jump on the bed and you have to try to catch me."

They proceeded to have a very fun, giggly playtime together, with lots of hugs and cuddles (this was a boy who ordinarily avoided hugs from his mom like the plague). This reflects one of my basic rules of Play-ful Parenting: *It works best when the adult provides the insistence on con-necting, but the child actually sets the terms of how the two are going to connect.* Notice how this mother pointed out the need to connect but didn't impose any particular way. Instead she listed some vague possibilities, just to explain the concept, until her son jumped in with an idea.

—UNLOCKING THE TOWER OF ISOLATION—

I was getting ready to leave a boy's house after a great first session of play therapy, when he called after me, "You're a stinker." I came back around the corner and he stepped back, worried that I would scold him. I whispered to him, "Shhh, don't tell anyone my secret name—only my closest friends call me Stinker." He replied, as expected, "Mommy! Larry's secret name is Stinker!" I said, "Hey, you gave away my secret name, waaah!" He laughed, then got suddenly serious: "You're a stinker, and I hate you."

By this time I had figured out that he just wanted me to stay longer. I've noticed that, for some reason, most people don't recognize "You're a stinker" as a child's version of an engraved invitation to be close. It really means, "I like you." I guess it's the same language junior-high boys use to show they like a girl. So I said, "Oh, I had a great time playing with you, too, and I really like you, too. It's hard to say good-bye." He thought about this for a moment, then said, in a very relaxed tone of voice, "Could we just do the sock game one more time?" I said that we could. After we played that game again, he proudly walked me out to my car and waved wildly as I pulled out, saying to his mother, "He's coming back again next week." The key to unlocking the tower was just translating his insult into a request for some connection.

In this next story, there was literally a locked door between the child and myself, but nevertheless a connection was reestablished. I was starting a play-therapy session with Gerry at his house. As soon as we started playing, he ran into his room, closed the door, and locked it. Now a lot of people would think that's the end. How can you keep playing after that? You can either force the door open, or you can leave. In Playful Parenting, however, there is a third option. Keep inviting the child to connect, but offer to do it their way, on their terms. In this case, after a few minutes of confusion and futile knocking on the door, I wrote love notes and passed them under the door. Gerry couldn't read yet, so I would write them and then read them out loud to him. I would say, "I love you; please come out and play," and stick it under the door. He'd rip it up and throw it back under the door at me. The one word he could write was "Boo," so he'd write "Boo" on a piece of paper and slip it out; then I'd scream "Aaagh" and act real scared. Then I'd come back and write a new note, again reading it out loud as I slipped it under the door: "I'm scared, but nothing can keep me away from you." This was a very fun game, but the emotional issues involved ran deep.

I had been asked to come play with Gerry because he was refusing to go to his grandmother's. His parents were planning to leave him with her for a few days so they could have more time to pack for an upcoming move. His little sister, though, was going to stay with the parents because she was still nursing. Obviously this stirred up a cauldronful of feelings in him: sibling rivalry, unfairness, the upcoming transition of the move, being left behind, and so on. Let me stress that this was a happy, well-loved child. He loved his grandmother and usually couldn't wait to go visit her. His feelings were strong but totally normal.

When he first locked himself in his room, Gerry insisted that he was not going to his grandmother's and I couldn't make him. And besides he hated me and I was stupid. After a half hour of note passing, Gerry called through the door, "Okay, I'll come out, but no hugging." Since I had never mentioned anything about hugging, I took this as my cue, and implored, "Oh, please, just one little tiny hug." He giggled and ended up spending the last fifteen minutes of my visit cuddling in my lap.

I told him I had to leave, but I'd see him after he came back from his grandmother's. He yelled, "I'm not going!" I said, "Oh no, does this mean we have to do the whole door thing again?" We both laughed. By the time I got home, a few minutes later, his mother had left a message on my answering machine. As soon as I left the house, Gerry started planning his visit to his grandmother's. He began to pack and made a list of toys he would bring. His cup of attachment, emptied by the strain of feeling as if he were going to be left behind by his parents, was filled by a round of play that addressed this theme directly.

Reconnection takes persistence. One of my nieces and I have a little ritual when I see her. I say hi to her, and she ignores me. I keep saying hi, in a relaxed and cheerful tone, until she says hi back. We then laugh about how many times it took. Sometimes I'll try saying it in funny voices. I insist on contact, but it is a gentle insistence, not a harsh and punitive one. This is a good game for us because I love her feistiness (her favorite expression last year was "I don't want to, I don't have to!"), but I also want to make sure we connect. Eventually, we always do, and we have a great time together. Often by the forty-seventh "hi," her siblings and cousins are gathered around, wondering how long it's going to take, and everyone is giggling. Of course, this amount of persistence can't be achieved all the time, or else with some children you would be doing nothing else. But now and then it is important to stick with it.

Any play can be the doorway to connection. When a child pretends to shoot you and says "You're dead," try falling over dead, in a dramatic death scene, right on top of him. Grab his leg and beg him to bring you to a doctor. If the child squirms away, go into even more dramatic death throes that bring you right back on top (as long as the young person giggles and enjoys the game, of course). If your daughter calls you a stupid idiot, try being so stupid you can't tell her from a pillow, and try to take a nap on top of her. I sometimes refer to this aspect of Playful Parenting as "it takes a village idiot to raise a child."

When preteens act cool, pretending you don't exist, ask them if you can have the gum they are chewing so you can get close to them any way you possibly can. That's guaranteed to get a rise out of them. (You don't have to really chew it if they do hand it over, unless you are a stickler for full authenticity.) Or start a pillow fight with them, or a wrestling match. Even the most disconnected behavior usually leaves some window open somewhere for connection.

If reconnecting is so great, then why is it so hard? When people disconnect, they often have to struggle through a pile of bad feelings, like terror or abandonment or loss, in order to restart a connection. Reconnecting can thus be very painful emotionally, so children tend to avoid it. Adults often shy away from reconnection for the same reasons. The intensity of the feelings may be too much for a child, so they lock themselves deeper in the tower of isolation. Better to be lonely than to face directly all those tender feelings.

In the last chapter I talked about the value of tuning in to your children. In terms of connection, tuning in to a child fills her cup, and tuning out empties it. So even if we don't like what we see when we tune in, we still have to tune in first. They need to feel connected and confident before they can make any positive changes. So once again, *get down on the floor and play what they want to play*. With older children, tuning in may mean sitting with them and listening to the music they like and watching the movies they rent. Yuck. But do it.

—WHO IS THAT HOLDING YOU? MOVING FROM CASUAL CONNECTION TO DEEP CONNECTION—

Besides play, being close also involves many types of nonplayful interactions between parents and children, such as comforting and holding children when they are crying. The title of this section comes from an ongoing series of episodes between my wife, our daughter, and myself. When Emma was two, Anne began her internship in family medicine, meaning that she was at the hospital all night every fourth night. This went on for a few years. When she would come home, Anne would be totally exhausted from working thirty-six hours; I would be tired from single-parenting, and Emma would act as if nothing had happened. She would say hello to Anne and then go back to doing whatever she was doing before.

At first, nothing seemed amiss, but it was. It became apparent only on the days Anne was less tired than usual and she tried to get Emma's attention and play with her. At that point, Emma would studiously ignore and avoid her. When Anne picked her up, she would look anywhere but into her mother's eyes. Watching Anne try to make eye contact while Emma squirmed around was both funny and sad. At the same time, we noticed that Emma wanted only *me* to put her to bed, give her a bath, read to her, and so on. Many times, given how tired Anne was from being up all night, we just went along with this. Sometimes, even the next night, she wanted only me. Slowly, we began to put the pieces together and realized that the two of them needed some concentrated attention on reconnecting. My job, as the relatively well-rested parent and the one whose connection hadn't been disrupted, was to help them.

What we had was a *casual connection* between parent and child rather than a *deep connection*.[5] Children who have not been terribly traumatized can generally go about their business fairly well for a while with only a casual connection, and the effects of the lack of deep connection may not be seen right away. So Emma could say hello and keep on playing happily, though she was, in fact, disconnected from her mom. The pain of this disconnection was buried, and we saw what was happening only when Anne insisted on connection.

Our first step was to have family cuddles, with my encouraging Emma to look at Anne and notice that she was back. Often Emma would cry for a while, and then she would seem much happier and more relaxed. At first we thought that meant we were done, but gradually we realized that the connection was still not fully restored. No, she'd be eager to get back to playing, but she *still* wouldn't look at Anne. She had released some of her sadness about missing her mom, enough to be able to play, but not enough to allow a deep connection.

One time, Anne was holding Emma, who was saying she wanted me to give her a bath and put her to bed. Emma was ignoring her mother so blatantly that I asked, "Who is that holding you?" She said, "Daddy." Anne and I both said, "What?" Emma looked right at me—from Anne's lap—and said, "Daddy's holding me," and then gave a big smile. Anne and I looked at each other, halfway between bewilderment and indignation, while Emma laughed and laughed. Finally she said, "Mommy's holding me," and put her head on Anne's shoulder. Sigh. Over the next few months this question—Who is that holding you?—began to run like a thread through our efforts to reconnect. We could always tell where things stood by Emma's answer. Sometimes just asking the question let her hold on to Anne and cry about having missed her. Other times, she would say "Daddy" or "Nobody," and then look over her shoulder to see if Anne would give up, or if she'd keep insisting on connection. When she said, "Googoohead is holding me," we knew we were in for some serious giggling. Whichever way it went, if we persisted (which was hard, given how tired we adults were), it would always end with Emma saying, "Mommy's holding me," and looking deeply into her eyes. Connection reestablished.

I think this interaction played out the way it did because the traditional roles were reversed. Because Anne was the mom, she wasn't going to let their connection slip away so easily. Because I was the dad, I knew I didn't want to have the "honor" of always being the one to put her to bed, read to her, change her diaper, and on and on. I started wondering how many fathers, who come home tired after work, just say "the hell with it" when their children push them away and resist connection. It is easy to miss the fact that children really do want to connect when they look as if they want to be left alone. The child thinks, Dad cares more about work than he does about me. Besides, I miss him so much it hurts. So I'll play it cool and make him come after me. Dad thinks, I'm just a paycheck. The hell with this. If he wants to play with me, he knows where to find me.

In more ordinary, everyday types of interactions, play creates an opportunity to express love and nurturing, gently repairing the wounds of earlier conflicts or upsets. One mother I worked with started a routine with her daughter of tenderly putting all the Beanie Babies to bed each evening. On days when this mother and daughter had been fussing and whining at each other, this ritual was especially poignant and sweet, as it seemed to relieve the tension for both of them. The mom could say things to the stuffed animals she might not be able to say directly to the child, such as, "We had a hard day; I hope you have sweet dreams." The child might say to one of them, "You've been very naughty; you have to sleep under the bed," allowing her mom the chance to say, "Oh, I think she feels real sorry and she could be in bed with the others; what do you think?" There is no end to the ways people can use play to mend a relationship that matters to them.

CHAPTER 4

ENCOURAGE THEIR CONFIDENCE

"I will never give up!"
—EMMA COHEN, AGE FOUR

One day I was wrestling with my daughter when she was around four years old. We were playing a game we had played a few times before, in which she would try to get past me to the couch and I would try to stop her. I tried to get her to plow through me, making contact and using her physical strength instead of trying to trick me and sneak around the side. As we wrestled, I added more and more resistance, making it harder and harder for her to push past me and get to the couch. She had to use more and more of her strength, and she was wrestling hard.

At the same time that I was trying to get her to exert her power and build her physical confidence, I was also encouraging her. An important part of wrestling with a young person is playing both of those roles, not getting so caught up in the competition that you forget whose side you are on (theirs!). I could see her beginning to get a little frustrated and starting to think about giving up. I tried increasing my encouragement, but that didn't seem to help. My next thought was to try to push her into a powerful position, by getting her annoyed with me just enough to fight her hardest, while still knowing that this game was for her, that I was on her side. I started pretending to taunt her using an exaggerated, obnoxious voice, saying, "Why don't you just give up? You'll never make it to the couch."

At that she stopped wrestling, stormed out of the room, and disappeared around the corner. I thought for sure that I had blown it; I had pushed too hard or gone too far. Perhaps I hadn't made it clear enough that I wasn't really teasing her, but rather egging her on in a friendly way. All those thoughts were racing through my head as I thought about whether to chase after her and apologize, or give her time to cool off. Before I could decide, she came back around the corner with her fists raised triumphantly in the air and a wide smile on her face. "I will NEVER give up," she shouted, as she tackled me and used twice as much strength as she had before to try to knock me over.

She had an easy time getting past me, because I was bowled over by her burst in confidence. I asked her what happened, and she said, "I went to the power room and got more power." Later she explained that she had pretended to put a special lotion on her that would give her more power. Like Dumbo the elephant, who discovered that he could fly even without his magic feather, she had discovered a self-sustaining source of confidence and power.

For months after that day, we would both get a big laugh out of my pretending to forget her magnificent line as she entered the room. "I will *sometimes* give up? . . . I will *kind of* give up? . . . I will give up only if it's too hard? . . . What was it?" She would throw her fists back up in the air and say it again, radiating self-confidence, "I will *never* give up." Years later, she still returns to the power room when she faces a special challenge, particularly physical challenges like being tired on a hike with a long way yet to go. And when playing is hard for me—when I get bored or tired or frustrated—I often duck into the power room myself and decide again never to give up. Then I can go back to playing with heart.

—POWER AND POWERLESSNESS—

The power room is an example of using play—in this case, wrestling—to promote confidence. Sadly, when I look around at children, I see too little of this quality. I see children who are scared, timid, and intimidated. They are fearful of speaking their own minds or even thinking their own thoughts. I also see plenty of recklessness, bravado, violence, nastiness, and bossiness, but none of those is really self-confidence. Where is the true power? Why is it so rare?

The answer starts with our society, which is ambivalent about power. We seek it and admire it, but we mistrust it. We are especially ambivalent about power in children. We applaud the "good" kind of power, like when a child stands up for a friend, but we don't really want them to stand up to us. We want them to be assertive, self-assured, and poised, but not abusive, bossy, or pushy. We admire physical strength and gracefulness, courage and self-confidence, while we punish aggression and bullying. Adding to the confusion, mothers are often accused of letting their children have too much power—by spoiling them and not disciplining them enough. At the same time, *empowerment* is a buzzword in psychology, and all efforts are supposed to be made to empower children.

We use the same word—*power*—to apply to vastly different things. To avoid confusion, unless it is obvious, I generally use the word *confidence* to refer to the positive side of power—the power to stand up for what is right, the power to be adventurous (within safe limits), the power to know your own inner strength, the power to achieve a goal, the power of happy play. On the other side is powerlessness, which often looks like passivity, inhibition, timidity, fearfulness, whining. Another type of powerlessness, what I call pseudo-power, offers up a hollow imitation of power. This category includes biting, hitting, threatening, bossing, stealing, intimidating, and reckless disregard for safety. Playful Parenting helps children out of the traps of powerlessness and pseudo-power, tipping the balance in favor of true power, confidence, and competence.

Fortunately, development is on our side, since most children experience waves of the healthy kind of power as they meet the world and make it their own. The first wave of confidence comes from the infant's power to get his basic needs met. The baby exposes his vulnerability and love and cuteness; the caretaker responds with food, shelter, love, and warmth. At first, infants experience themselves as all-powerful: *I cry and milk arrives at my lips. I smile at a face, and it smiles back.*

But then, frustrations and disappointments inevitably start to mount for the infant. *I cry, and nothing happens. I cry some more, and still nothing happens. I smile, and nothing happens. I want something, and it doesn't appear. Mom wants something different from what I want.* A little of this frustration is necessary for a child to develop, but too much leads to powerlessness. Infants also face an enormous number of things that are out of their control: when and how their needs are met, whether their caregivers are happy or sad, where they go and what they see. Of course, they have some power—they can cry or fall asleep or close their eyes or reward good parental behavior with a smile—but they clearly don't call all the shots.

Infants learn just about everything through interaction. It has become a cliché to say that the parent is the baby's first and best toy, but I think it is true. Physical closeness, with lots of eye contact and an animated tone of voice, teaches babies about the most important element of their world—other humans. These everyday playtimes also allow the child to process the nonstop streams of information coming in through their senses. Swinging, rocking, and riding in the stroller teach them about gravity and motion. Making the rattle shake and then stop, making it disappear and reappear—these simplest magic tricks teach the baby the basic rules of the universe, things we take for granted.

The second wave of confidence is the toddler's power to say no, to assert herself as a separate being. If this power is respected but safely contained (with firm, loving limits), then the growing child can assert her own identity without hurting anyone, including herself. The toddler also continues the infant's incredible pace of learning about the world, and making it her own. Just watch a toddler with a busy board, or on a climbing structure, or in a play group, and you'll see minute-by-minute strides in developing competence and confidence.

When parents are scared or annoyed by this growing independence and assertiveness, they may crack down too hard, squashing the child's spirit. One consistent finding of research into child abuse is that physical abuse increases dramatically when children reach eighteen months to two years in age, right when they are starting to have a will of their own. Instead of seeing toddler willfulness as a child's healthy drive toward independence, these parents interpret it as defiance and disrespect and so-called willful disobedience. The response is excessive punishment or violent outbursts. If parents don't provide any limits, and the toddler rules the roost, the child can feel out of control, a different type of power-lessness. The middle ground is to recognize and even enjoy the burst in independence, while providing the safety and structure of clear limits.

The third wave of confidence is the child's power to make his or her place in the world, including in the world of other children. Starting in preschool and extending into adolescence, children learn to play games, to swing on monkey bars, to make friends, to read and write. Their world explodes with new things, new people, and new ways to feel either power-ful or powerless. For some children, winning and losing become emo-tionally charged. All children experience frustration as they go through school—whether it is the strain of mastering fractions or the anxiety of not fitting in with the group. As adolescence approaches, young people are sucked into the youth culture, which offers them a complex mix of empowerment and disempowerment. They choose a style of music and clothing that horrifies their parents, but are they truly exerting their own power, or just slavishly following the dictates of the fashion and enter-tainment industries?

Powerlessness creeps in as a result of the setbacks children experi-ence as they strive to feel confident and self-assured. They can't do things as well as their older siblings or their peers, so they feel frustrated. They are criticized and punished and given grades, so they feel judged. They are flooded with messages about how they are supposed to behave, how they are supposed to look, what they are supposed to buy, so they feel inade-quate. The combined effect of these feelings leads children to retreat to the fortress of powerlessness, either down to the hidden dungeons (pas-sivity), or up to the battlements (aggressive pseudo-power).

The Playful Parenting approach to confidence and powerlessness helps children and parents at every stage of this developmental sequence. All of these healthy aspects of power, these opportunities for competence and confidence, can be fostered through play and playfulness. No one slides through childhood without some feelings of frustration, helpless-ness, and powerlessness. When powerlessness rears its ugly head—and it inevitably will—Playful Parenting can help children back to confidence and competence.

—EXPERIMENTING WITH POWER:
PLAYING THE POOPYHEAD GAME—

I wish I had a nickel for every time I've been called a poopyhead. I've been called many other names, but that one best captures the overlap between the young child's two great loves: bathroom humor and name-calling. These are both very much related to power: the power to control one's bodily functions and the power to hurt someone's feelings. I have developed two simple games to play with these themes. When I am called a poopyhead, I say, "Shhh, don't tell everybody my secret name!" Like clockwork, they shout out, to whoever may be listening, "Larry's secret name is Poopyhead!" I say, "Ha-ha—I was just kidding, my *real* secret name is Rice Krispies Cake" (the sillier the better, since the object is to break the tension about name-calling with some serious giggling). "Larry's secret name is Rice Krispies Cake!" "No, no, I beg you, *pleeeease* don't tell anyone!" I've played this game with some children for hours.

The other game is just as simple. The child says some word that mom or dad doesn't want him or her to say—usually a body part or a bathroom word or an obscenity. I say, "Well, you can say that all you want, but if you say Bobbledyboo you're gonna be in big trouble." "Bobbledyboo!" "Oh, ho, ho," I say, "now you're in trouble." I say this lightly, not in a mean, scary way, as I chase the child around the room. Occasionally, an inhibited child needs a whispered hint that it really is okay to say Bobbledyboo, that I will just *pretend* to get them in trouble. Simple, huh? It always works. They not only giggle like crazy and love the game, but they actually stop being so obsessed with saying those other words.

These games are not simply reverse psychology. It isn't just a matter of manipulating children's rebellion into getting them to do what you want. The poopyhead game lets children experiment with power—the power of words and the power to break rules. Instead of having them experiment on other children, which always causes hurt feelings, let them try out that name-calling and bathroom humor on you. This helps us step out of the power struggle and into play.

Speaking of power struggles, a man in my fathers' group told me about a game he invented for his daughter when she was little and didn't want to have her fingernails or toenails trimmed. My friend discovered that trying to force her didn't work, because she would fight and squiggle around. Either she'd get hurt or he'd be too afraid of hurting her to get near her with the scissors. The new game was called stop and go, and it went like this: Dad started a few feet away, holding the nail scissors. He told her that when she said "stop," he would stop immediately, and he wouldn't go again until she said "go." If she didn't say "go" after a short while, he could say it himself, but he would still have to stop when she said "stop." She couldn't just say "stop-stop-stop-stop" real fast (this rule was added later, as she tried to test the limits of the game). When she said "stop," he would stop in his tracks as if he were frozen, which always brought a giggle or two (already they were way ahead, since nail-cutting had never been associated with giggles before). When she said "go" he would inch toward her.

Eventually the nails got cut, and, even more important, they had fun. Stopping on a dime when she said "stop" built the trust that he wouldn't hurt her or force her. Putting her in charge of his coming forward loosened up the whole situation. He decided when it was nail-cutting time, but she was in charge of how fast it would be done. Parents often groan when I tell this story, saying, "Where am I going to find the time to play a game every time I have to cut fingernails, or change a diaper, or give a bath?" They conveniently forget the amount of time they are already spending fighting or pleading or being annoyed. I believe it is always worth the investment of time up front, even if your ultimate goal is to have to spend less time on these mundane activities. Actually, though, it can become such a fun game that it no longer counts as a chore.

—PREPARING YOUR CHILD FOR THE WORLD—

Bill Harley, a children's entertainer, said about his third-grade teacher:

> Mrs. Nottingham was from the old school. She was very strict. . . . She taught us all sorts of things, math, spelling, reading, but what she really taught us was, *it's a cold, cruel world.*[1]

Many parents subscribe to some version of this cold-cruel-world philosophy, believing they have to prepare children for the hardships of life by getting them used to it. But if life is really that difficult, then we don't need *more* beatings and humiliations and losses than we will get anyway. What children really need is to be secure and self-confident, and that comes from being loved and well cared for. Not protected from every little bump and bruise, but not toughened up either. Toughening people up in order to help them face the world's dangers hasn't worked too well, as we can see from the epidemic level of violence among boys and men, who get the cold-cruel-world message relentlessly. The ones who take the message to heart seem the most prone to violence. I still remember vividly the first time I saw the slogan on a Vietnam-era military cap: "Kill 'em all; let God sort 'em out later." I think that is the logical end point of the cold-cruel-world training. Be prepared for that world out there where you can't trust anyone and you're totally on your own and danger lurks behind every bush.

Of course, some people go too far the other way, trying to protect their little angels from the world, cushioning them from every blow. That doesn't prepare them for life either; it just creates fearfulness and timidity. We prepare children best by both *nurturing* them and *challenging* them. My metaphor for this combination is bricks and mortar; you can't build a strong wall with just one or the other. Children gain an inner strength— the mortar—from being loved and nurtured, having their needs met, knowing they are loved no matter what. They get a different kind of confidence—the bricks—from being challenged and playing their hardest. If they are treated with tenderness and respect while they overcome increasingly difficult challenges, they are truly prepared for the world. For example, I might keep encouraging children to try something new, like Rollerblading, but offer to hold their hand for as long as they want me to.

A group of four-year-olds were asked if they'd rather play with playmates or parents. Most of them chose their parents. Are you surprised? With their parents, they said, they could win, they could be in charge. Other children don't usually give in to make the playing field more level.[2] By bossing their mom or dad around, or beating them at basketball, they

get a refill of their attachment needs, and then they can go out and manage the more-or-less level playing fields with peers.

The idea of preparing children for the cold, cruel world is a significant factor in the realm of winning and losing at games. The effect is
strongest in sports, but it is also present in games like chess or checkers.
Fathers tend to take the cold-cruel-world approach more than mothers,
and especially with their sons. Many fathers insist to me that they *never*
let their sons win, because boys need to be prepared for competitions
with peers, who won't throw the game to them. But a grown man going
full out against a child isn't exactly fair either. What does that prepare you
for? Oh yeah, the cold, cruel world.

Take the question that I am asked over and over again, "When do I
stop letting my child beat me at checkers?" This is one of my favorite
questions, even though there isn't a simple answer. You want to accom-
plish so much with a simple game of checkers. You want him to enjoy
himself; you want him to improve his skills; you want him to be a little
competitive but not too competitive; you want him to be a good sport
when he wins and a good sport when he loses; you want him to know that
his peers aren't going to let him win like you do.

In general, you start out letting them win, and then slowly play
harder and harder. But it may go back and forth for a while, and even
when children can beat you fair and square, they may still want to play by
the "special rules" now and then. Sometimes they want to win; sometimes
they want a challenge. I think the best thing is to follow their lead. You
may have switched to fair play, or maybe you've started playing medium-
hard, and then a game comes along and the child signals that he or she
wants to win. Or maybe it's the other way around. You've been letting the
child win, and he or she starts to signal that more of a challenge is in order. Children probably won't come right out and say it, so be alert for
subtle signals, like, "This is boring." Or, "Did you let me win?" You can
answer, "Well, I didn't play my hardest; do you want me to?" Maybe they
gloat over winning, even though you let them win. You could say, "Should
I play my hardest so you don't win all the time?" Then see how it goes. If
it goes well, over time they will balance the enjoyment of winning—even
unfairly—with the enjoyment of a challenging match—even if they lose.

You may also need to spend some time directly on the child's feelings about competition. Children will signal that they need special attention to these feelings about winning, losing, and competition by being very upset over losing a game or very obnoxious about winning. In that case, switch gears from playing the game to playing with these themes. For example, set up a game where they will always win, and pretend to be a ridiculous figure of a sore loser. Or brag about how great you are, then miss every shot—whatever helps them laugh and release that feeling of life or death over the outcome of the game. Make up a game with a funny rule, like, "No hitting me with this pillow," and then act goofy when they—surprise—hit you with it. "You cheated! Waaah!"

Kevin, age five, had just started playing soccer, and he was very excited about it. I arrived for our play-therapy session, and he had on his shin guards and cleats and was holding his ball, waiting to play soccer with me. We went outside, and he marked off the goals. Before we started to play, he said, "Be easy, I'm just a kindergartner." I said, "Okay," and I took my cue from this—he didn't want too big a challenge, at least at first. He wanted to gain confidence. So I didn't play very hard. I let him score goals and didn't score any myself.

When I started trying a little harder on defense, he got nervous. He said, "Freeze," and I froze in place, while he dribbled around me and scored. I said, in a pretend-outraged tone, "Hey, how can I defend the goal if I'm frozen?" He said, "That's the rule, you freeze when I say so until I unfreeze you." Then he kicked the ball backward through the goal and said, "I get another point if I kick it backward through the goal." I said, "Oh, do I get that, too?" "No, just me!" Big pretend tantrum from me: "Waaah, that's not fair." Big giggles from him. Eventually, he started letting me get the ball once in a while, but I made sure at first to be bumbling and incompetent. I would dribble up near his goal, then pretend to be spending a lot of time lining up my shot, bragging about how I was going to score a goal. I would take so long that he would come and kick it away from me. I would pretend to be surprised and upset, and he would giggle like mad. Finally, one time he came down the field and didn't tell me to freeze, so he actually had to get by me in order to score.

After that, I think he felt a little more confident, because instead of looking nervous about the game, he started taunting me. He'd say "Nanny-nanny-boo-boo" when I had the ball and "Ha-ha-ha-ha-ha" when he scored a goal. Children do this to each other all the time, trying to spread out their feelings of humiliation and incompetence. Usually everyone ends up feeling bad and spreading it around even more. Sadly, some coaches and parents add fuel to the fire by yelling at or humiliating the children. I assume since Kevin was not a strong player that he had either gotten this treatment or feared getting it. When children pass on this cruel teasing to me, my favorite response is to pretend to cry, in a very fake way, "Waaah!" Kevin laughed a lot when I did that. We played a while longer, and he announced the score was seventeen to three.

I played dumb. "Wait a minute, who has seventeen?"

"Me!"

"And who has three?"

"You!"

"Aw, I was afraid of that."

Kevin called a pause in the game to take a break, shouted "Huggy!," and ran over to me. This was our tenth session and the first time he hugged me, so I think it must have been because he felt so safe and confident from the way we were playing soccer. Before that, he would always show affection in more subtle ways, like stomping on my shoes (so I couldn't leave) or taking my watch (so I wouldn't know it was time to go).

I think the key point of this story is that there were actually two games going on simultaneously. One was the soccer game, and one was a confidence-building game. The power game involved playing with the themes that were important to him: competence and incompetence, humiliation and self-esteem. Through this two-in-one play, he had the chance to feel powerful and strong. He giggled away his feelings of inadequacy. A different child may have wanted me to play my hardest so he or she could master the game of soccer by seriously practicing moves and skills. That's fine, too; you just have to take your cue from the child. As I explained to Kevin's mother after the soccer game, his rules, which tilted the game so unfairly in his favor, gave him the chance to play through his feelings about not being the best at soccer. At recess, being one of the least-athletic kids, he felt as if the deck was stacked against him; so, with me, he set up the opposite situation.

Rob, at nine years old, is very different from Kevin. An excellent athlete, he is extremely competitive and is devastated by losing. He can't handle it at all. He wants to play goalie in soccer, but only in the first half, because he knows he'd crumble if he were responsible for the team's loss. In terms of children's need to fill their empty cup, Rob is in a hard spot. He loves sports, but his cup is filled by winning and emptied by losing. He doesn't have his cup filled just by playing. He doesn't have a cover that keeps it from being spilled when he loses. He needs some Playful Parenting play in order to get his cup refilled—the cup of confidence and feeling good about himself, the cup of feeling as if he's part of a team, part of the world, lovable and admirable, able to play his best but not devastated by losing.

I suggested to his dad that sometimes, instead of playing soccer or basketball or whatever sport, that they play "the winning and losing game." This is a game where the focus is on playfully addressing the emotional layer underneath. It can be any game at all, as long as there is playful use of the ideas of winning and losing.

For example, flip a coin, heads or tails; if you lose, go into a Shakespearean death scene because you lost. "Alas, my life is over henceforth, for it hath come up tails. . . ." If you win, announce that you are the greatest coin-flipper in the history of the universe; do a little victory dance, and then act real surprised when you lose the next toss. Or, if you can't think of any way to play with those themes of winning and losing, competence and incompetence, just say, "We're going to play the winning-losing game, so I can give you a hand with how hard it is for you." "How do you play that?" "I don't know, you got any ideas?" "How can I have ideas, I don't even know what you're talking about." "Any game where the idea is to have fun with me losing or you losing or pretending it's real important who wins and who loses." They'll eventually come up with some great ideas. Try them out. If they don't come up with anything, say, "I lose, I couldn't think of anything. Your prize is a cuddle," and then give them a big cuddle (or at least chase them around the house trying to give them one).

—QUIETING THAT CRITICAL VOICE—

Unfortunately, an extreme emphasis on winning, losing, success, and failure has pervaded childhood, even childhood play. Free play has all but disappeared in this time of lessons, team sports, paid indoor playgrounds, television, and computers. Once the experts discovered that play is good for learning, our society has started to take play and make sure it is always educational, productive, and competitive.

> Nickolder's parents gave her swimming lessons at ages 2 and 3, but each lesson was met with resistance. By the time she was 4, she still did not know how to swim, but did like to dabble in the water at the wading pool. Her parents arranged private lessons with a favorite preschool teacher. With each lesson, Nickolder grew more reluctant to return to the pool. The more external pressure put on her to learn, the more resistant she became. By Nickolder's fifth summer, her parents gave up their goal and decided to just let her play and be with friends in the shallow end of the pool. Soon, Nickolder started to really enjoy playing in the water. Then she began to imitate others who could swim. Within a few days, she could swim for six feet.[3]

Adults are famous for taking all the fun and playfulness out of learning swimming or math. Even worse is our tendency to criticize children. It happens so much we don't even notice it. Criticism is a nasty habit, difficult to break. We feel as if we are being so helpful, but it is really no help. All it does is install a little voice in their head—or sometimes a very loud voice—that will criticize them ruthlessly and relentlessly for the rest of their lives. You may have a voice like that in your own head. I was in a writing workshop, and the teacher, Kathryn Deputat, read us pieces from an old letter she found in the attic of the old farmhouse where we were having the class. The letter was beautiful and still rang true after a hundred or so years. At the end of three pages, the writer of the letter apologized, "This is a brief and stupid note." Kathryn wanted us to notice how persistent the critical voice is.

Children do this all the time—putting down their own work or their own abilities. And they often criticize each other mercilessly. (Of course they do—they learned it from us!) Sometimes, if we're lucky, they just need a little encouragement, a smile or a nod. This lets them ignore the critical voice and go on with their creative flow or their learning process. But if the critical voice inside stops them from even trying, if it convinces them to give up on drawing or soccer or math or horseback riding or writing poetry, then we have to do more. We have to insist that they keep at it, that the critical voice is *not* the truth or the last word. Faced with a firm contradiction—"I know you can do it . . . you're a great artist"—the critical voice will often make a last gasp for control. When we say this to children, they often cry or yell at us or insist they are stupid, they are bad at drawing, they hate math, they will never be good at sports.

All we have to do is listen, and maintain our confidence in them, while they release these feelings. This may not sound too playful, but listening patiently to these outbursts is a crucial part of Playful Parenting. The process of growing up and learning things and mastering new skills brings lots of frustration, and this frustration is released by giggles (when you're lucky) or by tears (when it's too strong a feeling to come out in laughter).

Too bad children don't come up to us and say, "I'd really like to pursue my interest in sculpture, but there is a voice in my head that tells me I'm no good at it. Will you help me?" Instead they say, "I'm just not interested in it anymore." We, therefore, need to be detectives and sniff out the difference between a real change in interests and giving up because of feelings of powerlessness. "We have to find ways for [children] to tell their own stories, paint their own pictures, construct their own worlds, act out their own scenarios, and keep their own dreams alive."[4]

—RECOVERING LOST CONFIDENCE—

Child psychologists have noticed for many years that play serves an especially important role in children who have been traumatized. When children have been in a car wreck, or an earthquake, or live in a violent home, they act out these traumas in their play. Barbara Brooks and Paula Siegel, in a book about helping scared children, write the following:

> They make toy cars go through endless collisions or make blocks fall down over and over or have one doll hit another doll. . . . Following Hurricane Andrew, the very young children played London Bridge . . . over and over. . . . Play is one of the few tools that young children have to express their feelings. . . . In the aftermath of the Northridge earthquake . . . preschool kids . . . built great towers of blocks on the table and then gave the table a powerful shake to knock over the blocks.[5]

On a smaller scale, these kinds of games are repeated every day by children everywhere. Most children gravitate automatically to play that helps them master the big and little upsets of their lives, just as we adults like to talk to our friends about the aggravations in our own lives. When children seem to be struggling, adults can facilitate their recovery of confidence by playing with them.

Let's say you and your spouse have been arguing a lot, and you're afraid it is affecting your child. But your child doesn't want to talk about it, and you're not sure how to bring it up. Next time you're playing house, you can make the mom and dad dolls argue with each other, in a kind of silly way. That gives the child the chance to pick up the theme, or drop it, whichever she wishes. She may have another doll tell the parents to make up, or she may say that she's running away from home, or give some other hint about her feelings. For an older child, whom you think may be struggling at school about rejection by the "in group," you might say, "Let's start a Beanie Baby club and the other dolls want to join." Anything the child needs to master, playing a game about it can help.

In a wonderful book on toddlers, Alicia Lieberman notes that play "gives the child a safe space where she can experiment at will, suspending the rules and constraints of physical and social reality." For example, the child (helped by the parent, if necessary) can give a story a happy ending, or make himself the victor or the hero. This process is called mastery because the child is now "the master rather than the subject."[6]

Lieberman gives the example of Cecelie, fifteen months old, who was upset that her parents were going out, even though she was being left with a well-liked sitter. Cecelie made up a game of hide-and-seek and played it over and over with the sitter. Playing with the ideas of disappearance and return helped Cecelie remember that her parents would come back. In another fairly typical scenario, Lieberman describes a twenty-month-old boy, upset after hearing that girls don't have penises, who covers and un-covers his with a cup—to master his fear that he might lose his.

There are some things that are so predictable and inevitable, faced by almost all children, that it is hard to call them traumas. Nevertheless, they are painful and they sap a child's confidence. Losing a friend, having a secret betrayed, and being teased are just a few examples. As parents, we want desperately to help children escape these hard lessons of life, or at least master them when they do happen. We know that lectures don't really work, but we keep giving them anyway, just in case, because we aren't sure what else to do. A playful approach is much more helpful.

Take keeping a secret—not an easy task for most children (or adults). Emma and Ted were in the backseat. They were nine and had been good friends since kindergarten. Ted said to Emma, "Do you want to know a secret? It's something Eric told me and made me promise not to tell."

"Umm, okay," Emma said.

"You can't tell anybody because Eric will kill me."

I jumped into the discussion at this point, because I could see the in-evitable disaster looming down the road better than they could. But I re-sisted the strong temptation to give a lecture about secrets and betrayal and friendship. Instead, I said, in a very lighthearted way, "Soon *everybody* will know the secret, because they only tell it to people who promise not to tell anybody." They both laughed. I thought they were getting the point, but I wanted to switch to play mode. So I opened my window and pointed to a person walking down the street, saying to Ted and Emma, "Should I tell that person a secret?" They laughed and said yes. I said out the window, "Hey, I'll tell you a secret if you promise not to tell." They cracked up because I was saying this to a stranger out the car window. Soon we were all shouting out the window, "Wanna know a secret? Don't tell anybody!" and laughing. Now, don't get me wrong: These two children, like all their peers, were still going to experiment with telling secrets, even when they had promised not to tell. But at least they had a chance to laugh about the tense burden of keeping a secret. A shared laugh is a big improvement over a moralistic lecture that falls on deaf ears . . . which brings us to the next principle of Playful Parenting: following the giggles.

CHAPTER 5

FOLLOW THE GIGGLES

In my mind there is nothing so illiberal, and so ill-bred, as audi-
ble laughter. . . . I am neither of a melancholy, nor a cynical dis-
position, and am as willing and apt to be pleased as anybody;
but I am sure that since I have had the full use of my reason,
nobody has ever heard me laugh.

—LORD CHESTERFIELD,
Letters to His Son (1774)

Despite Lord Chesterfield's advice to his son, sharing laughs together is essential to Playful Parenting. For a parent who wants to use play to build closeness and confidence, giggling is a sure sign that you're on the right track. Following the giggles means simply that if something makes the child giggle, then you do it again. And again, and again, and again. All kinds of laughs are wonderful, but there is something about the delighted and infectious nature of giggling that makes it a special hallmark of playfulness.

Getting the giggles started isn't all that difficult. You make funny faces at the baby. You play chase with a two-year-old and you stumble and fall right at the last minute and can't catch her. Or, you're running away from a six-year-old and you let yourself be caught, with howls of "Oh no, I can't believe you got me." You grab a pillow and start a pillow fight with your ten-year-old. You put on your teenager's clothes and jewelry and adopt her hairstyle, the ensemble that drives you crazy, and see how long it takes until she looks up from the TV and notices.

In general, when the adult exaggerates and really hams it up, that almost always makes children laugh. Being goofy and silly usually gets giggles, also. If you want them to get the giggles, don't talk in a regular voice if you can talk in a funny voice; don't talk at all if you can sing; don't stand up when you can fall over. With young children especially, funny faces, funny voices, and falling down are the key elements of getting the giggles flowing. If you feel self-conscious about being so goofy, pick up a stuffed animal or an action figure and make *it* say silly things in a humorous voice.

The older children get, the bigger the challenge they pose in the giggling department. You can't just fall over or make a goofy face for a guaranteed response—but don't be afraid to give it a try. You may get an eye roll instead of a giggle, but it's worth a shot. You can also experiment with being outrageous or with telling jokes. Since most older children try hard not to cry, or they feel badly if they do, I like to get giggles by pretending to cry, in a very fake way, especially if they hit me or insult me. "Waaah, I'm telling my mommy that you said I was bald."

The unexpected response is a basic technique of comedy, both in the theater and at home. So don't go into your preteen's room to tell her, for the tenth time, to clean it. Go in and scream, "Girl Power!" and sing a Spice Girls song (complete with dancing, of course). If you don't get a laugh, at least she'll say, "Okay, okay, I'll clean my room, just please *never* do that again!"

Pillow fights are good for inspiring giggles, though with older children, pillow fights may shift into more serious play about power and strength. Children from four or five up through teens often like the sock game. Each person tries to take off everyone else's socks while keeping his or her own on. This game is fun with two people, and a riot with three or more.

It is worth some trial and error to find what makes each child laugh—though all comics have tough audiences and days when they totally bomb. If you are having trouble, try being more enthusiastic, more energetic, more wild than usual. Remember that young children may not get subtle jokes or high-brow humor. They are more likely to crack up by just the mention of the words *fart* or *poop* or *butt*. (Of course, some of us adults don't have any trouble staying on that level of humor.)

Some children, even very young ones, do prefer more refined types of humor. The key is to know your children. Read books together. If they do watch TV, and I know most do, watch it with them, so you know what they are seeing. Then you can determine how it affects them, and you can crack jokes about it. I was watching cartoons at a friend's house with their four-year-old. Every time a commercial came on, she'd say, "I want one of those." I started beating her to the punch, saying, "I want *two* of those." We started outdoing each other with how much we wanted each toy, and we promised to buy each other everything we asked for. We had a ton of fun and laughed more during the commercials than during the cartoons.

Ask children to try to get *you* to laugh—you'll get a good picture of what *they* think is funny. A few of my favorite giggling games involve trying hard *not* to laugh. It's nearly impossible, like trying not to think of an elephant. The easiest game is a staring contest, where the first person to laugh or smile—depending on the rules—loses that round. Another one is called *the serious and solemn occasion*. Each person takes turns saying, "This is a very serious and solemn occasion," with a perfectly straight face, trying not to laugh. Good luck!

I'm sure most of the ideas I've just listed, about how to bring on the giggles and follow them, are old news. Everyone knows how to laugh and how to get children to laugh. The reason I am saying it anyway is that *we often forget the importance of laughter*. We are especially forgetful, or especially serious, when we are dealing with children who are being obnoxious or aggressive or uncooperative, and when we have run out of patience and good humor. Stress doesn't help much either. But these are the very conditions when Playful Parenting is most useful.

On one level, the association between laughter and play is self-evident. Play is fun, and laughter is the sound track of having fun. On another level, though, there are profound relationships between giggling and the deeper purposes behind children's play. Laughing can be a sign of connection between people, a sign of successfully completing a challenging task, or a sign that a child no longer feels miserable or hurt. Giggles and belly laughs are the natural way that children and adults release fears and embarrassment and anxiety. Parents can use this technique of following the giggles to lighten up a conflict or a tense moment.

Before moving on, here's one note of caution about giggles. Tickling may bring laughs, but *if it involves holding children down and tickling them against their will, don't do it*. It may bring giggles, but these don't really count because of the feeling of powerlessness from being made to laugh when you don't want to. It is too easy for this type of tickling to become a power struggle where the stronger person wins. This feeling of being overpowered is very different from the other kind of tickling, the good kind, like a little chuck under the baby's chin or the game where you or your child tries hard not to laugh while being gently tickled. Many men are fond of the hold-'em-down-and-tickle-'em game, because when we were young, that was one of the only games we got to play that allowed us to have close physical contact without outright violence.

—LAUGHING TOGETHER—

Sharing a giggle is a basic way to join and connect with children. Laughter automatically brings people closer. My friend Margaret, who is from New Zealand, always laughs as a way of saying hello, and it instantly bridges the cultural divide and the time since we've seen each other last. So laughing together makes a connection, and making a connection often brings a laugh. In other words, laughter is a key to the fortress of isolation. Indeed, one of the hallmarks of depression in children is the inability to find humor and enjoyment in life.

I have already described the staring contest, where two people stare at each other and see who laughs or smiles first. This game combines eye contact with giggles, two of my preferred methods of connecting. Another game, which I call *the tragic Shakespearean death scene*, combines giggles with physical contact, the other great way of being close. In the death scene, a child pretends to shoot you, or hits you, or sticks out his or her tongue, or says "I hate you, you're stinky," and you grab your chest and fall over—right on top of the child, in a highly exaggerated and drawn-out death scene. Falling over makes them laugh, while falling (gently!) on top of them brings the closeness and usually escalates the giggles.

Another game inspired by Shakespeare is the love-potion game, based on *A Midsummer Night's Dream*. Titania, queen of the fairies, is given a love potion in her eyes, which makes her fall madly in love with the first creature she sees, no matter how monstrous. That's exactly what children need: they feel monstrous sometimes, and they need to feel loved regardless of what they say or do. When we engage with them on their terms, they can take off the monster mask and return to their true selves, cooperative and joyful. So one way to induce heavy giggling is by singing corny love songs, reciting corny love ballads, and making up corny compliments. Being on your hands and knees looking desperate helps with this one. Yes, I know it sounds horribly embarrassing and undignified, but no one ever said parenting was going to be like having tea at Buckingham Palace. I like to use the love-potion game when children are trying to be gross—like when they're showing their half-chewed food or saying bad words. "Oh dear darling, that is the most beautiful sight I have ever witnessed. May I please get my sketch pad and draw a picture of it to have forever . . . ?" Sometimes all you have to do to get giggles is say "thank you" when you get insulted. I remember my niece Sarah, when she was about seven, saying to her mother, "I told Larry he was weird, and he said thank you! That is so weird!" Then she ran back over to me laughing, ready to tell me I was weird again.

If there are two adults available, pretending to fight over the child is always fun. "I've got the head." "Ha-ha, I've got the feet, that's the best part." "No, he's all mine, I love him so much." This human tug-of-war is another example of a game that combines physical closeness and laughter, as well as exaggerations of affection. The funny thing about children is that in spite of how well we may love them, they often feel unloved or unlovable. Maybe they don't feel unloved all the time, and maybe they are not devastated by it, but almost every child feels this way some of the time to some degree. Funny exaggerations of love and affection are a good way for many parents and children to express their deep feelings for each other. It fills the empty cup, because the goofiness of it catches them off guard.

When children are together in a group, they will often sail off into waves of giggles or gales of laughter. For some reason, adults usually refer to this as infectious laughter, as if we are afraid of catching it. Cherish these times. They build a powerful bond between children, and with us if we share them. Think of the contrast between this wonderful kind of group glee and the horrible kind of group laughter, which is aimed brutally at an outcast or scapegoat.

The first kind is inclusive; it draws everyone in. The second kind uses laughter as a weapon of rejection and exclusion. In the same way, fun imitation of children brings giggles, but its mean counterpart is a nasty kind of teasing that hurts feelings. We have all watched children imitate one another in both fun ways and hurtful ways. Imitation, if it is done thoughtfully, can bring a terrific sense of closeness. If done in a mean-spirited way, it builds walls between people. You can tell which way it is leaning by whether the child giggles or not. Don't imitate children to annoy them or teach them a lesson. Instead, do it to join them, to follow their lead and express your deep desire to be close to them. Laugh together.

—UNLOCKING THE TOWER OF POWERLESSNESS—

Children sometimes laugh when they successfully complete a challenging task, like climbing a mountain or riding a bike the first time without training wheels. They also laugh when they are scared—but not too scared. They laugh at things that are a little bit naughty—but not too naughty. Sometimes children, and adults, laugh when they aren't supposed to, such as at a funeral, or if someone trips on the street and hurts himself, or during a lecture on war crimes. This is a natural response, a release of fear, embarrassment, and tension through laughter. While we do need to be sensitive to other people's feelings, and no one likes to be laughed at or to hear someone laugh at things we hold sacred, we also need to understand the nature of human emotion. Laughter is a spontaneous way to release strong emotion, even when something isn't funny. When Charlie Chaplin slips and falls on his butt, with that pained expression on his face, everyone laughs; it is human nature. If we invite children to laugh at *us* during playtimes, they are less likely to laugh at other people in a rude way. So fall down a lot and pretend to cry loudly, "Waaah!"

Using Playful Parenting, we can help children release all this emotion in ways that aren't hurtful to others. We do this by just spending lots of time giggling together, but also with some specific techniques. To help children with fears, for example, it often helps to play as if *you* are the one who is scared, and really exaggerate it. Make sure they don't feel mocked or humiliated. It helps if you don't imitate them exactly, but just take the general idea and exaggerate it.

With an eleven-year-old boy who is fearful, I pretend that I am scared of everything. And I do mean everything: pencils, the letter Q, lightbulbs, video games, anything that happens to be in the room. He'll ask what time it is, and I'll say that I don't know because I'm scared to look at my watch. He thinks this is hysterical. This type of play lets children get some distance from their fear, and the distance allows them to release the fear through giggles.

A less dramatic way to act incompetent is to play chase and let the child have one narrow escape after another. This game is even funnier if you pretend to be shocked and confused. "How did you do that? I had you! This time I'll *really* get you." Then you miss again, of course, unless they laugh harder when you catch them and then somehow accidentally let them slip away.

Why is this so funny? The outrageous claims make the adult into a fool, which is funny enough, but especially since it helps them feel more powerful. Children often try to make each other feel helpless, powerless, stupid, or incompetent so they don't have to feel that themselves. That usually ends in conflicts and upsets. No one comes out ahead when one child tries to feel powerful at another child's expense. This is another reason adults need to participate in this kind of play—so that children won't do it to one another.

By making their escape harder and harder, but still letting them get away in the end, I am *playing at the edge of the child's development*. This edge is usually a very funny place. Let me explain: If you can get things just right, where the task is neither too hard nor too easy for the child, then he or she is really amused by it. My favorite example of this is from a film I saw in graduate school about stages of child development. In one clip, children of different ages were shown a large doll, which was wearing a blindfold. The psychologist asked, "Is the child easy to see or hard to see?" Younger children looked very serious and said, "It's hard to see." Older children looked annoyed at the stupid question and said, "It's easy to see." At just the right age, children laughed and laughed and laughed. Right on the edge of understanding this linguistic mix-up, they found it very funny. In the same way, with a baby just the right age, if you show them a fork, then put it behind your back and bring out a spoon, you'll be rewarded with happy surprise and a signal to do it again. Too early, and they just reach for it and say "gah-gah." Too late, and they look at you sideways as if to say, What are you trying to put over on me?

A few years later, as children learn that some words have a special power to freak out grown-ups, you can get big laughs just by saying certain words or by pretending to be horrified when you hear them. You know the words I mean. If the real bathroom words or swear words bother you, make up your own words, make them "forbidden," and then play at being shocked and horrified when you hear them.

Moving up a few more years, I get big squeals out of kindergartners and first-graders by saying I want to marry Barbie, or Barney. Again, playing at the edge of the issues that are developmentally "hot" for them at that moment gets the big laughs. We never grow out of some of these developmental edges. Look at magic—it plays with the basic ideas of reversibility, object constancy, and object permanence. Tying a knot is reversible, while cutting a string isn't, so magic rope tricks are funny. Object permanence means a scarf should stay a scarf and not change into a dove. Object constancy means that something that disappears under a cup should be there when the cup is lifted. Even though we learned these basic ideas when we were infants, we still enjoy magic and sleight of hand because they play with this edge.

—LIGHTEN UP THE SCENE—

One thing I do when I start to get a little bit frustrated with a young person, as an alternative to saying "I'm going to send you to your room" or something like that, is to make a *mock* threat that lightens up the situation and turns it into play. When this works well, I feel like an alchemist who has taken a block of lead and turned it into gold. Here's a sample threat: "If you do that one more time, I'm going to pour water on my head." I pick up the glass of water, put it above my head, and they laugh. I don't actually pour it! They say, "Yeah, do it, do it!" But by then the whole tone has changed. Now we're both laughing instead of being frustrated and locked in combat.

But it's important to remember that this is a *mock* threat. Real threats and angry tirades lock in frustration by scaring children, practically ensuring that they will shut you out. Funny mock threats, especially if they are aimed at yourself, release frustration. Once that frustration is released, cooperation is much more likely. Real threats communicate: I'm mad at you, it's your fault, and you had better shape up. The predictable result is defensiveness and conflict. Mock threats mixed with humor can communicate: I'm not happy with how things are going between us and I want us to fix it. The result this time is a relaxing of the tension and a willingness to meet each other halfway. Many parents say, "I can't play like that when I'm mad." Well, if you are too mad to play this little game, you are probably too mad to be making real threats, also. We don't do our best parenting when we're that mad, so we may as well lighten up. Take a break so that you can cool down (maybe pouring that water on your head will help, after all!).

To turn tense situations into play, try being light and a little outrageous. I find that it helps to *pretend* to scream when I want to *really* scream. There is a subtle but important distinction between a pretend scream of frustration and a real one. The real ones scare our children and make us feel worse. Pretend ones can delight our children and pull them back together with us into a team. I can't really describe it without a sound track, so just try faking an overly exaggerated but not scary scream.

—MAKING UP AND PLAYING DUMB—

Giggles can also be a part of making up if you have not been able to avoid a conflict. Often it is the adult who doesn't want to let go of the struggle. We want endless remorse and reparations and apologies from our child before we are willing to connect again. We refuse to laugh, as if our lightening up would be a reward to the child for bad behavior. But *laughter is healing.* Remember, for most difficulties between parents and children, the real problem is lack of connection, so the solution is more connection. Punishment, as we'll see in a later chapter, locks in the bad feelings, while laughing together is a great way to let them out so parent and child can find each other again.

Playing dumb—which is easier for some of us to pull off than others—lightens up tense moments. For example, I was walking up the stairs behind two boys at an elementary school. The bigger one was dragging down the other one's backpack in a highly annoying way. He thought it was funny, but the other boy was getting more and more upset. I could see that the boy being annoyed was faced with a bad choice—either suck it up and take it, or start a fight he'd probably lose. I said to the annoying one, in a calm, matter-of-fact voice, "It doesn't look like he's enjoying this game as much as you are." He stopped. Now, I knew that he had no intention of the other boy enjoying himself. Nevertheless, my playing dumb instead of scolding him got him to notice the other boy and notice his own behavior. Meanwhile, the boy being harassed was protected, but not in a way that would get him beaten up later for being a tattletale, which might have happened if I had marched the bully down to the principal's office.

When an older sibling is being mean, I say to the younger one, in my "gee-whiz" voice, "Gee, that looks like it hurt. How do you get back at her when she does that?" The younger siblings may not be able to tell me, but they always get a little glimmer in their eyes. Or I say to the older one, again in a happy voice, "Boy, that was awfully mean. What's going to happen next?" If I play the heavy and give a lecture, they are going to forget what I have said in microseconds. They are taken by surprise with the village idiot approach, so they might stop and think about it. And they usually laugh instead of escalating the violence or the conflict.

—LOSE YOUR DIGNITY TO FIND YOUR CHILD—

Children often feel stupid—either secretly or not so secretly—and they long to see someone else look stupid for a change. One of my favorite ways to reach children is to lose my dignity. This lets children be the more powerful one in playful interactions, and lets them heal their bruised egos by seeing me lose my dignity a little. I have found that nothing lets children laugh more than my pretending to be a dolt. (Adults laugh at this as well.) I do this by singing funny songs, falling a lot, dancing around, and otherwise looking quite foolish. Becoming an expert at losing my dignity has required a great deal of practice.

Here's one example, which I call *Captain Lex von Vader Hook*. I was playing once with a six-year-old boy, and he said he was Luke Skywalker and I was Darth Vader. That was fine, but before we could begin to play he changed the characters on me. "No, I'm Peter Pan and you're Captain

Hook." "Okay." "No, wait, I'm Superman and you're Lex Luthor." I think he would choose a good-guy character and feel powerful. Then he would assign me a bad-guy character and feel threatened. So he switched to a different character, and so on. We never got to play. He really wanted to use this superhero play to overcome his fears, but the game itself scared him too much.

In other words, if play can be a vehicle for healing from fear, ours was stuck in a snowbank, with the wheels spinning. Eventually this kind of play just fizzles out, usually because the grown-up gets bored. I decided to help things along. I combined all my roles into one, so he couldn't flip from one to the next, and addressed the powerlessness issue directly by making myself incompetent and goofy. When children play the good guy, they don't want the bad guy to be *too* powerful. So I started singing a song: "I'm Captain Lex von Vader Hook, I'm the dumbest bad guy in town. . . ." I made it clear that no matter what powers I had, or no matter what character he was, I would *try* to get him, but he would *always* win. I had the bluster of all these bad guys combined, with none of the bite. He loved this game and for months wanted to play it over and over every time we were together. The second or third time we played it, he made up a new song for me, escalating my loss of dignity: "I'm Captain Lex von Vader Hook, I love to poop and pee. . . ." I would sing this, and we would both laugh. I would pretend to be horribly humiliated, and he would feel like the king of the world.

I realize I am asking a lot of parents when I suggest that we lose our dignity. A lot of adults have a hard time just loosening up. We're expected to be serious at work and just about everywhere else, but our children are begging for us to snap out of it and have some fun. When adults aren't sure how to start having more fun playing with children, I ask, "What's the most outrageous thing you could do? Would the sky actually cave in if you did it?"

Harville Hendrix, the well-known marriage and relationship expert, suggests that couples play the ha-ha game. This involves standing very close, face-to-face, heels off the ground, bouncing lightly on the balls of your feet. Each person takes a turn saying "Ha!" in a friendly voice, back and forth, until both are howling with real laughter. Hendrix's basic idea is that "face-to-face high-energy fun" is invaluable for reconnecting. Adults often act as if there were only one way to have face-to-face high-energy fun (I won't go into details in a family-oriented book), but children know lots of ways. We need to learn from them . . . and practice.

Cosby Rogers and Janet Sawyers write that "adult play (such as bridge, tennis, or fishing) has aptly been described as . . . not fun, lacking spontaneity; deadly serious—very literal; and focused on doing it correctly and well."[1] Therefore, to play like a child, *bungle*. Blunder. Stumble. Be unable to figure out why the square piece won't fit in the round hole. Risk looking silly, sing, fall over. Exaggerate everything. Lighten up. *Try* to have fun.

Switching gears after work is one of the hardest parts of parenting for many of us who work outside the home. Most jobs fall a bit short in the giggling department. The same can be said for switching gears after the chores part of child care and homemaking. It is hard to create a giggly space for playtime. The most common ways that adults unwind—TV, alcohol, and naps—are not part of the Playful Parenting agenda and don't take into account the child's needs. Of course, the parent has needs, too, but if the children are merely an aggravation after work, then something needs to change. Setting aside time for high-energy fun, complete with giggles, can be a new way to meet everyone's needs. The hardworking mom or dad gets to unwind, the child gets some exuberant playtime, and everyone gets to reconnect.

Parenting is hard work, and being unhappy makes it harder. Most parents are a little uptight; a few are more seriously depressed. Depressed parents have an especially difficult time following the giggles, using humor to lighten up a tense situation, and loosening up. You might have just barely enough energy to make it through the necessities of life but not have any energy left over for fun and play. Perhaps you don't even realize you are unhappy until you try to join children in these giggle-fests, and you can't do it. *If the ideas in this chapter are out of reach for you because of your own feelings, then please face those feelings squarely.* Take a good hard look inside, talk to other parents, get professional help. Your children will be forgiving and patient, but they do want you to loosen up.

—FROM GIGGLES TO TEARS: WHEN
GOOD PLAY LEADS TO BAD FEELINGS—

When my daughter was five, she was playing one day with our friend Tim. Since Tim didn't have any children, Emma saw him as fresh meat, an adult who might actually want to play. Emma was making mazes for him to try, and they were having lots of fun. But when Tim made one for her, she had difficulty, and her frustration increased with his attempts to help her. She said, "I hate you" and some other nasty things and stalked off. Later she came back, acting happy and ready to play, but I could see that Tim wasn't ready. She seemed surprised that he was still upset at having been dumped on so badly.

Children sometimes overestimate the ability of an adult to handle their strong feelings, especially adults who take the time to play with them. Tim was surprised at Emma's sudden shift from giggles to angry outburst to smiling. I suggested that the two of them might need to re-connect first, maybe by shaking hands or sharing a joke or deciding to-gether to be pals again. She stuck out her tongue, said she hated me, too, and stalked back to her room.

Her mom, Tim, and I were talking in the kitchen when Emma came back with a big smile and proposed a game for us all to play. None of the adults were much in the mood to play by that point, since adults tend to take these types of insults personally. I again suggested reconnecting first, and she rolled her eyes at us and went back to her room. We could hear her playing by herself. I said, "She's over saying she hates us, but we're not." Saying this out loud eased our tensions, and we laughed about it. Two or three more times Emma came out with a game idea; I responded with a connect-first idea, but she ignored me and left. At one point I tried to hug her, and she screamed and squirmed away.

The next time she came out, she had a piece of cardboard and a plas-tic spoon that she said was her "two-sided date pad and pencil." She sat down on the couch and we all went over to join her. She pretended to write on it and handed it to me, saying she had written me a message. I asked her what it said, and she "read it" out loud: "I love you, Daddy, but I don't want to hug you." I asked if I could write her back. She said *she'd* write my response for me. She proceeded to pretend to write again, and then read it to me: "I want to hug you, but I still love you." Then I asked if she had anything to write to Tim. She wrote on her pad and said, "Sometimes I pretend that I hate you, and you get confused." Tim said, "Yes, I do get confused." She wrote some more, then read to Tim, "I pretend that I don't like you, but I really do." Tim said, "That's an amazing two-sided date pad," and she said, "Yes, it is."

There were no major giggles in that story, but I include it here because it illustrates the way emotions can instantly shift during play. Perhaps after a giggly wrestle, the child will stub his toe and release a torrent of tears. Maybe after an hour of being the horse, carrying kids around on your back, you finally say no more because you're exhausted or you've had enough. Instead of "Thanks, Dad, that was fun," you may get a furious protest: "You *never* play with us; your back *always* hurts."

These sudden shifts—from giggles to tears or tantrums—happen because the child has a pile of backed-up feelings. She keeps the door to these feelings tightly shut. The fun play opens the emotional door to let out the giggles, and a flood of other feelings come pouring out after. Once the tears start, they may last a long time. Very few parents realize how healthy it is for children to get this chance to shed some of that backed-up supply of uncried tears. We make the mistake of fussing or yelling at the child, because the tears or outbursts seem to be over nothing. But old feelings latch on to the littlest excuse to come out from hiding, especially after a long fun playtime. If we can just sit with them while they are releasing these feelings, they will eventually emerge happier children.

This flow from giggles to tears, tantrums, or aggression is puzzling to adults, but it is really quite normal. All the child needs is to be cuddled (if she is crying) or listened to quietly (if she is tantruming), or held gently but firmly (if she is kicking and fighting in a way that might hurt somebody). If you are prepared for these feelings, you can just relax and let the child express them and be done. If you aren't prepared, it is easy to get mad: "How dare you talk to me like that? I've been playing with you for an hour. Quit crying, don't be a baby." But these feelings aren't about *nothing*, they come from deep inside, and one of the great side benefits of giggly playtime is that it can let children feel safe enough to share them with us.

Because the shift from giggles to tears is often triggered by a slight (or imagined) injury, parents often misunderstand what has happened. They say, "You're not really hurt." It may be true that the child is not really injured, or that she is overreacting to a tiny scrape or bump. But that's the idea. She is using that bump as an opportunity to release old unfelt feelings, now that she feels safe and close from all that giggling. Maybe those tears are stored up from previous injuries that were more serious, but you weren't around to hold her when they happened. Now she is making up for it by pretending to be injured so you will cuddle her. Maybe she feels as if she has to be physically hurt in order to be held and comforted. Either way, there is no need to tell her she isn't really hurt. Just love and cuddle and comfort her and welcome the release of feelings, which may be happening just because she feels so safe and secure with you.

Some parents, instead of dismissing the child's tears, overreact, ending the play with, "No more roughhousing; I *told* you someone would get hurt!" But if the child is just using a very minor injury as a chance to release old feelings, then there may be no real danger to the game and no real reason to end it. Often, all that is necessary is a brief pause to pay attention to that burst of feelings, then back to fun play—which becomes even more fun now that the child is no longer carrying that load of painful emotion.

Playful Parenting's emphasis on giggling does not mean that every moment has to be filled with giddy excitement. There are sad times, scary times, and lonely times, and even aside from those, there are times when the child is content but not in a giggly mood. Following the giggles does not imply a crusade to cheer someone up or cajole her out of her feelings. The child may in fact be quite serious, but nothing is wrong and she doesn't need to be pushed into laughter. The difference between contented seriousness and grim misery is what I call engagement. Is the child engaged in what she is doing? Is she focused, relaxed, interested? Or is she bored, listless, or bouncing off the walls?

Cosby Rogers and Janet Sawyers say, when you want to figure out how children's play is going, the first question to ask yourself is: "Are children happy, with twinkles in their eyes?"[2] That twinkle may reflect a giggle or a belly laugh just waiting to come out, or it may be a sign of a more serious contentment, or the satisfied feeling of finishing a challenging task, like building an amazing Lego spaceship, or sewing clothes for a Beanie Baby, or taking the training wheels off a bike.

Lighthearted play that brings laughter may set the stage for success in the more serious side of life, and vice versa. Alexandra was three when a new baby sister arrived. After the "honeymoon" period, Alexandra started asking her mother over and over, "Why are you always looking at her?" She would say this in a tone of resentment and jealousy. Kristin, her mom, was frustrated that none of her rational explanations to Alexandra seemed to have any impact, and she was starting to get annoyed by this repeated question. She would explain why she spent lots of time looking at the baby and would ask Alexandra if she felt jealous, but nothing really changed. Kristin was telling me this as we sat having tea in her kitchen, while my daughter and Alexandra ran around the house. Every few minutes they would race through the kitchen laughing.

After hearing all this, I called Alexandra over and said, "Alexandra! I'm going to look at you!" I proceeded to put my eyes close to her elbow and her head ("So I can look at you really closely"), and to make my eyes bug out from the exertion of looking at her so hard. Both of us giggled the whole time. My daughter came over to watch. The girls ran out, and then Alexandra came back and asked to play that game again. When Kristin or Emma tried to talk to me, I'd say, "I'm sorry, I can't talk now; I'm looking at Alexandra." The next time we went over to their house, Kristin told me that Alexandra had stopped asking why she always looked at the baby. Instead, she started coming up to her mother and saying, in a very serious voice, "Look at me." Kristin would look at her, gazing intently, while Alexandra soaked in the attention like a thirsty flower. She would stand still, with a serious expression, until she decided to run off and play. I think that the brief "follow the giggles" playtime we engaged in earlier had allowed her to express, in a direct, nonplay way, what she needed and wanted from her mother. The indirect question—about why she looked at the baby so much—was confusing to Kristin. But this direct request for attention was not. Unlike many older siblings, Alexandra did not have to escalate her behavior into hurting or threatening the baby in order to get her mother's attention.

—

Is there enough giggling going on in your house? At the playground? At your child's school? In my opinion, a good school is one where you hear giggling and laughter in the halls and in the classrooms. We often forget that children learn best when they are happy. In the frenzy to evaluate schools and students, no one asks whether children are happy. Many parents and child-development experts have lamented the loss of free play and the way it has become replaced with lessons, competitive sports, structured activities, and watching TV. I say, let's quit moaning about it and follow the giggles.

CHAPTER 6

LEARN TO ROUGHHOUSE

Paul had to display extraordinary restraint when he played
with his brother Patrick. . . . Paul roared up to the infant,
then screeched to a halt, contorting himself in order to get
down to Patrick's level. Paul held his strength in check for
nearly fifteen minutes as he wrestled with his little brother.

SHIRLEY STRUM,
FROM A DESCRIPTION OF BABOON PLAY[1]

Whenever I talk about the topics in this chapter—wrestling, rough-housing, active play, and aggressive play—I am immediately interrupted. Parents, especially mothers, insist that they don't wrestle, they won't wrestle, they couldn't possibly wrestle. So I've decided to start this chapter with a special invitation: *Even if you don't think you ever want to wrestle, or even if you think you already know all about wrestling, read this chapter anyway.* It's full of ideas that are useful even if you don't wrestle—and maybe you'll even change your mind.

Many animals wrestle, including humans, and we seem to do so for a variety of reasons. Children wrestle and roughhouse as a way of testing out their physical strength, as a way to have fun, and as a way to control their aggression.

Boys and girls—rambunctious children and quiet ones—all benefit from thoughtful physical play with adults. The active ones, who are going to be in the thick of the rough and tumble in school and on the playground, need a chance to do it first with someone who can give them undivided attention, help them deal with their fears, hesitations, impulses, anger, etc. That's our job, because we won't call them names if they cry or if they give up, and we will stop for a rest when the child needs one. Other children are not going to hold back very much, and they certainly are not going to encourage expression of feelings. Meanwhile, children who are less physically active need roughhousing with adults so they can explore their physical power and develop their confidence and assertiveness. So I make a distinction between the kind of wrestling a Playful Parent does with a child, the kinds of play fighting children do with one another, real aggression, and physical play. All of these types of wrestling are discussed in this chapter, starting with a set of guidelines that help make wrestling the kind of play that brings closeness, confidence, and healing from emotional hurts. In other words, we are not talking about professional wrestling here.

—LARRY'S RULES OF WRESTLING—

Remember the love gun game (page 50), which transformed aggressive impulses and disconnection into play? Well, in this chapter, we can see how wrestling and other forms of roughhousing can transform powerlessness into confidence, and isolation into human connection. The problem with a great deal of wrestling is that the stronger person wins while the weaker person gives up or gets hurt. Sometimes two young people figure out how to avoid these problems when they wrestle each other, but often there is a definite need for adult involvement to make sure it goes well. Don't worry, I'll provide a few ground rules to follow.

In the biblical story, Jacob wrestles with a man who turns out to be an angel. Jacob hangs on, despite being injured, until the angel will give him its blessing. The Buddhists have a similar story, in which a holy man, Milarepa, is not upset or scared by the presence of demons in his cave; he just casually offers them tea until they disappear. When children show us their wild and scary sides, we need to be as persistent as Jacob and as calm as Milarepa. If we can stay with them, physically and emotionally, we will find the cooperative, loving, joyful human being who may have been buried under a pile of angry or scary or sad or lonely feelings. Wrestling with them can help them find their true selves again.

There is an endless variety of ways to wrestle. You try to pin their shoulders to the floor, or they try to pin you. They try to get past you, or you try to get past them. They try to knock you down. You hold them, and they squirm to get away. They may need you to lose your dignity and be totally incompetent so they can feel powerful. Or you match your strength to theirs, like the older baboon did with his little brother.

And if they are bigger or stronger than you—you may want to set it up so you have an advantage, and let them fight their hardest before they can win. For example, arm wrestle where you can cheat (you can have your elbow off the table and use two hands), and they can't. Or they are allowed to use only one hand, or one finger. Or, you just fight your hardest, showing there's life in the old bird yet, even if your child ultimately wins.

To help you get started, I have come up with ten rules for wrestling with your child.

LARRY'S RULES OF WRESTLING

1. Provide basic safety.
2. Find every opportunity for connection.
3. Look for every opportunity to increase their confidence and sense of power.
4. Use every opportunity to play through old hurts.
5. Provide just the right level of resistance to the child's need.
6. Pay close attention.
7. (Usually) let the child win.
8. Stop when someone is hurt.
9. No tickling allowed.
10. Keep your own feelings from getting in the way.

---

1. *Provide basic safety.* See to it that nobody gets hurt. To make sure that it's safe, set up ground rules. *No hitting, no biting, no punching, no kicking, no head locks.* Besides being safer, pushing and holding are more helpful in building confidence and connection than hitting. Your commitment to *no one* getting hurt, including yourself, builds feelings of safety that allow for effective wrestling. Watch out for emotional injuries

also. Don't tease or humiliate the child. Since wrestling often involves saying "ouch" and "stop" when things are actually going fine, agree on a code word that means that everyone will stop immediately (it might be something straightforward like "halt," or something silly like "banana cream pie," but it shouldn't be a word that the wrestlers are likely to say otherwise). Always stop right away when someone says the code word or if there is an injury.

Children may need to be reminded about these ground rules many times. If safety permits, it is best to keep reminding them, or holding them gently but firmly so they can't hurt you, instead of stopping the play as soon as they break a rule. See if you can stay engaged, continuing to play, while still maintaining safety. This gives us the chance to help children who are impulsive or aggressive to gradually control these feelings. The reason wrestling often gets out of hand between peers is that no one is in charge of safety, so the play fighting turns into a real fight or ends in bitterness and hurt feelings.

2. *Find every opportunity for connection.* Take cuddle breaks. Insert as much connection as possible, wherever possible. If the child avoids eye contact, you might say, "Before we battle to the death, let us do the ancient warrior custom of looking each other deep in the eyes." If he likes to say, "You're dead!" then you can fall down dead, but fall slowly in a protracted death scene (think Shakespeare) *right on top of him*, pulling him down with you in a big hug. There is a huge difference between wrestling and punching a punching bag, and that difference can be summed up in two words: human connection.

Make setting limits, if necessary, an opportunity for connection and empowerment. Adults often end play sessions abruptly when the child crosses a threshold of what the adult can tolerate. These thresholds may be perfectly legitimate (if the child is beginning to hit or bite, for example) or may be simply our adult limitations on what we can handle (such as getting our feelings hurt or wondering what the neighbors would think). Either way, the child's crossing the line may not have to mean an end to the play. Rather, it is another opportunity for connection, a chance to talk about limits and feelings. With practice, it is often possible to set the limit in a relaxed way, then return to the game or the wrestling.

If verbal limits don't work, and the aggressive or dangerous or destructive behaviors continue, see if you can wrestle in such a way that no one gets hurt, while remaining engaged and connected. Some children, especially those who have been victims of violence themselves, may need a special setup in order to be able to wrestle as hard and as wildly as they want without anyone getting hurt. Of course, ending the play is perfectly reasonable if it is the only way to maintain safety or if the adult is unable to keep from getting angry.

3. *Look for every opportunity to increase their confidence and sense of power.* Mostly this is done through giving the right level of resistance (see number 5) and by encouraging them. It can be tricky to be simultaneously the coach and the sparring partner, but above all the goal is to encourage and challenge them. I frequently tell children during wrestling: "No tricks." Using their physical strength provides them with much more of a sense of their physical and inner power than does winning by tricking you. Sometimes, though, they may need to show off their superior intellect rather than their superior physical strength, in which case tricks are fine. In general, the basic message in wrestling combines the themes of connection and confidence: "Your power is welcome here. There is a place for you to be strong *and* connected, without hurting anyone."

4. *Use every opportunity to play through old hurts.* For example, if a child faced a difficult challenge earlier in the day and was not pleased with the outcome, she can replay it with you, through wrestling, with you representing the obstacle or the bully or the difficulty. The object is not necessarily for her to *win* this time around, though that can be helpful, but more important, to fight *all out* with you cheering her on. This fight provides a means of playing out the frustration, humiliation, and helplessness of having lost or given up the first time around. The key to a successful replaying of an old hurt is that it must remind the child of the initial incident, but not so much that she is paralyzed with fear or powerlessness. She may need reminders that this time around she is in charge, she has you on her side, she can be strong, she is safe.

5. *Provide just the right level of resistance to the children's needs.* The whole idea of wrestling is to provide resistance. The goal certainly isn't to win or even necessarily to let them win, but to let them use their inner power fully, in a way that does not hurt anyone. They need enough resistance to know you are there and to get a sense of themselves being powerful, but not so much that they are overwhelmed or feel obliged to give up. Some children—very young children, children who have been traumatized, who have been exposed to a lot of violence in their lives, or who feel especially fearful—may need to just touch you, and then have you fall over howling in mock pain. That might be as much resistance as they can handle. If that game makes them giggle, you know you are on the right track.

As children get older or feel more comfortable wrestling against you, they might need more resistance. You may need to push back, to set it up so they really have to work hard to pin you. And as they get still older and stronger and more confident, you may need to give even more resistance so they can go all out. Children who try to hurt you when they wrestle need a great deal of resistance; they need to be held gently but firmly so they cannot hurt anyone. Held or wrestled this way, they can struggle hard, releasing the painful feelings that have been leading them to be aggressive.

6. *Pay close attention.* How do you know whether to be watching for opportunities to connect, or to build confidence, or to play something through? Well, you may never know for sure, but you can increase your odds by paying close attention. If they hesitate about making any kind of contact, try asking them to touch you gently with one finger, and then fall over dramatically—see if that gets a laugh. Maybe they need a big boost of confidence like that before they can connect. Or if they are punching and kicking and biting with no eye contact, try getting their attention, or slowing things down, in order to get some contact first before settling into rough-and-tumble wrestling.

There are two signs that wrestling is on the right track: one is giggling and the other is sweating, straining, and exertion. Sometimes these go back and forth, as the wrestling shifts from having fun to struggling against a deep feeling of powerlessness. The signs that something is amiss are lack of eye contact, giving up, blind rage, or the child's actually trying to hurt you. Pay more attention to connection, confidence-building, working through, or finding the right level of resistance. Watch for escalating anger, from you or them. Then take a break to cool off.

You may need all your strength to make sure no one gets hurt when children kick and fight hard. They aren't wrestling anymore, but releasing a huge pile of terror and anger. They may be only dimly aware that you are there, holding them and making sure no one gets hurt. Hang on! Talk to them gently. This happens because children have been hurt and scared, and you may be shocked that they have these emotions inside of them. The wrestling opened the door for the release of these heavy feelings. When the feelings are done—and I have to admit that they can last a long time—then most children exhibit a remarkable change. They look deeply into your eyes, they smile and laugh, they want to try something that before they felt was too difficult. They seem to have dropped a load of worry or tension off their shoulders. At first, parents tend to be scared and confused by these tantrums and outbursts, but once they see how happy and relaxed children are afterward, they realize that the wrestling and the outpouring of emotion really works to build closeness and confidence.

7. *(Usually) let the child win.* Most often, the best end to an episode of wrestling is victory for the child. As I described in number 5, every child will need to engage in a different level of fight before ultimately winning. In some situations, however, children may need to know that you are fighting your hardest, even though it means you might win. The same is true when playing checkers or chess or any game with children— usually you start out letting them win, then you offer more and more resistance. Ask them if they want you to try your hardest, and ultimately enjoy their triumph as they beat you fair and square. Often there's no winning or losing at all in a good wrestle, just a lot of physical play.

8. *Stop when someone is hurt.* Stop immediately if someone's hurt, even if they seem to want to go back to wrestling. Interrupting wrestling— or any activity—to pay attention to physical injuries is especially key for boys, who are often encouraged to be stoical and keep playing. Playing on when you're injured, "sucking it up," does not build character; it builds *armor.* Then we wonder why boys and men have a hard time with intimacy and feelings! We have a strong temptation to want to give our boys armor, but that is not the real way for them to be safe in the world. As girls now are allowed and encouraged to be more athletic, they are unfortunately also getting the message to ignore pain.

For other children, both boys and girls, the challenge is not to quit after an injury, but to go back to playing after taking a break. A very minor scrape or bump can make some children (and adults) want to give up. They need respectful and gentle encouragement to give it another go. Even if you think the child is pretending to be hurt, it is still important to stop—in this case, to regroup and go slower or provide less resistance. The fake cries and whimpers of pain are signs that the child feels overwhelmed and that things need to be toned down a notch or two.

9. *No tickling allowed.* No holding others down and tickling them against their will. Tickling can be fun, but it can also feel to children as if things are out of control. Tickling can be confusing; the laughing seems to mean children are enjoying it, even if they may not be. So best to avoid it when you are wrestling. If children ask to be tickled, try a quick little poke, then back off until they stop laughing, instead of continuously tickling them. Or move toward them as if you're about to tickle, and then back off—you'll get the same laughter without the out-of-control feeling. Or try offering a different type of closeness instead. One way to think about "good" and "bad" tickling is to compare the way you tickle an infant—just a little chuck under the chin, followed by a torrent of giggles—versus the way your uncle or big brother tickled you, holding you down until you screamed for mercy. If they have been tickled a lot already, they may want to tickle you. You can either let them, or say, "No tickling"—whichever makes sense at the time.

10. *Keep your own feelings from getting in the way.* When adults first try to wrestle with children this way, they are often flooded with old feelings left over from their own childhoods. They may feel an impulse to humiliate, tickle, tease, or dominate the child, reflecting what was done to them when they were small. Or they may feel weak and helpless. In fact, many people have an immediate negative reaction to the very idea of wrestling, either because they didn't like it as a child or because they have seen adults wrestle children while under the influence of old, buried feelings of rage, competition, powerlessness, or helplessness. The purpose of the kind of wrestling we're talking about is for the child to feel confident and powerful. Don't let old feelings of ours get in their way. Fighting against a much stronger adult who is out for blood, who desperately needs to win, is not terribly helpful for the child. This is *their* time, not your time. See the last chapter of the book for how to deal effectively with these feelings if and when they come up. In the meantime, just set them aside and focus on the goals and principles previously described.

Adults who did not get much chance to be physically powerful as children, especially girls who were discouraged from this kind of play or boys who were beaten up a lot, may feel physically timid and hesitant at first. They are often reluctant to do anything that even looks like hurting anybody, or reluctant to risk getting bruised or injured. So push yourself. Practice with a friend. Make loud karate noises in front of the mirror. Take a martial arts class. Go to the power room (see chapter four).

Another group, mostly men, was encouraged to be rough, aggressive, and competitive as children. Wrestling was a matter of survival. This leaves us ill-equipped to wrestle in a way that fosters a young person's confidence and connection. *Leave the competition and ferocity at the door.* Don't wrestle if you are mad or frustrated. Maintain eye contact with the child. Take cuddle breaks. Aim more for giggles from the child than for superhuman physical prowess. Many of us were brutalized as children, and when we wrestled or fought, no one was following these guidelines on our behalf. We needed this kind of play and didn't get it, and that can leave us feeling or acting like loose cannons or soldiers in combat.

If you have feelings that you can't set aside, be honest about them (but be humorously honest, not *brutally* honest). In fact, the best thing to do is exaggerate them. "I am so tired, I can't stay awake another second. You'll have to get me onto the couch. If I wrestle one more second, I will surely die." "Waaah, that hurt, boo-hoo! You stepped on my toe. I will never be your friend again. . . ." "If I don't win, I am going to sulk all day."

—GETTING STARTED WITH PLAYFUL WRESTLING—

How do you get started with wrestling if you've never done it with your child? Simple. You say, "Let's wrestle!" She says, "What's that?" You say, "You try to pin me down using all your strength—you try to get me on my back with both my shoulders on the floor (or, you try to get past me onto the couch, but you can't sneak around; you have to use all your strength to go right past me)." Start simple; later you can move to each of you trying to pin the other at the same time. Or you could kneel on the floor and say, "Try to knock me over." (Having mats or at least rugs there would be a good idea!)

At a young friend's birthday party, the boy's father pretended to be an ox, and each child had to drag him over a line in the grass. The dad made lots of loud moans and groans, while he used exactly the right resistance for each child to feel he or she had really accomplished something.

Here's an example of a time when less resistance was needed, rather than more; when the child didn't need an all-out wrestling match but an experience of victory. My role was to be a bumbling, incompetent fool. You see, Emma and I were at her grandparents' house, and she was very antsy. It was just before her fifth birthday. You can easily imagine, I'm sure, the agony of spending days waiting until presents could be opened. She wanted to wrestle. Given her frustration level, I expected it to be an all-out fight, where I would have to use lots of my strength and get her to use all of hers. Instead, she set up a game where she tried to get past me without any actual wrestling. I reached to grab her and she said, "Let me get past you." In other words, this time I didn't have to fumble around until I figured out how much resistance to put up; she told me straight out what she wanted.

This is because after a few experiences of wrestling, children get pretty savvy about it and tell you how they want it to go. I once asked a girl, around seven years old, if she wanted to wrestle. She said, "Okay, but no punching, no head locks, no kicking, you have to stop when I say stop, and you have to start on your hands and knees." I said, "You've done this before." She had an older brother and somehow the two of them had figured out how to make their wrestling fair, instead of her getting clobbered all the time. She was a mighty wrestler.

My job with Emma this time was not to put up a tough fight and encourage her to use all her physical strength. It was to let her win easily while still making it fun. If all she had to do was race past me, it wouldn't be much of a victory. After a few false starts (I was still thinking in terms of wrestling) we eventually hit upon a very entertaining game. I stood at one end of the room bragging about how strong and powerful and smart

I was, insisting that she could never, ever get past me. Then she would trick me and somehow get across the room. I acted shocked and went over to the other side of the room to do it again. At first, Emma used old tried-and-true tricks: She would say, "Hey, look over there, it's an elephant," and I would look and she would waltz past. I increased the resistance by making her come up with a new trick to sneak past me each time. Of course, if that had frustrated her I would have let her do the same trick as often as she wanted. I took her giggles and intense concentration as a sign that she wanted the challenge of thinking up new tricks.

Some of her solutions were very creative, like pretending to hypnotize me. When she would be stumped for a trick, I would give her a hint. For example, standing up very tall with my legs spread apart, I would say, "No one can get past me!," and she would crawl under my legs. Then, of course, the next time I would crouch down low ("You'll never trick me like that again!"), and she would jump over me.

You may have noticed that this example did not actually involve any wrestling. I include it here because the principles, especially getting just the right resistance, are exactly the same. Part of the fun of this game was my taking a few seconds to keep bragging after she had already gotten past me. Children love it when you continue to brag after they've beaten you, especially if you exaggerate a double take of shock and dismay that *somehow* they have once again eluded your grasp.

During a play session with an eight-year-old boy—with whom I had played once before, so I knew he liked to wrestle and he liked to win—I started things rolling by saying "Oh no! Now I'm in for it!" in a mock-horrified voice as soon as I saw him. He responded with a diabolical laugh and started to square off for a wrestle, but then he pulled away and went over to the toy shelves. I think maybe the wrestling was too much too soon. He was interested, but he wasn't quite ready.

I wanted to let him be in charge of the play, but I also wanted to pull him back into connection. I saw him eyeing the Lego box, and I didn't want him to spend the whole time building a Lego ship and not making any contact, so when he touched the box, I said, "Oh no! You touched the blue plastic part, now the house is going to fall down!" His eyes lit up, and he got that sneaky grin on his face again. He moved away across the room so that I was between him and the box, and then he tried to lunge for it. (As an aside, I am sure I have missed countless little signals like this, but happily I caught that one. He could have just stayed where he was and touched the box again. Instead, he set up a game, without a word, that required him to get past me to touch it.) We had a long fun game of his trying to get to the box and my trying to stop him. We did end up wrestling, but it was on his terms. I have no idea why I said that touching the box would make the house fall down. It was just the first thing to come out of my mouth, to get a rise out of him and get him back engaged in the play. But I think it was actually the right touch, because it seemed that the reason he avoided wrestling at first was because he was afraid of his own aggressive impulses. The idea of the whole house falling down just from his touching a box of Lego pieces exaggerated this fear and made it funny. That, in turn, let him play out the feelings through wrestling. Children who don't get the chance to wrestle may have to bottle up those aggressive impulses until they explode.

—AGGRESSION—

When we see National Geographic specials with shots of lion cubs play fighting, we assume that they are practicing their hunting and fighting skills. What we may not see is that they are also learning how to *control* their aggression, how to modulate it. When male mammals fight each other for dominance of the herd or the troop, they almost never fight to the death, or even to serious injury, which means they hold back some of their strength. Though we might expect that it would be better for them to fight their hardest, apparently it is useful for animals to learn how to fight with the equivalent of one paw tied behind their back. The result is a complex dance to see who is strongest without *really* putting it to the test. The same is true when young humans, especially boys, play fight. They aren't just practicing aggression, they are practicing restraint and control as well. My favorite examples of this come from baboons, who are uncannily similar to us in many of their social relations. In some ways they may actually control their aggression better than many humans.

One adolescent male baboon "liked to join groups of smaller baboons in wild free-for-alls in which three or four monkeys would gang up on one. But just when the situation started to get serious for the victim, they'd switch to another target. Once in a while the overexcited youngsters would get carried away and the playful melees would turn aggressive, but since everyone wanted to continue playing, the aggression was usually controlled and short-lived." And Paul, the baboon mentioned in the quote at the beginning of the chapter, restrained his aggression impressively when he played with his baby brother. Even though Paul outweighed Patrick, thirty-three pounds to six, and male baboons have been described as "fighting machines," Patrick was never seen to get hurt.[2]

When children in the United States play war, they are usually doing the same thing that lion cubs are doing when they play fight: testing their muscles and their "claws," and exploring the complex world of conflicts, alliances, and strategies.

But war play takes on a wide range of different meanings for different children; this is especially true as you don't have to live in a war-torn country to witness violence. We are all exposed to images of real and imaginary violence every day—in movies, cartoons, and so on. Real children are killed or injured every day in fights and shootings and accidents. Some parents think war play is perfectly fine, a way of working out feelings. After all, children—especially boys—have been playing these games for centuries. Other parents are appalled, fearing that gun play will lead to real gun violence, that cartoon deaths will numb children to the reality of pain and suffering. I think that both groups are a little bit right.

[Note: When children who live in a war zone play war, it has a very different meaning. They are using play to recover from the trauma of what they have witnessed and experienced. Since the adults around them are often either unavailable or traumatized themselves, this play can easily turn into real aggression without any effective healing.]

There is a good kind of fantasy war play, which may include pretend guns or other pretend weapons, complete with sound effects and elaborate death scenes. Pretend guns (the kind you make with your finger or a cardboard tube or a stick) allow children to create games and rules and play out the themes important to them, including themes of warfare, violence, and weapons. Adults do have roles in this kind of play, to keep it lighthearted by dying in extravagant death scenes when the child says "Bang bang, you're dead," or to introduce themes of nurturing (the army medic) and caring (the devoted soldier buddy) into the play.

On the other hand, toy guns, especially realistic ones, tend to restrict children into playing in very limited ways. What else can you do with a Star Wars Death Star besides blow up a planet? Yet when you get tired of making your cardboard tube into a light saber, you can make it a rocket or a conductor's baton. When you get tired of your fake Uzi, you're not likely to play a game of Mideast peace talks. And in the most extreme situations, play violence can simply be training for actual violence, rehearsing what to do with a gun when you are angry at someone.

I don't believe you can or should ban all aggressive play. Children need to come to terms with aggression—their own and others'—and if we don't let them do it through play, they will do it in real life. Still, it is fine to negotiate until you find a happy medium that lets them express themselves but does not violate your own values. For example, some parents allow magical weapons such as wands and dragons' teeth, but not imaginary guns and bullets. Trying to eradicate all aggressive play always backfires. Unable to play out the aggressive feelings that they have inside, they may think that something is wrong with them, because they aren't ever supposed to feel angry or violent. They may become obsessed with war and weapons, because these are forbidden playthings. Good creative play, however, especially if you get on the floor with children to play with them, does not make children violent, no matter what kinds of aggressive games they are playing.

When people talk about aggression, they usually talk about boys, but girls have to figure out this aspect of life as well. A friend of mine sent me an e-mail: "Laurie's interested in aggression right now, and I'd love ideas for how to help her do this in a healthy way. She talks about how she and her friend Lily at preschool like to 'push each other.' She loves books with monsters in them. One of her favorite imaginative games is playing Billy Goats Gruff—she takes great delight in butting and kicking the troll off the bridge. If we talk about fish and animals that live in the ocean, all she wants to know is whether they bite. Anyway, none of this disturbs me too much—but maybe you'd suggest games or forms of play that would let her explore her own power?"

In my answer to this mom, I first commended her for not getting freaked out about her daughter's natural experimentation with power and aggression. It's healthy and normal for her age. I then explained that Laurie, like most preschoolers, was exploring several new things—new things her body can do (push someone hard enough so they fall over) and new ideas about how much control she has over her own aggression and how much control others have over *their* aggression. So she and Lily have fun pushing each other at school, and she wants to know whether fish bite.

Next I discussed games that play with these ideas. Games like Simon says, red light/green light, and so on aren't about aggression, but they *are* about control over impulses, so they are classic games for this age (and up to age six or seven). Another idea is to have her bite something like a rag or a doll. Then the parent can say, "Okay, bite harder, bite softer, bite quickly, bite longer," and so on. These rapid shifts that teach self-control are also fun. This idea is discussed in more detail later (pages 109–110).

Another game I suggested was a classic role reversal, where Laurie's mom or dad could play the part of someone who is figuring out how to handle aggression. This family lives on Fox Street, so I made up a game called the Fighting Foxfish of Fox Street, where the parent is the biting fish who chases after Laurie in a clumsy, undignified way, always missing, maybe biting him- or herself instead of Laurie (using fingers or arms as pretend jaws), or chomping on the chair and pretending to spit out yucky splinters. The foxfish might say, "I just have to bite something right now. Look, a worm. Ouch! That was my toe." You don't want to imitate her aggressive behaviors exactly, but make them close enough to bring the giggles.

—THE BENEFITS OF ACTIVE PHYSICAL PLAY—

Not all physical play involves roughhousing or wrestling. Some of it is just climbing and swinging and running around. All children need this kind of play, and most need way more than they get. One problem with TV is that after hours of sitting in school, children don't need more hours of sitting in front of a screen. In rare instances, TV can be a simple resting spot, and then the child can return to more interesting and creative play. My friend Charlie told me about his son, Davy, who loves sports. Davy will sometimes take a break from playing some sport outside to come in-side and watch sports on TV. After a few minutes, he is eager to shut off the set and return to actually playing. Back on the field or the court, he incorporates some of the moves and the commentary he has just seen into his ball-playing. Unfortunately, that way of using TV is rare; more often, it saps the energy and enthusiasm and creativity out of children and leaves them semicomatose on the couch.

One difficulty for many parents in the area of physical play is how to balance safety with adventurousness. We often have a tendency to be ei-ther overly worried or not worried enough. I usually hover too much. When Emma was little, I would stand right underneath her when she climbed on a play structure, my face contorted by worry and anxiety. Her mother would let her climb as high as she wanted, a confident smile on her face, trusting Emma's judgment. At the time I thought this was hor-rible, but she was right. No broken bones. And I know, as a therapist, that even if she had broken a bone, bones heal faster than timidity and fearful-ness. Emma is now confident and athletic, and I no longer cringe when she climbs a tree. Janusz Korczak—who was the Dr. Spock of Poland be-fore he was sent to the Warsaw Ghetto—wrote about how much better psychologically it was to give children piles of sand, sticks, hammers, nails, and wood, instead of games and store-bought toys (he would surely have railed against TV), despite the risk of injury.[3]

Physical play is extremely important to children's development. From newborns' first gentle tosses in the air to kids playing organized sports, children learn by using their bodies. Because some of us adults would rather sit and think and talk, we often make the mistake of trying to talk through parenting problems that are better dealt with physically or through play. Here are just a few examples of how active physical play can help children:

● *Self-soothing.* Self-soothing is the ability to comfort and calm yourself even if you are alone, and it is a major accomplishment of in-fancy—though many of us still have difficulty with it. Contrary to a com-mon belief, young children do not learn to self-soothe by being left on their own to "cry it out," or by being sent to time-out. They learn it from being soothed by someone who cares about them, then over time they take that comfort inside and are able to soothe themselves.

When children have a general difficulty in calming down or recovering from an upset, they need lots of cuddling time. But look at what happens: If children can't settle down, they can't get the cuddling they need. Boys are especially unlikely to get all the comfort and cuddling they need because they don't sit still for it. Wrestling often helps them, since active children may do better with active cuddling than the sit-quietly-on-the-lap type of cuddling.

When children have a hard time calming down, parents are often hesitant about roughhousing. They are afraid that it will escalate, and that children won't be able to settle down. But these are the children who need it most. You can't learn to settle down if you never get revved up. Children with lots of energy who never get to roughhouse end up going wild when they do get the chance, because they don't have any practice with calming down. If you start to wrestle regularly, both parent and child will learn to do a better job of winding down.

One thing I do is teach children how to take three deep breaths to relax. Not all deep breaths are created equal. I teach children to take a deep breath in through the nose, then let it out slowly. Let the exhale take twice as long as the inhale, so that the next breath has to be even deeper. Three or four of these make a huge difference. Make sure they don't just take rapid gulps of air, hyperventilating, when you ask them to take three deep breaths. I find it helps to do it with them. It helps them breathe more deeply, and it helps adults relax, too.

Children with difficulties in self-soothing also benefit from pretend play with dolls, where they practice soothing the doll when it gets upset, by cuddling it or laying it down for a nap. The parent can help by pretending to be the cranky baby, or by modeling nurturing, soothing behavior for children. It goes without saying that most boys miss out on this kind of play, so it is no wonder that so many seem to have short-circuited their dimmer switches (they can rev up until they crash, but they can't slow down).

● *Paying attention.* Parents and teachers tend to despair (or rush to the medicine cabinet) when a child has difficulty with attention and focusing. Stanley Greenspan offers some wonderful alternatives to despair or medication. He recommends setting aside several periods per day for a certain kind of play that he calls self-regulation. The basic idea is to have the child jump, run, swing, dance, do jumping jacks, or engage in any repeated rhythmic movement. Then you call out frequent, rapid changes: "Go faster, slower, slower, faster, superfast. . . . Go right, go left, go right, go left. . . . Hop on your left foot, now hop on your right foot, now hop on both feet." This game, which most children find fun and which works very well in groups, is one of the best ways to make up for deficits in emotional regulation, deficits that many children, especially boys, seem to have. There are innumerable variations. Hand a child a pile of blocks and say, very fast, "Sort by shape. Now sort by color. Now use your left hand." If they like to sing, say, "Sing louder, now softer." If they scream, ask them to scream their loudest, then a little softer, then a little softer, then whisper, and so on.

Self-soothing and paying attention are actually quite closely related. For example, it may look like Jed's problem is that he can't sit still in his fourth-grade class. He may join the ranks of boys diagnosed with attention deficit disorder. But perhaps the real problem is that he can't soothe himself when he feels anxious or frustrated. He has missed out on one of the earliest developmental achievements of infancy, and it's showing up years later. Unable to reduce his anxiety, he fidgets, kicks his neighbor, and gets in trouble. He may need a lot of connection-building play.

● *Motor planning and sequencing.* Some children have problems with what is called motor planning and sequencing, which may be seen in difficulty getting organized for school in the morning, or keeping track of assignments, or seeing a project through to the end. To help this problem through the use of physical play, create an obstacle course, starting simple and making it harder as children master it. For older children, make a treasure hunt, with clues that lead to more clues. Once again, some activities that are more commonly played by girls, like complicated hand-clapping songs or jump-rope games, are helpful in developing these skills.

● *Impulse control.* Children learn to control their impulses through play. We may try to teach impulse control by lecturing, punishing, and having friendly chats, but none of those are very likely to work. Psychologists Elena Bodrova and Deborah Leong describe a five-year-old boy who was unable to sit during circle time at school without interrupting the teacher. However, that same boy could be a perfect student when he was *playing school* with other children. Over time, he will be able to transfer this control he has during play into the classroom.[4]

So, play out the situations where your child is impulsive. Just say "Let's play school." "Let's play getting dressed and ready." "Let's play that you want this toy real bad, and I won't share it with you." "Let's play crossing the street—oh no, the little bunny almost got hit by a car." Take a real situation that is hard for them, label it as play, and let children practice gaining control over their impulses in ways that won't get them punished or humiliated.

CHAPTER 7

SUSPEND REALITY: REVERSE THE ROLES

*"Let's pretend that you're the dad and I'm
the daughter, and you're mad at me."*

—A FIVE-YEAR-OLD GIRL

TO HER ANGRY FATHER

In play, the ordinary rules of reality are suspended, and that is what gives it such power. A little boy can imagine himself a superhero; a young girl can wrestle her father to the mat and pin his shoulders down. Children playing school get to hand out the assignments and the grades and the punishments. The playing field is leveled, or even tipped a bit in favor of the child, to make up for the frustrations of being smaller and weaker and less competent than the bigger folks.

Even if no one shoves them around or takes advantage of them, children still feel powerless sometimes. They can't always feel as if they are the king of the mountain. After all, at the doctor's office, who gets the shot? In school, who has to sit still and keep quiet unless called on? At home, who makes the rules, and who is supposed to follow them? Who has to go to bed at a certain time? Who has to say please and thank you? Of course, children should get medical treatment and learn math and have bedtimes. But they also need lots of playtime that reverses the roles, suspends reality, and lets them be in charge. They need to take on the more powerful role—the hero, the princess, the perfect student.

The most common way for children to cope with these injustices and upsets is by using play to come up with a new script and create a new, improved reality. In this new reality the roles are often reversed. They play the part of the doctor, the teacher, the parent, the *Tyrannosaurus rex*, the Power Ranger. Preteens take on the role of the teenager, and teenagers try on adult roles.

—REVERSING ROLES—

In the middle of a soccer game, Daniel, age seven, said he had to go to the bathroom. He said, "Don't touch the ball," and then he tucked the ball away inside a box. I said I wouldn't touch it. He thought for a minute, then said, "I don't trust you, come inside with me." This was a new theme in the play that I hadn't seen before, but it certainly made sense. Daniel tends to wander off in school and get in trouble a lot, so he was playing out the theme of someone not being trustworthy. In the play, he reversed the roles so that I was the one who couldn't be trusted, and he could be the one who was in charge of enforcing the rules.

Role reversal is especially helpful for restoring children's sense of confidence—escaping from the tower of powerlessness—and for overcoming fears and inhibitions. At times, children play out these roles on their own, and all they need from us is to be their stage manager or producer—providing the play space, the toys, the refreshments. Other times, they need us to be a responsive audience. As they begin to engage in fantasy play, they may also need us to participate as a fellow actor, or even occasionally as a director. A popular philosophy of child rearing suggests that the more we leave children alone the better; benign neglect will allow them to blossom and develop on their own. That might be fine if it weren't for the intrusive influence of our culture and the media. It's a paradox: because of the pressures on children to limit their imaginations and creativity, they actually need active adult help in order to write and star in their own stories. Benign neglect doesn't empower children, it leaves them at the mercy of the best marketing money can buy— marketing that doesn't just tell children what toys to purchase, but also how to play with them.

—FROM TRAGEDY TO COMEDY—

In a comedy, things are turned upside down for humorous effect. In a tragedy, things start out upside down ("There's something rotten in the state of Denmark") and the play drives toward setting things right. Both of these are applicable to children's play and the roles they take on. If you think about what makes children giggle, often it's when reality is suspended and roles are reversed. These are giggles of liberation as they are freeing themselves from worries, fears, and especially from feeling powerless over their lives. They laugh, and their world is set right again.

Playful Parenting helps this natural process along by making sure that this time it is the adult, not the child, who is in the less powerful position. Daniel, the seven-year-old who didn't trust me with his soccer ball, had been having problems at school, mostly for being defiant and not listening. In our play-therapy sessions he often liked to play the part of a kid who breaks rules and gets in trouble, while he assigned me the role of the authority figure, chasing after him to punish him.

This game, however, didn't bring on the giggles. He was easily upset while playing it; nothing was ever quite right. After all, it was just a replay of his school day, and even though I tried to liven things up by being a bumbling goofy authority figure, the play didn't go anywhere. So one day I decided to give a little push by suggesting a role reversal. First, I asked Daniel what happened in his school if someone got in trouble. He said they might get a time-out. I asked about what happened if it was something really bad, and he said they would be sent to the principal's office.

"What does the principal do?"

"She *talks* to you!"

"Eek! That sounds really scary."

Daniel leaned over and whispered to me, "Do you know the principal's name? It's Miss Sternly."

"Oh yeah? That's a good name for a principal."

"Just kidding, it's Mrs. Atkins."

"I'll be the kid who gets sent to the principal, and you can be the principal," I suggested, trying to set up the role reversal.

"I'll be *Mr.* Sternly."

"Okay," I said, then I put on a child's voice. "Excuse me, Mr. Sternly, the teacher sent me here, I'm not sure why; maybe because I turned everything in the classroom over, including the teacher and all the desks and the fish tank."

"And the kids?"

"Yes, and the kids, I turned everything over because I didn't get to use all the blue markers like I wanted to. What's my punishment?"

"If you do it again, you will be sent out of the school *forever*." Daniel took the role reversal idea and ran with it.

"Oh, no, that would be terrible."

"And you have to fix everything *with your own money*. Now go back to the classroom and fix everything up."

Unlike our play together when he was the troublemaker, this simple exchange with him as the principal was accompanied by a great amount of giggling and clowning around.

Even though children learn at an amazing rate, they still often feel incompetent, especially when they see others doing something they can't do yet. Role reversal can help with this, too. The first time my daughter tried cross-country skiing, she whined and complained bitterly. It seemed to me that she was doing fine and would enjoy it if she just let herself, so I tried to talk her out of feeling miserable. Guess what? It didn't work. I got so annoyed at her complaining that it took me a long time to realize that she felt incompetent and was frustrated by how often she fell (or almost fell) and how hard it was for her to get up. All I could see was that she was doing great for her first time. All she could see was that she fell and I didn't. So I made a big show of falling myself, all four limbs and ski poles and skis up in the air, aiming in different directions, shouting about snow getting in my underwear. She laughed and laughed, then proceeded to enjoy herself immensely for the rest of the time, and even asked if we could ski again the next day. In other words, I reversed the roles and became the less competent skier. That left her in the position of being relatively good at it, which gave her a burst of confidence that let her enjoy it. Unfortunately for my wounded dignity, lectures and coaching didn't help at all. It took a more playful response to cut through her feelings of incompetence.

Reversing roles usually means that the child is now in the one-up position, but not always. Sometimes older siblings need something very different. They are used to being the boss, and they may need a role reversal that puts them down a notch. But in a *playful* way! In frustration, parents often try to reverse the roles by showing the older sibling who's *really* boss, but that usually just leads to more conflict between the siblings. What I usually do with older siblings, or any older or stronger children who are picking on smaller ones, is to say to them, in a mock-threatening voice, "Hey, pick on someone your own size." And I put up my fists in a parody of a fighter's stance, waiting for them to come after me instead of their victim. Of course, I never beat them up! More often I run and hide under a pillow, or let them flip me over, or do something else to get their giggles going. Other times, I wrestle hard with them, giving them more of a run for their money than could the smaller child, who could only whine or tattle or scream to get even. Underneath the aggression, bigger children usually feel powerless, so I often have to reverse the roles once more, letting them be more powerful than me (in play) instead of their taking advantage of being more powerful than their little brother (in reality). It is important to be clear that you are joking around and are not going to clobber them (even if they've just finished clobbering a littler child). Give them, in a gentle, playful way, the idea that they are not the boss of the world. And at the same time, give them the idea that they can be powerful without hurting anyone smaller. You can be someone they can fight with where they can go all out and no one gets hurt.

—STORYTELLING TO HEAL FEARS—

Scared children need a way to heal from their fears. One way that helps is to tell the story of what happened to them, either in words or by acting out the story in play. Often they play the same scenes over and over, scenes that are closely or loosely based on their own experiences. Unfortunately, children sometimes forget the details of scary events or refuse to talk about them, because it is too painful. They may need some gentle reminders of the incident from an adult, in order to finish dealing with it and put it away. Adults, like children, often wish they could just forget about terrible things that happen. But shoving it under the rug is not the same as really dealing with it and putting it behind us. According to Barbara Brooks and Paula Siegel, "The point of having the child tell the story is to allow her to discharge the feelings connected to the memories and experiences. Without this venting, the feelings leave a residue in the child's mind that will haunt her later."[1] As I describe in greater detail in the last chapter of the book, adults also need to tell their own stories. Parents need to talk to each other about the joys and difficulties of parenting, and especially to share the incidents and feelings that seem too painful or embarrassing or scary to tell.

Telling stories is also a way to tap playfully into the themes that are important in children's lives. These stories work best when they are thinly disguised versions of the truth—close enough to make a connection between the story and the real events and feelings, but different enough to make it safe. Storytelling is a wonderful way to introduce themes that a child may avoid thinking about (or playing about) directly. A friend of mine, whose son had a very bad time at his first preschool, noticed that he hardly ever talked about it and never played school when he was at home, even though usually he was very verbal and very imaginative in his play. Even after he started a new school, which he loved, he never seemed to deal with the difficulties he had at the old one. His mother couldn't believe he didn't have any feelings about it, and she assumed he must have buried them.

Not wanting to force him to face these feelings (and, of course, you really can't force a child to talk or play about something if he doesn't choose to), but wanting to help him with these feelings somehow, she decided to tell a story. She made up a story about a little mouse who was in a very leaky boat on a storm-tossed sea, but then was picked up by a sturdy boat with a wonderful crew. She never mentioned that the leaky boat represented the first school and the sturdy boat represented the new school. At some level though, he made the connection. He wanted to hear this story a dozen times the first day she told it to him, and then spent the rest of the day acting out the story, adding numerous details that the mom could see were representations of what had happened in the old school. After this, he was even more enthusiastic about his new school, and he was much more confident there about trying new things. Did he realize the story was about his school experiences? She didn't know for sure, but it didn't really matter.

One of the basic ideas of Playful Parenting is finding just the right distance, and I think this is part of why children love stories so much. In physical play, like running around in the park, finding the right distance is simply a matter of how close or how far to be from the child. Distance is the very essence of the game that I play with a four-year-old friend. She likes to play with me, but she is pretty shy. She never lets me come nearer than about six feet. If I do, she hides behind her mother's skirt. So we play a version of chase or tag where I chase her, but I never invade her invisible force-field range. I stay at least six feet away. Sometimes I shift gears and start running away from her, and she chases me, maintaining the six-foot distance. We never get closer than our fixed distance, but we are still playing a game that is all about connection. Meanwhile, she spends the whole time smiling so big I think her face is going to split open.

In the case of stories, it is the *symbolic distance* that is important. Talking directly about a troubling topic may be too difficult, but sharing a fictional version of the same topic may make it possible for the child to tackle it. With a little practice you can make up stories that touch on the right themes and feelings without hitting too close to home. Of course, some stories are just stories and don't have to be related to the child's life.

Good stories are just the right blend of fact and fiction. They hit the themes that are important to the child, but they do it in a disguised way, with animal heroes or fictional characters. For example, a three-year-old with a new sibling may not want to hear any more lectures to "be gentle with the baby. . . . I know you feel jealous sometimes. . . . Blah blah blah." She may, however, want her mom to read her a funny picture book about a bunny rabbit with a new sibling, and read it over and over and over. On the other hand, many children like hearing true stories, especially the story of their birth or adoption.

As children grow older, we can shift from telling them stories to listening to their stories. With children who are around ten or twelve, I love to ask them to tell me their life story. They may need a lot of encouragement, but I try to let them tell it themselves. Resist the temptation to butt in with your own perspective on the story, or with extra details that you remember, unless they ask you. If their story is sketchy, ask them to tell it again, adding some more details this time. Keep asking for the story, and for more details, for as much time as you have available. It can be a very powerful experience for both of you. This storytelling idea is easier when it isn't your own child, since when you know all the details, it is tempting to add them or correct the child—both of which inhibit the child's ability to tell it his way. For younger children you can start the story for them, and ask them to add whatever they remember, or imagine.

Telling stories *together* is a great way to make sure the story is neither too far afield nor too painful. Joint storytelling simply means that every once in a while you ask the child for ideas on how the story should go. Or sometimes children will forcefully offer their own ideas in a jointly told story. My friend and colleague Sam Roth told me about a boy whose favorite game was joint storytelling, where the child would create terrifying dangers for the hero, while Sam would have to figure out ways to save him. The boy was symbolically finding the right distance for talking about fears and worries he could not talk about directly; Sam was symbolically talking about safety and security.

Children use this idea of symbolic distance all the time in their own play, especially dramatic play where they make up characters and act out scenes. It is important to let them be in charge of this emotional distance, because they are deciding how much they can handle. Lawrence Hartmann, whose parents were both psychoanalysts, tells a story about a drawing of a prince he made when he was four. He was showing his parents the prince's sword, and they said, "That's a penis." "No," he said, "it's a sword." "No," they insisted, "it's a penis."[2] Even if the sword *was* symbolically a penis (which perhaps must be assumed in a family of psychoanalysts), his parents were not allowing him to be the one to decide whether to play it safe and call it a sword.

—ACTING AND DIRECTING WHEN NECESSARY—

When children are dealing with feelings of powerlessness, they often engage in role-reversal play on their own initiative. They may need us only to be an eager audience. Other times, this kind of play does not develop spontaneously, and more adult thought and planning are necessary. We must be prepared to be actors in the drama, or even directors and playwrights. Children who have specific fears, for example, are likely to need our help. Most children will not make up pretend games on their own to deal with these fears; instead, they will just avoid the thing they fear. If they are afraid of bees, or the water, they may stop wanting to go outside, or refuse to go swimming. Parents may get annoyed and frustrated, and even force children to do these scary things, but sometimes the fears remain in place anyway. The reason children often avoid using play to heal fears is that fear leads people to avoid whatever scares them, which makes it hard to use play for its healing purpose. Unfortunately, no one ever got over a fear by avoiding it, only by facing it. If an adult initiates a fun game about it, children can gain confidence that their fears can be overcome.

So if a child is afraid of bees, you might say, "You be a bee and I'll try to run away from you." Let yourself get "stung," and then scream. Or you say, "I'm a bee and I'm going to sting you," but you play the part of a klutzy, incompetent bee. Somehow you end up stinging yourself every time, instead of the child. Or you keep bumping into walls and falling over on the floor. Anything to get the child giggling about something that used to be too scary even to think about.

I see a boy in therapy who is afraid of bugs, and he always makes me be the one to fetch the ball or Frisbee when it goes into the bushes. I close my eyes and stumble into the bushes, pretending to be too afraid of bugs to look. I ask him to direct me, since I can't see, as I bumble around. He laughs and tells me which direction to go and slowly builds up his confidence. If I just went and got the ball for him, he might be happy to have avoided the bugs, but he wouldn't have made any progress on his fears. If I had made a big deal about his fear, he would have been humiliated. Contrary to our models of military training, people don't learn best when they are humiliated. Taking on the fear myself seemed to unstick the fear a little bit, like putting oil on a rusty hinge. Finding the right symbolic distance isn't always easy though, since it may change from day to day. One day I tried my trick of pretending to be afraid of bugs, and instead of playing that game with me, he walked away. After a minute of standing in the middle of a bush and feeling like a dope, I changed to being loudly afraid of *thorns* in the bushes, instead of bugs, and he came running back over to coach me through it so I could get the ball.

I have seen many parents allow fears like this to go unchecked forever, limiting the child's activities, out of an effort to protect them from feeling scared if they are forced to face the scary thing again. Other parents ignore the fear, forcing the child to sink or swim. Playful Parenting provides a middle ground, a more effective solution than either of these. Naturally, it involves a playful attitude and attention to closeness and confidence.

Fernando, age three, was scared of swings. He usually wouldn't go on them at all, but one time he went on because his best friend, Ned, was on and he wanted to do everything Ned did. He was enjoying himself, but at one point he got scared, let go of the chains, and fell off. Fortunately he wasn't hurt, but, not surprisingly, he became more afraid of swings than ever. His father asked me for ideas about how to approach this problem.

One option, I said, is to reverse the roles, to be the incompetent one who can't swing. I find that it is often better to play at being incompetent instead of pretending to be fearful, since that seems to let the child loosen up and laugh about it more. So, you say, "I am the best swinger ever, no swing is too tough for me, I know everything there is to know about swings," and then you act as if you can't tell the difference between a swing and a slide. Or you can't even get on it properly. Or you fall off. Meanwhile, hopefully, the child is laughing his head off, and/or giving you instructions on how to do it properly, which, of course, you bungle. As always, be on the lookout for signs the child is feeling teased or made fun of, and if this seems to be the case, apologize and switch gears right away.

Unfortunately, my brilliant advice fell flat and didn't work at all, because the child refused to go to the park. We went back to the drawing board. My next suggestion was that Fernando's dad announce that they are going to have a special playtime to work on going on swings. We guessed that Fernando would say, "I don't want to go on a swing" or "I don't like swings." That's okay. Dad could answer, "I know, we may not go on a swing today, but we are going to work on *getting over the fear of swings.*" If you don't ever mention swings, he'll never look scared, and it may look as if the problem is solved. Maybe it's no big deal to be afraid of swings, but who needs a life filled with restrictions like that? On the other hand, if you say, "You're going on the swing and that's final. If you cry about it, you're never going to the park again," you may win the battle, but you're on the way to losing the war. Children who end up being reckless daredevils—mostly boys—have buried their fear and have to continually prove to themselves that they aren't afraid, so they do increasingly dumb things.

The middle ground is to mention casually that you want to help him get over his fear of swings. You have become the director and stage manager, overriding his avoidance of swings, but not so much that he freezes up or shuts all systems down. At the right distance—which may be just outside your front door or twenty yards from the swing or right beside them—there is an invisible boundary that represents exactly the border between avoiding the fear and being flooded by it. This is the edge (it may not always be at the same place even for the same child). This is where the work of using Playful Parenting to heal fears takes place. At this edge, when you say, brightly, "Let's go on the swing," the child's response may be trembling or screaming or laughing. They may burst into tears, or break out in a cold sweat. That's the signal you're at the edge. That's good! Don't panic. Listen to the feelings, but don't force them forward or let them give up. Just keep relaxedly saying, "Let's go on the swing. Let's go one step closer. How about if we touch the swing?" The child has to trust that you won't trick him and make him get on before he is ready. Be prepared. This may take a few minutes or a few hours, and it may all happen at one sitting or over the course of several playtimes. Gradually, you inch toward the goal, with lots of encouragement. In Fernando's case, it took a couple of times. Now Fernando is king of the swings. This technique isn't exactly a role reversal, but it involves balancing different roles—the boy who is paralyzed by fear, the boy who never wants to go to the park again, and the boy who really wants to be able to swing.

Sometimes there's a different outcome to a scary experience. Instead of avoiding the thing they fear, or playing a game about it, children compulsively seek it out. They may *try* to use play to deal with the fear but can't figure out how to do it in a way that works. Instead, they just keep scaring themselves all over again. Horror movies and overly violent television often have this result. They may want to watch the show over and over not because they liked it but because they are locked in a cycle of feeling scared. They try to overcome their fear by watching the show again and again. They may not even look scared, and they may actually start acting out the stuff they see on the screen.

To get over their fear, some children may just need to watch the show a few times, until it gets less and less scary with each viewing. This is called desensitization. Or they may need to watch it in your lap, or next to you, so they can face the fear in a safer setting. If you are watching a movie like this with children, it's a good idea to take what I call scream breaks. Pause the movie and give a pretend scream, which will usually be followed by giggles. This break lets some of the feelings out, like the valve on a pressure cooker.

Occasionally, when children play out what they saw, or watch the show over and over, instead of desensitizing they get totally scared all over again. When this happens, the answer is once again for the adult to initiate role-reversal play, with the adult playing the role of a bumbling, incompetent, and not-very-scary monster. It's a fun challenge to develop a monster or a bad guy who is just the right mix of scary and goofy, in order to get children to laugh. The laughter helps them out of the cycle of aggressive- or horror-oriented play.

—FANTASY PLAY—

In the epigraph to this chapter I referred to the time my daughter said to me, when I was very frustrated with her, "Let's pretend you're the dad and I'm the daughter and you're mad at me." This isn't role reversal, and, in fact, it was funny precisely because she assigned roles for the game that were *exactly the same* as our real-life roles. What made it playful, and eased the tension between us, was the way she took the real situation and made it into fantasy play. This technique is even simpler than role reversal and can be just as effective. If children are having trouble with friends, try simply saying, "Let's pretend that we're friends." See what happens. Let them decide whether to make you a good friend or a bad friend. The fantasy play might be close to the real situation, or only loosely related. With one young boy, I made up a game called Larry's School of Nonsense and Goofiness, because he never would have wanted to go along if I had said, "Let's play kindergarten." He loved to play the nonsense school game, and we made up all kinds of silly rules and punishments and difficult challenges that provided a dramatic (but humorous) link to the real-life difficult situations facing him at school.

Another way to look at this idea is to see that children may get their sense of power from *controlling the game*, in the same way they get it from reversing the roles. For instance, when a client of mine—an only child—was eight and waiting eagerly to hear about the birth of her new cousin, I expected some "sibling" rivalry to appear in her play. Sure enough, she set up a game with me where I was the father, she was the older sister, and there was a new set of baby twins. I was supposed to pay attention only to the twins and not to her. She proceeded to have a pretend temper tantrum. I thought she would want me to nurture her in the game, but she wanted me to ignore her and give all my time and energy to the babies. In other words, she knew better than I how she wanted to use the play—not to have her cup filled by playing the part of the cherished baby, but to take on the role of the discarded older sibling in a playful way. We played in this vein for several weeks, and it was very effective in helping her deal with her feelings of jealousy and rivalry. You'll notice that she did not reverse the roles, making herself the baby (which is the most common response to a new child in the family). She kept the roles intact but fictionalized the situation, twisting the roles a bit. However, even though she retained the role of the displaced older child, she did reverse the roles in a more basic way—no longer was she the helpless victim of her own jealous feelings; instead, she could use play to master those feelings. She may not have been able to control the amount of attention the new cousin would soak up, but she *could* control the game we played.

Another painful theme that children will often try to introduce into a game is the feeling that no one likes them. Unfortunately, when children try to reverse the roles with this theme, adults get confused. The play often runs into a dead end. Children say, for example, "I hate you," or "You're stupid." The parent feels outraged or rejected. But the children are not going to curl into your lap and cry, "No one likes me," even though that's what they really mean. We have to read between the lines and understand that they are telling us—in their own way—how much they hurt inside and how we can help them. So instead of yelling at them for talking to us that way, and sending them to their room, we might say, "Waaah, Joey called me stupid. Waaah, no one likes me." Or, "You can call me stupid, but you'd better not call me Wiener Schnitzel."

One boy, who liked to play catch in his sessions, gave me a clue about this theme of not being liked. Once when I dropped the ball, he said, "That ball doesn't like you." I knew he was struggling with not having many friends at school, but he never talked about it. So I took advantage of this opening to get him to giggle about how upset I was that the ball didn't like me. Another child had a trick where she would tell me to sit down on the couch, and then push me off so I couldn't sit down. She would say, "The couch doesn't like you." Since she often got in trouble for hitting other children in school because she felt as if they didn't like her, I started hitting the couch and yelling at it while she laughed. I acted real surprised that the couch still didn't like me even after I punched it a bunch of times.

Psychiatrist Stanley Greenspan writes, "The transition to pretend play is one of the most important leaps your child will make."[3] Fantasy play requires, and fosters, symbolic thought, abstraction, and creative imagination. Some children leap right into fantasy play on their own. Others need a little push from adults. Try picking up a doll or stuffed animal and making it into a character with a funny voice. Call the climbing structure Mount Everest. Start playtimes with the phrase, "Let's pretend . . ." Once a fantasy game has started, play your part with gusto, and thicken the plot. Introduce conflict or challenge. Narrate the story. If a child doesn't ever seem to engage in fantasy play, try adding a fantasy element to the games they do like to play. For example, Ken and I play chess a lot in our sessions, and he almost never does any kind of fantasy play. So sometimes, during chess matches, I say, "I'll be Bobby Fischer and you be Gary Kasparov." That lets me exaggerate feelings of anxiety and nervousness—feelings that Ken tries to manage by denying them—through my pretend character.

Whenever a child is struggling with an emotion or a confusing concept in their lives, it helps to give that role to a fantasy character. For a child obsessed with fairness, for example, the parent might pick up the child's second favorite animal or toy and make it say, "That's not fair! You always play with Tigger!" You might develop characters who are sad, or experimenting with being naughty, or aggressive, or unable to solve a problem similar to one that is facing the child. "All the other animals teased me when you were at school today. I don't know what to do." "I'm scared when you turn the light out." Don't be surprised if the child is very mean to this puppet or doll that represents him; it's his way of showing how bad he feels about whatever problem he is having. He may also show you exactly what he needs from you, by helping the character in a very smart way. This technique lets the child have some perspective on feelings and problems. It helps parents, too, who often feel helpless when their child is struggling with something, but can't or won't talk about it.

Among the many fantasy roles that children take on in their play are good guys and bad guys. Once known as cops and robbers, this kind of play is now more likely to involve superheroes or fantasy characters from TV and movies. The main thing for parents to remember about this type of play is that it isn't as destructive or as horrid as it may seem. Remember Paul, the baboon in the last chapter who restrained his aggression in order to wrestle safely with his little brother? Well, superhero or good guy/bad guy play is a human way of practicing control over aggression. Some children prefer to be the bad guy, experimenting with being frightening or dangerous. Actually hurting other people isn't helpful, but playing at it can be both fun and educational—in the sense of learning to manage aggressive feelings and impulses. Other children prefer to be the good guy. They like to be aggressive in a way that is socially acceptable—by being Batman, for example, or a soldier. That is, they get to exercise their aggression but only at acceptable targets.

Some parents love this kind of superhero play and get into the characters along with their children. They understand that if they are playing the role of the bad guy or the monster, they need to be not too scary—powerful enough to be interesting, but not overwhelming. Maybe a little bumbling or incompetent (like Lex Luthor in the Superman movies). Other parents hate this kind of play and would love to ban it. Sorry. Children who want to play these games *need* to play them, and if they aren't allowed to, they will go underground and do them anyway. It is much better to join in and play with them, which then lets you shift the play a little bit if it gets too violent or out of hand.

—FINDING AN ORIGINAL SCRIPT—

Who writes the scripts that children act out when they demand a new toy they've seen advertised on TV, when they tease one another, when they play Pokémon or Power Rangers, when they go on a date, when they sneak behind the school to smoke a cigarette? Not our children, and not us. These scripts are handed down year after year, enhanced by television and movies. These prescripted scenarios kill imagination and creativity. In contrast, good fantasy play is spontaneous and free. It follows an imaginary script that is continually evolving and changing, a script "written" by the child or a group of children. This script may be inspired by characters or situations or scenes from a movie or TV show, but it quickly leaves that starting point to explore new territory of the imagination.

But look around at children playing; for the most part, you will see them acting out someone else's script instead of their own. Their own imagination is overpowered by the intensity and the repetition of what they see on the screen. If they break away from the screen at all to play, the game follows the prescripted story line exactly, or it fizzles out to boredom, or else the game becomes violent. This violence is not the playful use of fantasy but true aggression, reckless and dangerous. Toys that are spinoffs from movies and television and video games keep the play locked to that script. What else can you do with a gun besides shoot with it? On the contrary, a simple cardboard tube can be a light saber, a sword, a tree, a trumpet, and on and on and on. Of course, some children will get creative even with the most uninspiring toys, but often it takes some adult help to get the play unstuck from the same exact characters, scenarios, and outcomes. Although children love repetition, they need to change things a little in their play. They need to repeat, but with a little twist. Most toys are junk, by which I mean they can do only one thing, over and over. Great toys, like good dramatic play, allow children to make the world their own and allow full expression of their creativity.

On the other hand, most play experts agree that you can't success-fully ban games based on TV shows, especially war play or weapon play. You can try to ban it, but they are very likely to become obsessed with the idea of it, because it is forbidden. Beyond that, though, they *need* to play these games in order to figure out what those images and stories mean to them. By playing with them, we can help children rediscover their own stories, their own characters, their own source of imaginative play.

But if we just let them run wild with violent play, that does not leave children free to make their own choices. It actually leaves them in the hands of the media, who are exerting constant pressure on children, espe-cially boys, to fill their play and their imaginations with weapons. So if you can't ban it and you can't ignore it, what do you do? By now you won't be surprised by my answer: Play it with them. When they shoot you, fall down dead—preferably on top of them. Or pretend you were shot with the love gun (see chapter three). Pretend to be wounded and see if you can get the child to be a nurturing medic for a minute instead of a soldier or superhero. Exaggerate the mayhem in a way that brings on the giggles.

In the same way that toy guns can inhibit children's creative play, graphic images of sex and violence can overwhelm children's imagina-tions. These images replace children's own creations, the ones they come up with in their own minds, with a mass-produced and overly stimulat-ing imitation. You can see the results in their play. I can often tell just by how children play how much television they watch, or what types of things they are allowed to see. Shows that mix sex and violence, from slasher movies to professional wrestling, are the worst.

Many toys come with their own prepackaged scripts for how chil-dren are supposed to play them, and, in fact, our whole culture writes scripts for children (and adults) about how to behave. We are rewarded for following these scripts and punished for deviating from them. Boys are supposed to act one way, girls another way. Teenagers are told exactly how to rebel, and especially what rebellious products to buy. Children are programmed to watch a commercial and say, "I want one of those." Chil-dren need help with all this.

To counteract these prescribed roles, one thing we can do as parents is, together with our children, examine these images. Watch TV and movies with them, and stop to discuss the things you see. Play games based on what you've watched, but twist things around a bit. Play the role of the cheerful idiot who is entranced with Power Rangers, or who tries to imitate the dancers in heavy-metal rock videos.

Through billions of dollars in marketing, the corporations of the world write a master script for our children, with one and only one role for them to play: the consumer. When this role is assigned to them, and they go along with it passively, they are just locking themselves in the tower of powerlessness. One great way to take a step out of this tower is to understand how television influences people. Years ago, my daughter saw a video at a children's museum about truth versus deception in television advertisements aimed at children. Ever since, she has been wisely skeptical about claims made in commercials. This is another type of role reversal, because it puts children in the driver's seat, as decoders of the media message, instead of in the role of passive consumers.

Do you know who the true experts are in tuning in to children, understanding their motivations, their themes, their feelings? These are experts who put my fellow child psychologists and myself to shame. They spend hour after hour, day after day, paying attention to children and trying to figure out how they think and what they feel. Too bad they work for Disney, and Cartoon Network, and Nickelodeon, and MTV, and ad agencies, and toy companies. They have an interest—their profit—in knowing what makes children laugh, what scares them, what they like to play. We have to do at least as good a job as they do. Our stake in paying attention to children—tuning in—is much greater than a simple profit motive.

These corporations are tuning in to our children, and our children are tuning in to TV and magazines. The media aimed at children are so much more exciting and enticing than we'll ever be. So children tune us out, and we respond by tuning them out. David Elkind, famous for his book *The Hurried Child*, talks about the way this media-driven consumerism affects our children. "What characterizes contemporary capitalistic societies, particularly the United States, is the exploitation of children as consumers. Toy and clothing manufacturers and the music and movie industries now view children and youth as a vast market.

Indeed, teenagers have the highest percentage of disposable income of any age group in our society. And as children and youth become markets, their health and welfare become secondary to the accumulation of capital as they did at the time of the Industrial Revolution [when their labor was exploited]."[4] Elkind believes that this trend explains why there is less and less truly free play in the United States and other Western countries these days. It is replaced by play that brings somebody a profit. Just compare street games of hide-and-seek and kick the can with contemporary products such as Pokémon and American Girl dolls. Some children barely know how to play if they don't have a store-bought toy with them. Meanwhile, school days contain less and less play time, even in kindergarten, and more academic preparation for becoming a productive member of society.

One thing I love about visiting New York City is that there are so many ads that are geared to advertisers, as opposed to consumers. I usually find these marketing strategies fascinating yet disturbing. On a recent trip, I noticed two of these ad campaigns. One was for Nickelodeon, the other for MTV. It seemed that one or the other of these ads was on nearly every bus kiosk. The Nickelodeon ads all described a typical child, focusing on that child's unique talents. They all ended with some phrase about how these children made their own decisions about what shoes to buy, or made the decision for the whole family about what sports drink to buy, or had an average of so many dollars allowance each week. The idea was that Nickelodeon could deliver those consumers to any advertiser smart enough to advertise on their network. I was appalled. The ads were pretending to celebrate child power, then undermining it.

The MTV ads were more subtle. They didn't even come out and say that they were aimed at advertisers. The whole ad was a word or phrase that seemed to be some new teenage slang. Underneath was the definition and the MTV logo. I thought these were ads for some hot new show that I didn't know about, because I'm an old guy who doesn't watch MTV. My niece, who lives in New York and follows the advertising world, informed me that there was no new show. In fact, there was no new slang. These phrases were made up in the MTV marketing department, and the ads were supposed to make people think: I don't understand kids today, but I don't have to, because MTV does. I just have to hand over my money to them, and they'll do the rest, making their viewers into my customers. Scary. As if it isn't hard enough to bridge the gap between the generations, now we have advertising designed to make adults feel as if we will never understand young people.

Unplug and play.

CHAPTER 8

EMPOWER GIRLS AND CONNECT WITH BOYS

A three-year-old boy to his father:
"Dad, you're a man. And Mommy is a woman.
And George is Curious."

Parenting has been described as the process of giving our children both roots and wings. In the language of Playful Parenting, filling a child's cup is a metaphor for watering the plant so the roots will grow deep, and also a metaphor for nurturing the bird so her wings will soar. Every child needs a full cup; every child needs both roots and wings. Unfortunately, boys and girls are treated in ways that damage their roots and wings. One goal of Playful Parenting is to help correct some of this damage. Because of the way girls tend to be inhibited from exploring, they need help in spreading their wings, exploring the wide world, and discovering their own power room. Because boys are so often left alone with their feelings and deprived of the comforts of cuddling and nurturing, they need extra help in putting down roots.

The story of the love gun (page 50) was about using playfulness to help a boy connect on a human-to-human level instead of repeating the same tired script about shooting and killing. Though I have played variations of the love gun game with girls, I play it much more often with boys, because boys are more likely to need that added push to reconnect. By the same token, though I wrestle with boys and do my best to encourage their confidence, I make sure to pay extra attention to the themes of power and confidence in girls.

One of the few things I remember from graduate school is a set of studies that I call the tabletop experiments, which are about the different ways people treat an infant depending on whether it is a boy or a girl. Everyone was shown the same baby, but half were told it was a boy and half were told it was a girl. That way, the researchers knew that the subjects in the experiment were not just responding to subtle differences between boy babies and girl babies. In some studies, a crawling baby, dressed only in a diaper, was left on a large table in a room with a stranger. In others, the subjects heard a tape recording of a crying baby coming from the next room. The researchers secretly watched the scene, and measured how much the subjects let the child explore, how soon they went to get the baby when it "woke up," and how much they interacted with the baby.

If the adults thought the child was a girl, they went to get her sooner when she cried, and they interacted with her more. If they thought it was a boy, they waited much longer to comfort the crying baby, but they encouraged more exploration and more gross motor activity. In other words, only girls were given roots; only boys were allowed to spread their wings. The actual sex of the baby didn't matter at all.[1] Another of these tabletop studies is especially relevant to girls and power. John and Sandra Condry[2] showed adults videotapes of a nine-month-old baby responding to different toys. Some were told the baby was a girl and some that it was a boy, but in fact, all subjects saw the same videotape. The adult subjects were asked to rate the intensity of pleasure, anger, and fear that they saw displayed by the baby. The biggest effect was found with the jack-in-the-box, which made the baby in the videotape cry. The raters described this cry as *anger* if they thought it was a boy, and as *fear* if they thought it was a girl. Also, the people who thought they were watching a boy described the baby as being more active and more potent than those who thought they were watching a girl. It's no wonder that later on, boys are more likely to be punished while girls are more likely to be overprotected.

These tabletop studies illustrate my basic idea about how boys and girls are treated differently—almost from birth—and what they need from us as a result. They are not merely treated differently, they are each limited, blocked from their full potential. Girls are comforted, but are not usually encouraged to explore or take risks; they need Playful Parenting that builds empowerment and confidence. Boys are allowed to explore and are actively encouraged to be daring, but they are left alone when they are scared or lonely or sad. In fact, as they get older, they are not just left alone but punished for expressing these feelings. So boys need Playful Parenting that pays extra attention to connection and feelings.

When I talk to groups of adults, I often ask what annoys or aggravates or bewilders them about boys. It is no wonder that the answers, especially from women, come back loud and clear: "They don't talk." "They're closed up." "They don't share how they feel." The answer is simple: connect, connect, connect. Do it as playfully as possible, but do it. For girls, the answer is just as straightforward: empower, empower, empower.

In *Failing at Fairness*, an influential book about girls being short-changed by schools, Myra and David Sadker tell a story about a tenth-grade math class.[3] A girl goes to the teacher for help and is told the answer. A boy goes to the same teacher for help and is told to go back and try to work it out for himself. The Sadkers argue that the girl is cheated out of the chance to think for herself and develop her mathematical ability. I agree. I think they miss half the point of the story, though, which is that the boy loses out, too. It's the tabletop experiments all over again—the girl is given warmth but is discouraged from spreading her wings by working hard at the problem; the boy is given high expectations about achievement but has to do it all on his own, without any emotional support, without roots. Instead, the teacher might have said to both students, "Let's work it out together."

On average, boys and girls do play differently. Boys more often roughhouse; girls more often play house. I hear over and over from parents: Give a girl a fire truck, and she'll wrap it in a blanket and put it to bed. Give a boy virtually anything, and he'll make a weapon out of it. Of course, like all sex differences, these differences are averages. Men on average are taller than women, but we all know short men and tall women. Some boys prefer playing house to roughhousing, and vice versa for girls.

The fact that boys and girls play differently, and that they start to play differently very early, is often taken as evidence that these differences are natural or normal. Others insist that the differences are all learned, drilled into children by a sexist society. They are both sort of right. Many years of research can be summarized in one sentence: *Inborn sex differences are real, but they are quite small.*[4] Parenting, culture, and education can either minimize or exaggerate these small biological differences. In our society they tend to be exaggerated.

Both closeness and confidence should be every child's birthright. But girls are discouraged from being too powerful, and they are encouraged to be overly "nice," to care more about relationships than about achievement. If they don't fit this mold, they are called names that suggest they are not proper females: bitchy, pushy, bossy, dyke. Meanwhile, boys are discouraged from being too close. In place of closeness, boys are taught and pressured to overemphasize competition, assertiveness, achievement, and strength. Look at the insults a boy hears if he is connected instead of disconnected. If he has a close connection with his mother, he's a mama's boy; if he likes to play with girls, he's a sissy; if he wants to hug or hold hands with a boy, he's a fag; if he wants an equal, respectful relationship with his girlfriend, he's henpecked; if he likes school, he's a nerd.

In a world without these prejudices and without this differential treatment of boys and girls, would boys and girls still play differently? We don't know. We do know that now, in our current society, children play in ways that mirror the sex roles they see around them. Take a common example: the difference between the way boys and girls respond when they see a bug. Many girls, even after decades of feminism, will see a bug and go "eek, ooh, ugh!" and act out the famous helpless, pathetic, powerless, weak, damsel-in-distress scenario. A typical boy—even if his father is a diaper-changing New Age sensitive guy—will see the same bug and smash it, scrunch it, kill it. Preferably with sound effects resembling weapons of mass destruction. Neither of these is a very rational response. They are both exaggerations of sex-role stereotypes. Meanwhile, boys who act scared of the bug and girls who trample the bug run the risk of being teased for being so different from the norm.

A few years ago I was playing with my daughter and a friend of hers, a boy in her kindergarten class. They were playing a fantasy game about knights and princesses and dragons. Even though my daughter was physically stronger and more confident than her friend, somehow the knight kept having to rescue the princess. I remember thinking, Where do they get this stuff? I tried to get the princess to rescue the knight for a change, but eventually had to forget about it: children play to try on adult roles, and this includes sex roles—figuring out what it means to be male or female. In some ways, these roles have changed dramatically in the last few years. In other ways, though, they've barely budged since the Stone Age, certainly not since the age of chivalry.

One thing that has always puzzled me is why toy companies still package tea sets in pink boxes with pictures of girls on the cover. They know how to get boys to play with tea sets, and girls to play with robots, but they'd rather not. Even the chance to sell twice as many tea sets isn't a big enough motivation to get the marketing business out of its rut of toys for boys and toys for girls. Of course, it's not really a big deal whether a child plays with a tea set or not. Or is it? One study found that girls who engaged in more stereotypical feminine play as young children did worse than other girls in math and science in school.[5] We can only speculate about the long-term effects on boys of being limited to certain toys.

The Playful Parenting prescription, of course, is get down on the floor and play with children. No matter what games we play with them, we can make a special effort to connect with boys and empower girls, so that all children can grow roots and wings.

—WHY I PLAY BARBIE (AND ACTION FIGURES), EVEN THOUGH I HATE IT—

My daughter, the offspring of two ardent feminists, used to love to play with Barbies and dolls based on Disney-movie heroines. Thankfully, she's mostly outgrown it now. I hated playing this with her. It was boring, stupid, and against almost everything I believe in. Yet, sometimes, when my daughter asked me, I would play. Children play in order to figure things out about the world, and girls certainly have a lot to figure out in the areas of body image, clothing, makeup, looking pretty, romance, etc. The messages girls receive about all this are confusing and misleading and disempowering, and they need our help in sorting it all out. In the same way, boys need help figuring out all the messages they get about aggression and competition. That's why I also suggest that parents join in their sons' aggressive play (which many parents—especially mothers—hate as much as I hate Barbie).

Many writers have bemoaned the way our culture disempowers girls, especially as they approach adolescence. I think that what happens is that girls experience a disruption in their sense of the world and of themselves, especially about their appearance. The unrealistic and distorted expectations about how girls should look, and about what is pretty, lock many girls into a fortress of powerlessness. If looks are all-important, and they don't look the right way, then things are pretty miserable. Mary Pipher, author of *Reviving Ophelia*, talks about how girls experience a significant drop in self-esteem within minutes of thumbing through fashion magazines.[6] If your daughter reads those magazines, go through them with her. Don't let the images play out their seductive games without some input from you, some grounding in reality.

How can engaging in play help your daughter be empowered? If you sit on the floor and play Barbies with her, you can shake things up a bit. Be wild with the dolls: dance them around, dress them up oddly, make them say outrageous things. I like having one doll play up the sexist stereotypes that the dolls are based on, while another more powerful doll stands up to it. "I'm the femininity police, and you aren't being ladylike!" "Shut up and leave me alone; I like to run and jump, and you can't stop me." I try to introduce plots that are different from the love and romance and marriage scenarios that are the staple of girl-oriented games and movies. Have you ever noticed that Disney movies that focus on male characters are all about identity, like Pinocchio finding himself, while movies with female leads are all about romance—*The Little Mermaid*, *Snow White*, *Cinderella*?

To counteract the impact of what I have described in the tabletop experiments, we have to encourage girls to be adventurous, loud, strong, physically powerful, and assertive. We need to fight the notion that strong women and girls are not proper females. This may require, especially for mothers, that we take a close look at our own upbringing, and our own inhibitions about wrestling or rough-and-tumble play. All children can use a hand with being more confident and being powerful in a healthy and constructive way, but girls face extra obstacles to discovering this reservoir of strength.

If I play Barbies and Little Mermaid with girls in order to counteract the effects of what our society values and devalues, the same goes for playing war games and action figures with boys. I overcome my own pacifism and gentle nature in order to throw myself enthusiastically into games about killing and fighting and mass destruction. I insert a little reality into the play here and there—"Ouch, that must hurt!"—and I insert as much closeness as possible. I fall over dead on top of them if I get shot, cower behind them if an enemy is nearby, take any excuse to be physically and emotionally close. With both boys and girls, the Playful Parenting approach is to join in first, then gradually lead them out of the spot where they are stuck. If we lecture them, or refuse to play a game because it is too violent or too girly, they shut us out. Who can blame them? We wouldn't like it if someone told us our favorite activities were stupid. If we leave them alone to figure out all this confusing stuff about being male or being female, they really aren't being left alone at all. On the contrary, if we leave the scene, they are told how to behave and how to look and what to think by marketing departments, advertising agencies, and the entertainment industry. Corporations are eager to fill the gap that is left when we step aside.

Competition is an area that is confusing for both girls and boys, and for their parents. Girls may give up on trying their hardest, or may not be able to enjoy a victory, because they feel bad for the losers. Boys, meanwhile, are expected to care more about winning than about friendships or feelings. In other words, once again our society sets up boys to be isolated and girls to be powerless. Boys are supposed to sacrifice relationships and emotions in favor of competition and victory, while girls are supposed to sacrifice individual achievement in favor of not hurting anyone's feelings.

I saw this distinction clearly last spring in my daughter's soccer league. Her team was supposed to play against another team from the same school—in other words, against their friends instead of against strangers from other schools. The girls were dreading this encounter and wished for rain, snow, anything to avoid having to pit competition against friendship. I was mentioning this to another parent, who then told me about her son's baseball team. When they were scheduled to play against their friends and classmates, they didn't pray for rain. Both teams relished the coming encounter. For weeks ahead of the game they taunted and teased one another, divided along team lines at lunch, vowed to destroy each other on the field, and so on. This teasing among boys is very confusing for parents. Boys use teasing, and even hitting, as a way of being close to one another, especially since more direct ways of expressing affection are forbidden to boys after age three or four. On the other hand, this teasing and shoving can cause real pain and fear.

I am not arguing that the girls should be more like the boys or that the boys should be more like the girls. As with the bugs (squashing them versus running away screeching), the answer is somewhere in between. With our help, boys can be as well connected as they are powerful, and girls can be as empowered as they are connected.

For another example, look at children's artwork. Except for a few who have special talent or special teachers, most children become very stereotyped in their artwork. Boys will draw weapons and spaceships, girls will draw hearts and rainbows and maybe horses. I can't believe that this is a biological difference. I think it's a matter of being stuck in sex roles. Help them learn to draw more interesting things. Draw together to help them out of the lonely corner where the stereotyped drawings repeat in an endless loop. Exaggerating or playing with these differences also helps loosen things up. "Aw, you drew a love battleship; how cute. All those guns poking out of it are so precious. . . ." "Oh no! That rainbow shot me with a heart dart; I'm bleeding."

Since most boys have been pressured not to cry, or have gotten in trouble with their peers for crying, I made up a character called Never-Cry-Man. I say, with a dramatic flourish, "I am Never-Cry-Man; I never cry," and then I burst into fake tears at the drop of a hat. With girls I will play a character who is a parody of girliness, who lives and breathes for fashion and hair design. Or I play the role of a handsome prince who cares only about what the girl dolls look like. He's a very funny sexist pig who provokes laughter and lets girls reject the timeworn stereotypes. These games loosen up the absurd images that the media try to lock into our children's brains.

—CONNECTING WITH BOTH BOYS AND GIRLS—

Disconnection is natural and inevitable, and all children occasionally lock themselves in the tower of isolation. Some spend more time in that tower than others. As a group, however, boys face extra obstacles in reconnecting. Because of how boys are treated, they are more likely to have difficulty expressing feelings, showing that they've been hurt, looking vulnerable, maintaining intimate relationships, and giving or accepting tenderness. Unfortunately, these are exactly the ways to get out of that tower of isolation. The result is what Daniel Kindlon and Michael Thompson refer to, in *Raising Cain*, as boys' emotional illiteracy. That's a real problem, because emotional literacy is necessary for psychological healing and for real intimacy.

A repeated finding in research on childhood sexual abuse is that girls are more likely to be abused within the home, by relatives, while boys are more likely to be abused outside the home. In other words, those who prey on girls tend to manipulate the close relationship they have. Pedophiles who prey on boys tend to use the fact that boys are starved for affection and contact. In my work with adult men, I heard story after story of boys who were sitting ducks for pedophiles because these predators offered them "love," affection, respect, attention, and access to forbidden things like alcohol or pornography. The abusers were offering these things only for their own sexual gratification, but the boys were taken in because they were so desperate for connection. The emotional miseducation of boys leaves them lonely, which sets them up to be exploited and abused. Then, unable to freely express their emotions, this miseducation interferes with their recovery from those traumas. Many of these men came from loving, normal homes. Their empty cups weren't the result of negligent parenting but of our society's mistreatment of boys. Obviously, playing more with our sons isn't the only answer, but it is a significant start.

Look how hard it is for men and older boys to have any kind of physical contact that isn't violent, competitive, or sexual. We laugh at men's awkwardness when they hug each other, or when they don't know how to comfort a friend, but it is more poignant than funny. Cuddling more with boys is not going to reverse these powerful social forces overnight, but we have to start somewhere. We all know how destructive it is to maintain the archaic standard that boys don't cry, yet we still react differently to boys' tears than to girls' tears.

The starting place is *emotional connection*. Empathy, emotional intelligence, kindness—these are all learned in close relationships, not from books or moral lessons. And they are learned in play. Unfortunately— catastrophically—some of the things that would help boys connect are considered "girl things": cuddling; playing with baby dolls; reading and writing poetry; practicing music, art, literature, drama, singing, dancing. Some boys do these things, but they are much more common and much more encouraged in girls. Boys who do them may pay a severe price, and they often end up either giving up these activities or getting labeled as sissies. The ironic thing is that it isn't hard to get boys to play with dolls— many studies have shown that just watching a few videos showing men taking care of babies increases preschool boys' interest in nurturing doll play—but as a society we aren't sure if we want them to. We somehow want boys to grow up to be nurturing fathers without any risk of their becoming sissies.

There are games that we can play with boys to improve their emotional literacy and their ability to connect, games that won't be rejected as unmanly. Some of these activities focus on communication. In order to help boys to talk more, play simple word games and language games. One of my favorites is *fortunately/unfortunately*, where one person starts a story with, "Fortunately . . ." and the other person says the next line, starting with "Unfortunately . . ." You go back and forth telling a tale of disaster and rescue—two important themes for most children. Another great game, which doesn't require words, is squiggle. An old game that was popularized among therapists by D. W. Winnicott, squiggle is very simple. One person starts a drawing, making squiggles that don't look like anything in particular. The other person has to finish the drawing, making it into something. You take turns being the one to start. The idea of these play activities is to practice the building blocks of communication. Don't expect to leapfrog directly to deep conversations. For example, I consulted with some parents recently who were eager for their nine-year-old son to talk to them more. I suggested ways for them to listen to him on his turf—nonverbal communication. So rather than insisting that he tell them details about his school day, they asked him to give it a thumbs-up or thumbs-down. He loved that, and started adding more elaborate gestures. A former power struggle became a cherished family ritual.

Even video or computer games can be a basis for connection, and I don't mean just by plugging two Gameboys together. I was visiting a boy, age eleven, whom I see for therapy in his home. He often is finishing a video game when I arrive, and is torn between this activity—his favorite—and doing something more interactive with me. I like when he chooses to turn it off and play, but I also enjoy the challenge of figuring out how to connect with him when he is so transfixed by the screen. One day I came upstairs and found him going full tilt on the game, so I took off my coat and covered up the screen with it. At first he said angrily, "Hey, what are you doing, get that away." I said, "You are so good at this, I bet you can do it without looking." He was excited by this idea, and I told him I'd tell him which direction his enemy was and what was happening on the screen. We had a fabulous time, and it required more interaction than we usually had when we played chess or catch.

In fact, to help boys connect, you can play anything at all, especially games that require some interaction. Even better, play what they want to play. You can't communicate the idea that what they want to play is stupid and violent and antisocial, and then expect them to talk to you about their inner feelings.

Another set of games focuses directly on emotions. Make a facial expression, or find some good ones in a magazine, and play *name that feeling*. Ask them to make a scary face, a sad face, a scared face. Respond with a complementary face (that is, comfort the sad face, recoil in horror from the angry face). Get into fantasy play with them, and have your character express feelings through words and actions. Don't be subtle. Boys usually love it when a grown man pretends to cry in an exaggerated way.

Boys in our society are famous for having problems with paying attention and sitting still, as can be seen by the huge increase in the diagnosis of Attention Deficit Disorder (ADD). But I think many attention problems in boys are really *attachment* problems. They have more to do with the boy's cup being empty or leaky than they do with any inability to process information. No one can process information properly or pay attention well if they don't have the secure base of good attachment. Stanley Greenspan writes: "The active, energetic child soon learns to seek in stimulation the satisfaction he cannot find in intimacy."[7] Then, of course, all that racing around makes him hard to be close to. Thus, the impulsivity and scattered quality of some boys diagnosed with ADD may simply be a side effect of a deeper problem, an inability to connect. Most treatments for ADD don't address this underlying difficulty in attachment—the empty cup—and may even get in the way.

With young girls, concerns about closeness and connection often come out in fantasy play or playing with dolls, as opposed to fighting or play fighting. A child who feels mistreated might be extra nice to her dolls, or might play the part of a cruel mother. I'm not talking about abused children here—all children feel mistreated and misunderstood, at least some of the time. An adult can get involved in this kind of play by humorously playing the part of the mean mother, or by playing an incredibly obnoxious kid. As girls get older, they are often faced with significant challenges about making and keeping friends, and about finding a secure place in their peer group. Because at this point they may not still be playing with dolls, and in fact, they may be shutting their parents out of their lives, we have to figure out new ways to maintain our connections with them as they struggle through difficulties with connections. Play with them, hang out with them, do what they want to do, let them talk when they are ready. My favorite tactic with teenage girls is to say, "Okay, your turn." They ask me what I mean. I tell them that they can talk about anything they want, or we can go anywhere they want. Then I wait. We are usually so eager to jump in and offer helpful suggestions, but many children, especially teenage girls, need some space to sit and figure out what they want. If we wait patiently, they'll make good use of our attention and our confidence in them.

—BOYS, GIRLS, AND POWERLESSNESS—

It can be hard to get girls to put down their hairbrushes and ribbons and stop styling their dolls' hair long enough to wrestle or to play the part of the heroine instead of the damsel in distress. At least the goal is clear, though: to help them reclaim a sense of their own power. With boys and power, the goal is less clear. In some ways, power seems like boys' strong suit, but in other ways they are just as likely to be powerless. From what I have seen, it looks as if boy powerlessness comes in two flavors. One is straightforward enough: boys who are timid and fearful, passive and helpless. The other type is more confusing: the reckless boys who create havoc in their homes and classrooms. They don't look especially powerless.

The difference between recklessness and true power is connection. Like some attention deficits, recklessness comes from an earlier problem with attachment. I have had numerous experiences of seeing one child racing up a tree without paying any attention to the risks, while another child stands forlornly at the bottom, too scared to try. If a child doesn't see any risks at all, he can't explore safely, but if he sees only the dangers, he won't explore at all. One needs a soothing influence: "Slow down there, buddy; let's do this safely." The other needs encouragement: "Let's give it a try; I'll be right here to spot you."

In chapter four I described the power room, my daughter's name for a way she discovered to recharge her own batteries and wrestle harder. A lot of children, especially young boys, don't feel powerful, so they won't really wrestle. Instead, they will come and stand right in front of you and go "Hai, Ha, Hai, Ho Hai!" and do these Power Ranger/Ninja Turtle karate moves in the air. Or else they punch and kick and try to hurt you. In either case, there may be physical strength, but there's no emotional contact there, so it isn't real power. What I usually do, besides making sure I don't get hurt, is to say, "See if you can push me over. How about if we wrestle and we just use pushing." Pushing is a totally different kind of activity than a karate kick or a punch. There's a constant pressure, so there's a sense of contact.

A lot of boys who are really aggressive, who bite or punch or do these "Hai Hai Hai" karate kind of moves, will give up as soon as you really try to wrestle with them. If you try to just use pushing and pulling with them, they'll sometimes give up in two seconds because they are actually afraid of the real contact or of being truly powerful. Without a clear sense of a strong human connection, all they have left are the moves they've seen on TV. This is a clear indication that the aggression is a substitute for contact. Powerlessness in boys often masquerades as strength, because boys have to look tough and strong, no matter how they feel inside.

When children—most commonly boys—are not able to get their cups refilled consistently, they often become impulsive and inattentive. Other children, more commonly girls, can become timid and mousy because they are not allowed to be assertive or independent. It's the tabletop experiments all over again. The only thing some boys know how to do when they are frustrated is to be aggressive; the only thing some girls know how to do when they are frustrated is to sulk or follow passively along.

—BOYS AND FEELINGS—

I was listening to National Public Radio and heard an interview with the leader of the team that had just broken the land speed record, with a 750-plus-mile-per-hour jet-propelled car. He was talking about his team's success, and what it was like to drive that fast. After talking about the technical aspects, Liane Hansen asked him, "What about the emotional part?" He said, "We try to keep emotions out of it. Emotions are seriously dangerous." I had to laugh. The guy drives 750 miles per hour and it's *emotions* that are dangerous!

As a joke, I sent a friend a greeting card that said, "Sorry I yelled." Inside, it continued, "Next time I'll keep it all inside." Boys (and men) tend to get in trouble for expressing emotions, and we also get in trouble for what we do in order *not* to express emotions. Boys are teased for crying, and then everyone is surprised when they hit someone or break something instead of crying. In one preschool, researchers looked at every episode of crying. Surprisingly, boys and girls cried about the same amount. Other children usually ignored the crying, while teachers usually responded. The big difference came in the way teachers responded: With crying girls they were more likely to give comfort; with crying boys they were more likely to scold.[8]

When you're punished for having feelings and even more for showing them, it's hard to recover from an injury or a loss—big or small. You just don't have a chance to get it out of your system. I once saw a great video of clips from TV sportscasts. When a team won, there was incredible togetherness and shared joy among the men on the team. Hugs, claps on the back, slaps on the butt, and so on. When they lost, they each sat alone. The cameras would zoom in close for a shot, hoping like vultures to catch them crying. Why did they grieve alone, when clearly they had very close bonds with their teammates? Because if they shared their loss, they would probably have to cry. Faced with the sadness about losing, combined with the closeness and comfort of a friend, they just wouldn't be able to hold it in, because sharing suffering is what helps us release it. But they *could not* cry, certainly not on national television and probably not in the locker room either. You could see the facial contortions on these athletes, who were struggling emotionally *after* the game just as hard as they struggled physically during it.

I frequently hear about the boyhood version of these sports heroes. Parents will talk about their sons bursting into tears as soon as they get in the car after school, after holding it in for hours after a bad day or a bad experience. One mother told me about her nine-year-old son. The teacher had told her after school that he had a bad day, but he refused to be comforted and refused to talk about it. The mother asked him, "Were you afraid you'd cry if you talked about it, or if Miss Smith gave you a hug?" The boy nodded his head yes and let a lone tear trickle out. Of course, some boys are even more buttoned up than this, refusing to ever show any pain or sadness no matter what.

With a young boy named Lars, I invented a game called the designated screamer. This game is designed to help children who stoically tough it out when they get hurt. Lars and I were playing ball (of course that's what we were playing; he lived and breathed sports). He was about seven. He got hurt but immediately jumped up and started playing again. I could tell by his limping and his tight-lipped grimaces that his leg still hurt, a lot, but he denied that he was in pain and insisted on continuing the game. I started jumping up and down, pretending that *my* leg was in extreme agony. He asked me what I was doing, and I explained that I was the designated screamer. Just like in baseball, where there is a designated hitter so that pitchers can specialize in pitching, I made myself the one who would do his screaming for him. He laughed at this, while I jumped around on one foot making a fool of myself. Then he said he'd like to rest his leg a little before we played some more. That was a major accomplishment.

I once asked two six-year-olds, a boy and a girl, what the key was to popularity in first grade. The boy said, "Shoot missiles." The girl said, "Be nice." In other words, the fact that boys are given a heavy dose of "boys don't cry" does not mean that girls have full freedom to express all their feelings either. Instead of having to be tough, girls are encouraged to be nice. That leaves several key emotions in the unacceptable category, most notably, anger. No wonder so many girls become experts at subtle cruelty.

In their book about the educational system's shortchanging of girls, David and Myra Sadker also look at the way this same system miseducates boys. They interviewed a boy named Tony, who called the male role a prison, and said there were "five rules [that] must be followed by boys who want to fit the 'standard' code of behavior: Be a good student but not too good—any better than B+ is a nerd. Play three varsity sports—or two with weight training. Party and get drunk. Brag about sexual accomplishments and refer to girls as bitches in casual conversation. And never show your feelings. But as coeditor of his school's literary magazine, Tony said he was constantly surprised by the depth of the emotional side so many boys were hiding. 'Tough guys and jocks hand in these incredible poems. They're usually seniors who will never see anyone again—or they make it anonymous.' "9

—BOYS AND GIRLS, PLAYING TOGETHER—

I was driving my daughter and her friend Kent home from school. Kent started asking her, "Do you have Megatron?"

"No."

"Do you have Star of Death?"

"No."

I interrupted, "She doesn't have any of those violent computer games."

"Oh," he said. "Bummer." His voice made it sound like I had told him that she has no toys and has to live on bread and water. He tried again, "Do you know what a nuclear weapon is?"

"I'm not sure."

Kent proceeded to go into a lovingly detailed description of nuclear weapons and their destructive power. And how cool the game Megatron was. I turned on the radio, to protect my sensitive pacifist ears from this conversation. A song came on with a line about kissing. Kent said, "Eeew, gross." Emma agreed, "Turn it off!" I said, "Blowing up millions of people is cool, but two people kissing is gross?" They answered, in unison, *"Yes!"* The funny thing was that I think if Emma had been with a female friend, they would have giggled about the song instead of saying it was gross.

In general, boys and girls tend to segregate their play starting in kindergarten or first grade. As they split into separate groups, the style of their play becomes more and more different. They also start to think that the other gender is somehow drastically different from them. A few years before Megatron, Emma was going to Kent's house after kindergarten to play. Before she came, Kent's father told me that he ran around the house shouting, "What is Emma going to play with? I don't have any girl toys!" His father reassured him that they'd have no trouble finding things to play together, which was indeed the case.

Not that children always figure this out. In their book about war play, Nancy Carlsson-Paige and Diane Levin write about this gulf between toys for girls and toys for boys: "One parent described watching her daughter sitting on the front steps of their apartment building next to a male friend about the same age. Holly had her Barbie dolls, and Michael had his GI Joe figures and tanks. Each held their own dolls as they eyed those of the other. They looked as if they wanted to play together, but just ended up sitting there."[10] The authors make excellent suggestions about how adults can help, by offering neutral materials or art projects, or suggesting non-gendered games like having their dolls go to outer space. The Playful Parenting approach, of course, is to go downstairs and get down on the floor with them, maybe taking both dolls and initiating a fantasy game that tweaks these gender roles a little bit. For example, you could have the GI Joe say, "Hey, those high-heeled shoes would make a great weapon." And Barbie answers, "Do you think they make those green suits in my size? They are really fashionable."

In other words, *encourage boys and girls to play together.* This mixed-gender play gives boys the chance to have some play that builds connection and gives girls a chance to have some play that promotes confidence and power. Playing together helps boys and girls not be strangers when they rediscover each other in adolescence. They also seem to be more creative when they play together. In fact, they have to be more creative. Most girls expect more out of play than death and destruction, and most boys expect more than dressing dolls and combing their hair.

I was in the park and saw a father pushing his baby in a stroller. The baby looked to me to be about six months old. It was a heartwarming scene, until his wife showed up. As soon as he saw her, he started yelling at her, "Do you know what just happened? Do you want to know what just happened? Two different people said he looked like a girl. They thought he was a girl." He put on a sarcastic voice: " 'What a cute little girl. What's her name.' I can't f——ing believe it. Does he look like a girl to you?" He then put his face a few inches from the baby's face and yelled at the baby: "You do *not* look like a girl! How could *anybody* think you look like a girl."

I was half fearing (maybe half hoping) he would have a heart attack on the spot from this gender catastrophe. I found myself thinking of the men in groups I have led for batterers and sex offenders. Some of these men were so pressured to be masculine that it almost killed somebody. One man who grew up to be a violent bully toward his wife and children told a heart-wrenching story of being chased home by bullies when he was a boy. He ran inside the house, relieved to have escaped a beating, and his mother sent him back outside, locking the door, so he could go out there and fight like a man. A neighbor finally chased off the three older boys who were beating him to a pulp.

These are extreme cases, but every boy needs some help with the cruelty and violence that surrounds them and with the unrealistic expectations that they must always be tough and strong. We aren't just told that boys *will* be boys. Boys had damned well better *be* boys. A U.S. military officer, General Homer Lea, said in 1898, "The greatest danger that a long period of profound peace offers to a nation is that of creating effeminate tendencies in young men."[11] Heaven forbid!

All boys are affected by the taunts, insults, and violence against gay men and against boys who are labeled as fags, queers, and sissies. Even the boys who aren't being targeted themselves are hurt by this antigay, anti-sissy atmosphere, because they all have to prove their manhood constantly, or face the consequences. When boys taunt each other about being gay, they aren't referring to acts of homosexual sex. They are trying, not so playfully, to figure out masculinity. They are accusing each other of being less than fully male. As we can see from the man in the park, this is a dreadful disease. But we don't like it when boys are *too* masculine either.

Mike Tyson, the professional boxer who was convicted of sexual assault and later was banned from his sport for biting a piece off of Evander Holyfield's ear, is a good example of a boy who was pressured from all sides to be aggressive, who was rewarded for this aggression beyond his wildest dreams, and then—big surprise!—went too far. The response to his behavior reflects our ambivalence about male violence. He was vilified as a monster, but then he was given a short jail sentence, reinstated into boxing, and given another shot at the title.

As I hope I have made clear, comforting children, cuddling them and valuing them, does not make boys weak. It makes them emotionally strong; it makes them human. We are much less afraid than we used to be of girls being athletic and powerful and smart, though we still have room for improvement. Title IX, which required equal athletic facilities for girls in college, has changed things tremendously. Sports have become an acceptable way for girls to excel, to become confident and physically powerful. Now we need an emotional Title IX for boys.

CHAPTER 9

FOLLOW YOUR CHILD'S LEAD

"I want to teach people how to understand and love this miraculous creative state of 'I do not know' when related to children—so full of life and dazzling surprises!"

—JANUSZ KORCZAK[1]

Playful Parenting is a delicate balance between following a child's lead and stepping in as a guide. On one side, we let children be completely in charge of the play, in order to nurture their creativity and sense of confidence. On the other side, we actively intervene to help children get unstuck from situations that are repetitive, boring, or potentially harmful. I must confess that I have become an expert on this principle of Playful Parenting by repeatedly getting it *wrong*. One day I'll be sure I have to "do something" until I realize my job is to follow. The next day I'll follow along resentfully until I finally figure out how to lead us both out of a rut and onto a path that's fun for the two of us. This chapter is about following the *child's* lead; the next chapter is about times when it makes sense for the adult to lead the way.

I usually learn my best lessons about following when I try to lead, and things go nowhere in a hurry. One time my daughter and I were playing freeze tag. It's lots of fun with a big group of people, because one person freezes people and others can unfreeze them, so the game is constantly in flux. Playing freeze tag with just two people, my daughter and me, was less fun (for me). I ended up frozen most of the time. She would freeze me and then go off and do something else but expect me to stay frozen. I guessed that she wanted me to break the rules and come after her. Instead of following her instructions, I thought I would take the lead and focus on connection.

I guessed incorrectly. When I unfroze myself and chased after her, she was furious at me. I have to admit I made the same mistake a few times in a row. I was convinced (wrongly) that she needed me to push for connection even though it broke her rules. Also, it was boring for me to stay there frozen all by myself! Finally, I decided to follow her rules of the game precisely to the letter, no matter how boring or how much I wanted to come after her. I apologized for having broken the rules before and promised to freeze indefinitely. She froze me once more to check if I really meant it. I stayed frozen for a couple of minutes while she went into the other room. Every once in a while I would call out "I'm still frozen" so she wouldn't forget we were playing together. Once she saw I could follow the rules, she unfroze me and said *that* game was over. Now she wanted to play a game *together*, with me helping her balance on a big ball. I had finally gotten it right! The game she had wanted to play was not about connection. She wanted to see if I would follow her lead, and once I did, she could see I was on her side. Then she was ready to connect and do something fun together.

It isn't always easy to know how to follow a child's lead, especially if the child doesn't say much. Luke is eleven and not very communicative. Our therapy usually consists of playing chess or playing catch together, or of my watching him play video games. I ask him what's new; sometimes he'll say something, but often he won't. He isn't sullen about it, just reserved. He certainly never tells me about what's going on deep inside of him. One time I decided to push it a little bit. We were playing catch with a football, and I asked him what was new. He ignored the question. I tried again a few times; he ignored me each time. Finally, I said, "Is there nothing new, or you aren't going to tell me?" He gave the football a kick into the bushes and said, "That's what's new!" I loved that. When you are "listening" to a child's play, you have to treat *everything* as if it's communication, including throws and kicks of a football. Most children won't spell it out for you. Since I couldn't quite tell what he was trying to say, I decided to go with the funny aspect of this.

I said, "Oh, I see. You're telling me what's new in football language. Hmm, let's see, you feel stuck, like the ball is stuck in the bushes?"

"No." He laughed.

"You're flying high, but then you come crashing down?"

"*No!*" Luke kicked the ball again, and it hit the telephone wire.

"You sent a wire to New Zealand?"

"No! I mean yeah, I did." More laughing.

I kept making up translations of how the football could signify what he was thinking or what he wanted to say. Some of them were relevant to themes in his life; some were just funny. A few minutes later, when I was running after the ball, he said, "Ha-ha, you like that ball. Why don't you marry it?" Here was his clearest statement yet. His mother had told me that Luke was being teased at school about liking a girl, but he had never brought it up with me. Even though it was thinly disguised as being about me and the ball, I saw his teasing me as an opportunity to bring that theme into the play.

So, after I dropped a throw or kick, I'd say to the ball, "I love you, football. Why don't you like me?" He'd laugh at that. If I caught the ball, I'd say, "I think it likes me again," and pretend to kiss it. He really laughed at that. This technique is great for following the lead of children who don't volunteer much (or anything) about their lives.

The first part of this chapter describes some basic principles of following a child's lead, such as enthusiastically saying yes to whatever they want to do and setting aside specific occasions for what I call PlayTime. The second part of the chapter applies these principles to particular situations, such as PlayTime with siblings, with teenagers and preteens, with other people's children, and with hard-to-reach children.

HOW TO FOLLOW A CHILD'S LEAD

- Just say yes
- Do whatever they want to do
- Be safe (but don't worry too much)
- Set aside PlayTime
- Take time to recover

—JUST SAY YES—

Following a child's lead means that every once in a while (as often as we can handle it), children need us to be hugely enthusiastic, to say yes in a booming voice instead of the constant parade of no. Many of us have an automatic response to almost any request or anything we see a child doing—usually it's to say no, but sometimes our automatic response is to say yes. (Chapter thirteen, on discipline, will deal with the importance of setting limits as part of Playful Parenting.) Try counting how many times you say no to children in an hour, or in a day. I think you'll be shocked. We often feel compelled to jump in and say no when they are doing something or suggesting something that we know is a bad idea. Unfortunately, jumping in does not help them develop their own good judgment. They simply have to discover certain things for themselves, and the best way for them to do this is with our encouragement and support.

Of course, I'm not advocating anarchy. There must be limits. Children need adult supervision and adult help with decisions until they can make their own. But try breaking out of the automatic habit of saying no all the time. If they suggest something ridiculously dangerous, and you respond with an enthusiastic, "Hey, that's a cool idea, let's try it," *they* will probably say, "No! That's dangerous." If they suggest something that is harmless but seems impossible, try not to jump in and say so. Try saying, "Great idea. I wonder how we could make that work." They just might figure it out, to your surprise, and at the very least they will think it through for themselves.

One afternoon while I was waiting for my daughter after school, I started talking to Rebecca, the five-year-old sister of one of my daughter's friends. We were standing by her car while her mother was talking to someone, and she asked me if she could climb onto the car and ride on top while her mother drove home. *I* knew that *Rebecca* knew that this was, of course, not going to happen. But I also knew Rebecca, and I guessed that she expected me to say no, and that then she would start to climb up anyway to see what I would do. I didn't want to get in a power struggle with her, so I said, "Sure, let's climb up there; that'll be fun. We'll have to hold on real tight." And she said, "Larry! That's dangerous. We can't do that." I started to pretend to climb up, and she said, "No, no, we'll fall off." If *I* had been the one to say no, she may have kept alive the idea that this was a very cool thing to do that grown-ups don't allow because they are worrywarts. But by my saying yes, she got to figure out for herself how it would turn out. Of course, if she had said, "Okay, let's do it," I'd have played dumb and said things like "I wonder how we'll stay on when your mom turns a corner," or "I wonder what your mom will say when she sees us up there," nudging her judgment on a little bit.

Saying *yes* instead of *no* does not mean hiding how you feel. Saying yes to something doesn't mean you have to pretend to like it! If you hate a certain game, it is okay to say you hate it, but instead of just saying, "No, I won't play that with you," try humorously begging and pleading not to have to play it. I've seen so many parents, starting with myself, reluctantly agree to play some game they find boring or stupid, and then dragging through it on the verge of falling asleep. For me, this problem always came up when my daughter wanted to play Barbies, which I hate. Falling asleep during Barbie time was always my compromise between playing what she wanted to play and running as fast as possible out of the room. It was a compromise that didn't work well for either of us. She got a playmate who couldn't keep his eyes open, and I felt doubly awful—I was playing Barbie *and* letting her down. The solution was a different kind of compromise. I said straight out how I felt about Barbies, then kept on playing. I exaggerated my horror and repugnance and begged and pleaded not to have to play, making it clear that this was all in fun and I would, in fact, play them with her. Lo and behold, not only did I stay awake, but I had fun, and she did, too. The Barbie play was no longer the same old monotonous dressing and undressing the dolls, but turned into action-packed dramatic play, with tremendous bursts of giggles from both of us.

Just saying yes means having a basic attitude of acceptance rather than rejection, approval rather than disapproval. Be animated as you play: use gestures, your voice, and facial expressions. Be enthusiastic, racing after the ball if you're playing catch, throwing yourself into your character in fantasy play. Be sure to take stock of your own feelings, especially depression and anger, since these emotions make it hard to match children's pace and tone. Be warm, inviting, supportive. Now, I don't expect you to do this every minute you are with children; it would be nice, but it's a little unrealistic. My hope is that you will set aside certain times to really try on this attitude, even if it's just for a few minutes at first. Most of us—myself included—feel as though we are already giving so much, paying so much attention to our children. But hours of halfhearted, lethargic, resentful interaction is less helpful that a shorter time of full-throttle play. In fact, once they get some of this type of playtime, they will usually be less demanding of every minute of your attention the rest of the time.

I often catch myself saying "That won't work," or "That's impossible." What does that convey, besides that I'm an interfering grown-up with no imagination? I am trying to provide a shortcut for the child. I already know that it won't work, so they don't have to find out through experience, do they? Yes, of course we have to do this when it comes to things like touching the hot stove or running into traffic. But most situations in life aren't so drastic that children can't be allowed to figure them out on their own. It's like doing children's homework for them: the answers may be right, but they haven't learned anything. So instead of saying "That won't work," try saying "Let's try it and see." Either you will be surprised, or they will learn for themselves that it doesn't work. Whatever happens, they will see you as an ally instead of a naysayer. It isn't that you never say no when you are following children's lead, but look inside to see if you are saying no out of your own feelings of discomfort or because it is really necessary. As the next chapter will demonstrate, it is okay to try to unstick things that are stuck. Don't follow their lead, for example, when they tell you to go away and never come back. You may need to back off a little, but don't abandon them forever.

A few years ago I was with my daughter and some other families out in the country. Four of us—two dads and two six-year-old girls—were standing at the edge of a pond, and someone realized that the dock was just a raft tied onto the bank. One of the girls said, "Let's go for a ride." I immediately tried to put a damper on the whole thing: "It'll be too hard to untie. I don't think it's such a good idea." The other dad ignored me and said, "Sure, see if you can get it loose." I felt a glimmer of hope: They won't be able to get it untied. No such luck. They had it untied in no time.

I fought down my urge to panic and run screaming off the raft, leaving my daughter and the others to their fate.

While I was having visions of our makeshift raft sinking in the middle of a pond, which happened to be extremely cold, the other dad said—very calmly, I thought—"How are we going to steer it?" The girls snapped into action. They ordered me to jump off and hold the rope so the raft wouldn't float away. They ordered the other dad to stay on board and "keep a lookout," while they ran off to find some big sticks for steering. It worked! We had a great time on the raft. Later, seeing how delighted and triumphant the girls were, everyone wanted to try it.

I was happy for them, but inside I was stewing. Not because I had been proven wrong (I'm pretty used to that), but because I had been so quick to say no without really thinking. I had overestimated the dangers, underestimated their abilities, and let my own fears try to run the show. But it wasn't just that I had tried to say no. As usual, I had tried to take over, imposing my "better" judgment. I tried to convince myself that I was just being safe, but it wasn't really a matter of safety. It was a matter of my not wanting to risk getting cold and wet, but the girls were perfectly happy to take that risk in order to have such a great adventure.

—DO WHATEVER THEY WANT TO DO—

On several occasions I have had the great pleasure of watching Patty Wipfler lead play workshops for children and adults. Anyone who knows her work will easily see her influence throughout this book. She is the head of an organization called the Parents Leadership Institute, and a champion of parents, families, and young people. I recommend her writings very highly. Following children's leads and doing whatever they want to do are the cornerstones of what she calls Special Time. "The times when we can relax, play and connect with our children are at the heart of our precious relationship with them. But relaxed time for parent and child to share their love is always in short supply. . . . 'Special time' is an excellent tool . . . an active form of listening, in which your child's play becomes her vehicle for telling you about her life. . . ."[2]

Play, as Patty Wipfler suggests, is children's way of telling us about their lives. Playing what they want to play, how they want to play it, is our way of really listening. We have all had the experience of wanting to tell someone something, but they keep interrupting us or changing the subject or telling us what to do or how to feel. We hate it, yet we do it to children all the time. We say, "I hate that game," or we take over the game, telling them how to do it properly. That's not the best way to get a peek into our children's lives, to see what they really think and feel. Playing their way, on their terms, is what does it.

Of course, before we can play whatever they want, we have to play with them some in the first place. Unfortunately, when we say, "I don't want to play," they hear that as, "I don't want to join you in your world." No wonder they then say to us, "I don't want to go to school. . . . I don't want to go to Aunt Margaret's. . . ." They are just saying they don't want to go to our world either. The more we join them in their world, the more cooperative they'll be when we drag them along to ours.

And we can't just sit there like a lump while they play, either, much as we'd like to after a hard day. They need us to be active participants in the play, just like listening requires active attentiveness. We don't share our innermost selves with people who stare out into space while they are talking to us, or look constantly at their watch, or keep changing the subject. It can be a challenge to be an active participant in play, while still following their lead. It may mean that if you're outside playing basketball, you get to be an enthusiastic rebounder, and feed them the ball for another shot, instead of showing off your own three-point jump shots (unless they want you to show your stuff, or play your hardest against them, in which case you do that).

At workshops, I sometimes ask parents to tell me their most favorite thing to do in the whole world. I respond to each one, "That's boring . . . that's dumb . . . yuck . . . who would want to do that . . . you have to be kidding . . ." and so on. Before they tar and feather me, I explain why I have been provoking and insulting them in this way. I think we unwittingly give this message to our children all the time. I realized one day, in a painful shock of self-awareness, that when I told my daughter "I hate playing Barbies," I was really saying, "Your favorite thing to do in the whole world is something I find boring and stupid and sexist and a waste of time." Not exactly the message that a loving father (and child psychologist) really wants to convey. So as I described in the last chapter, I started playing Barbies with her, and together we figured out ways to make it fun and not quite so awful.

Why is it so important not always to say no? Imagine you had some scary or confusing or overwhelming things happen to you, and you weren't allowed to talk about them. Now imagine that you weren't even allowed to think about them. That's what it's like not to let a child play the way they want to play. Play is their way of talking and thinking.

Whenever I talk about this "do what they want to do" aspect of Playful Parenting, someone always asks, "If you always follow their lead, won't they always want to do the same thing, over and over?" Sometimes they do want to do things more times than we can stand (yet we say that children have a short attention span!). But the more we let them take the lead, the more children have room to try out new things. These new things might be physical challenges, like finally trying the monkey bars or the high diving board, or they may be emotional challenges, like asking someone to be their friend or talking about a bad experience in school.

—BE SAFE (BUT DON'T WORRY TOO MUCH)—

Talking with parents about following children in play, someone inevitably asks what I call the "run out in the street" question. "If you are following their lead, what do you do when they want to do something dangerous?" First, we have to separate our fears from actual danger. In these instances, perhaps we can say, "That scares me. Let's see if we can figure out a way to do it safely. If we can't, we'll have to forget it." Children have very good judgment when they are allowed to use it, but often they haven't gotten much of a chance, since we are always telling them what they should or shouldn't do. Most of us worry much more about danger than we need to, especially if we are going to be right there playing with them instead of sending them out to play on their own. You can always slow things down and help them think through the consequences, rather than jumping in to decide in advance that something is impossible or too dangerous.

Of course, as parents, part of our job is to pay attention to basic safety, but sometimes we use safety as a good excuse for our own insecurities and inhibitions. Like when I wanted to insist that the raft trip was unsafe, but really I just didn't want to get wet. The epigraph to this chapter, about finding the joy in the uncertainty of not knowing what will happen next, is especially relevant to following children's leads. We may feel as though we are concerned about their safety when we say no, but we may just be protecting ourselves from discomfort, embarrassment, and uncertainty. Not knowing where we'll end up is something that most of us adults find unsettling. That feeling of "I don't know" seems a lot like inadequacy and incompetence. If only we could relax and take a deep breath, sigh, and think, I've done a good job as a parent. Even with the mistakes we've made, even with the regrets, we have a lot to be proud of.

—SET ASIDE PLAYTIME—

When children choose what to play and how to play, their cup is refilled. This refill boosts their confidence and fosters their relationship with you. The best way to follow children's leads is to set aside an hour or two where the child is completely in charge. I call it PlayTime. If Playful Parenting is an invitation to join children where they live, PlayTime is an invitation to go a step further.

Playful Parenting is an attitude, a 24/7 approach to being more connected with children and having more fun with them, letting them learn and grow without pressure or fear. Parenting happens everywhere all the time; opportunities abound for play and playfulness, for filling empty cups, for comforting, for helping children heal, for sharing a tender moment. In addition to this general infusion of playfulness, connection, and confidence, sometimes children need something more structured. PlayTime is a detailed road map for going the extra mile into children's territory, in order to help them use play to build closer relationships, to explore the world, to heal from life's upsets, and simply to have more fun.

The basic format of PlayTime is quite simple. The parent or some other adult sets aside regular *one-on-one* time with a child. The adult offers the child *undivided attention* with *no interruptions* and with a clear *focus on connection, engagement, and interaction.* In a sense, PlayTime is just Playful Parenting Plus, where the "plus" means more enthusiasm, more joining, more commitment to closeness and confidence, more fun, a more welcoming attitude toward their feelings, more willingness to put one's own feelings aside, more active and boisterous play. In addition, you don't answer the phone or cook dinner or take a nap during PlayTime.

You may have noticed that what I call PlayTime is very similar to what play therapists do all the time: regular sessions of play that either follow the child's lead or push them to overcome some emotional block. While therapists tend to work with children who are more distressed, their techniques show the healing power of play for all children. If play can bring a child out of extreme isolation, or restore connection to a troubled family, surely it can help with "ordinary" distance and isolation, or "average" levels of aggression or frustration.

PlayTime is for every child, but it also has specific benefits for specific problems. If things are great, PlayTime will be a huge amount of fun for both of you. If things are fine, PlayTime will help make them great. If things are tough, PlayTime will make them easier, though it may be hard work along the way. If things are impossible, PlayTime just might make them possible, or even help heal a troubled child or repair a damaged relationship.

Parents who already spend a lot of time playing with their children often ask me whether there is any added benefit of setting aside specific time and calling it PlayTime. I think there is. Having a regular and scheduled time allows children to look forward to it and plan for it. They will often save up their feelings for it, which makes PlayTime a challenge but also helps them to be less demanding at other times. Officially setting aside the time also helps us to be extra enthusiastic and remember to say yes instead of no, to do what they want, and not to worry too much about safety and rule-breaking. I wouldn't expect anyone to do all that for more than an hour or so at a time! You might, in fact, just want to start with ten or fifteen minutes. But when you do set aside the time, this gives children permission to bring up emotional subjects that are generally not encouraged or allowed. The fact that you are choosing to play whatever they want—even Barbies or war games or Legos—is a big deal for children. The fact that you give them your full attention, no answering the phone or making dinner, is an even bigger deal.

Many parents think, Oh, I know just what Elmo will want to do for

PlayTime. But don't jump the gun and start doing or suggesting what *you* think they will want to do. Let them surprise you—and possibly themselves—by really making it a free and open choice. This point reminds me of the years that my father and I spent going to football games together. Neither one of us really wanted to go, or enjoyed them very much, but we each thought the other one wanted to do it as a way to have special time together. Like many parents and children, we put up with a lot for the sake of being together, but we both would have had more fun if we had figured out what we really wanted to do instead of guessing.

Another controversial area is whether to allow PlayTime to transcend the usual rules. If sugar is forbidden, children may want to go to the candy store during PlayTime. If war play is forbidden, then they may want to go at it with fake pistols and swords. If they are only fourteen, they may want to use PlayTime to learn how to drive. They aren't just trying to send us over the edge, they are using the safety of PlayTime to handle something new or something hard. They also use PlayTime to push us to rethink some of our rules and regulations. I don't have a set rule for this problem. Experiment and see what works for you and your children. I usually will try out the forbidden activity, with a five- or ten-minute time limit, but if it becomes a problem, then I call it off.

Angela, who was a participant in a mother's class I taught, faced a problem of this type with her sons when she tried to do PlayTime with them. They took advantage of the opportunity to do whatever they wanted to begin a wild game of pretend gunplay, which had always been strictly forbidden. This was a tricky situation, in which Angela had to balance her commitment to her sons' taking charge of the play with her commitment to her own antigun principles.

In order to untangle this knotty problem, the first question is: Is this kind of play or activity really dangerous (physically or emotionally), or do I just find it horribly uncomfortable? Angela decided her opposition to gunplay was mostly her own discomfort. Given her values and her parenting style, there wasn't much danger that her sons would become violent psychopaths. But she still felt unable or unwilling to endure that discomfort, even though she understood all the arguments for letting the children choose their play themes and play activities. I suggested a two-part approach, with the idea of respecting both the children's clear desire to figure something out about playing with weapons, and the mother's need to feel comfortable with the play they chose. The first part involved Angela taking every opportunity she could to talk with other parents about her concerns over pretend gunplay—to explain the reasons she hates it, why she is such a committed pacifist. Often such discussions help parents consider experimenting with loosening the rules somewhat during PlayTime. When you're experimenting with an unsettling situation like this, it helps to keep PlayTimes short; a half hour or less is plenty when you are going into uncharted territory.

The second part of the solution for Angela and her children was to discover some ways in which her sons could explore the themes they were drawn to, without making it too hard for her to stick around and play with them. For example, perhaps she could handle magical weapons or pretend swords in a fantasy game. These weapons might satisfy the boys' desire to play with guns without driving their mom up the wall. In the long run, the thinking we do in order to resolve these PlayTime problems ends up being very helpful in our parenting overall.

I think the reason children respond so well to PlayTime is not just that they get to do what they want and to be in charge, but because we are reaching for them, reaching for a close connection. They get to notice that we don't *always* act as if it's more important to talk on the phone, or protect the furniture, or stick to our many rules, than it is to play with them and have fun. As long as they see that we are aiming to follow their lead sometimes, they will accept that we are grown-ups with anxieties and rules (some reasonable, some not).

PlayTime—structured time set aside to enthusiastically follow a child's lead—can be helpful for just about any child. I recommend it for families where everything is going great as often as I do for families in crisis and turmoil. PlayTime can also help with sibling rivalry and other family conflicts, can help parents connect with hard-to-reach children, and can provide opportunities for parents and older children to have fun together.

Sibling rivalry, for example, often recedes if each child has regular one-on-one PlayTime with a parent. In big families, children often crave the chance to have the full attention of both parents, even if it's only for a few minutes. I know the time for this kind of commitment is very hard to come by, but it pays off. Children who desperately need attention have a way of getting it, and they'll get it by hook or by crook if they don't get it through PlayTime.

Younger children generally jump right in, raring to go, as soon as you explain the concept. Older children may need some time to think about this strange offer. "You really are going to do whatever I want?" They may not be able to think of anything at first, but don't be too quick to give suggestions. That just imposes your ideas. Just relaxedly say, "It's your special time; what do you want to do?" One important theme for adolescent and preteen PlayTime is romance—girlfriends and boy-friends, sex and dating. Pretending to be madly in love with a rock star or movie star can get them giggling. Sing ridiculously corny love songs, ask to chew the gum they've been chewing, promise never to wash the spot where they've touched you, and so on. They'll make fun of you for being such a dweeb (or whatever the word is these days). *Enjoy it.* That's their way of using play to deal with their experiences of being uncool, or their fear that tomorrow they may show up at school in the wrong clothes.

The mother of a twelve-year-old boy wrote about an unexpected con-nection they made.[3] She had a regular date with her son, every Wednes-day evening, to do something special together, whatever he wanted. Usually he wanted to go to the mall and hang out, and usually they had a good time, though he never talked much. She always thought they had a good, open relationship, and that she was a great listener for her son.

One week, a friend of the mother's died, and she decided to honor her friend's passing by not talking for three days. Before she began her si-lence, she asked her son if he wanted to reschedule their outing that was planned for the next day. He shrugged and said it didn't matter. After they got in the car and headed to the mall, he started to talk. He poured his heart out to her, saying things he had never told her before about school, friends, feelings, everything. She watched the road and kept quiet. After pulling in at the mall parking lot, he just stayed in the car and kept talk-ing. They never got out. When it got late, they drove home, with him still talking. Clearly her vow of silence gave him the freedom to talk with-out fear of interruption or judgment. Sometimes we just need to get out of a child's way, and the connection will happen spontaneously. The problem is, most of the time we don't even know when or how we're in the way.

Note: *PlayTime with other people's children is very different from PlayTime with your own children.* If children do not have a secure attach-ment figure at home, someone who consistently fills their cup, then they are going to want to make you one. They may cling to you so that you have to peel them off when it's time to leave. They may act as if they don't care if you come or go, but really the connection is very impor-tant to them. Or perhaps they will test you to see how much of their horribleness you can stand without going away. Too bad they can't just give us a written exam and not really have to test our tolerance for being punched or called names or ignored or yelled at or teased or shocked—all the things children do when they haven't had a full cup for a long time and you offer them a refill. Instead, they will show how much they need a friend by breaking your things and trying to hurt you. If at all possible, we need to maintain our connection, to stay engaged even when they go over the line and we have to set a limit. Children, our own and other people's, need us to be human and genuine, to be a home base, a source of refills for empty cups, leaky cups, and even broken cups. In my work as a play therapist, I encounter this kind of testing and this kind of confusion regularly. One girl, for example, in the course of fifteen min-utes, said to me: "I hate you.... Never come back.... Can you come every day? ... Can I be your daughter? ... If you leave, you can never come back."

If they do have an attachment figure, you are still valuable. You will have different areas of ease and difficulty than the parents or main care-takers. They may hate mess, while it doesn't bother you. You may get irri-tated by loud noises or wild play that doesn't faze them, and so on. Children quickly learn who can tolerate what. When my daughter was in kindergarten, I would often play around on the floor with her and her friends at pick-up time. They would climb on me as if I were a climbing structure, or wrestle with me. Other kids I had never met would get in line to play with me then, since most grown-ups don't go for that kind of thing.

—TAKE TIME TO RECOVER—

I probably should have mentioned right up front that PlayTime is harder than it sounds. If it were easy, I wouldn't have had to write this book. It isn't easy for me to stay focused on connection, to stay enthusiastic, to pay undivided attention to a child, to put off my own work or my plans to get dinner made early for a change. In fact, I haven't met anyone who really finds it easy. The main difficulty, of course, is our own unmet needs, our own piles of feelings (our worries, anxieties, and fatigue; our embarrassment about being joyful and playful). PlayTime, or any play during which we follow children's lead, can be hard because we feel as if we don't know how to play, or we feel as if we can't bear to play those boring, awful games they seem to want to play all the time. We often avoid it, and when we do play this way, we may need time to recover. The best way to recover from an emotionally draining PlayTime is to talk to other parents about it, especially other parents who are trying out the same thing. When we feel as if we don't want to play, because we're too busy or too tired or too bored, we need to push ourselves a little bit. Just like when we are depressed, we don't feel like exercising or going outside; but if we make ourselves do it, we feel better. And in the long run we are happier. So don't give in to those feelings of "I don't want to"; push through the inertia and play.

It is sometimes hard to stay actively engaged when you are just following. When I first started having PlayTime with my daughter, she would want to play a fantasy game in which I would be the king, or the little brother, and she would tell me to go to sleep. Unfortunately, I would really fall asleep, and she would get mad! I had a similar problem with Monopoly or other board games. When she was little she often wanted to roll the dice for me, move my piece for me, make the decisions about what I should buy. It was very tempting to tune out, to say, "You don't need me, I might as well go make dinner (or go take a nap)." But in her eyes, we were playing together, and that was important to her. My job was to stay awake.

Time for another confession. Most of the time I feel as if I'm terrible at PlayTime. I feel stupid, and I hate feeling stupid. I feel like a servant, and I hate feeling like a servant. I have a hard time just letting children lead the play. I get sleepy, lethargic, fatigued. If we're playing with Legos, I'll sort the pieces by color and shape, to distract myself. If we are building houses of cards, I'll build one better than theirs. I don't mean to humiliate them or frustrate them, I just get lost in my own feelings instead of following their rhythms and their needs. So why do I put myself through it?

First of all, even when I am not doing it as well as I'd like, it still has a powerful impact on the children and on our relationship. Afterward, I can usually see the positive effects it has had, as the children are calmer or less aggressive or less frustrated, and we can play together or sit together easily. Second, I can see that over time I am getting better at it, even though I still feel stupid or incompetent sometimes. Third, children keep asking for it, even if during PlayTime they tell me I am doing everything wrong. I guess that this complaining and protesting about my incompetence and ignorance during PlayTime is just their way of showing me what they need to play and what deep emotions they are using play to address.

—LETTING CHILDREN TAKE THE LEAD IN PLAY—

In my first session with Robert, I suggested to his mother that she try a technique of having him run faster and slower, right and left, etc., as a way of learning to regulate emotion better. This technique, which I wrote about in chapter six, was supposed to help him control his impulses and emotions so he wouldn't have so much trouble with his peers at school. He tended to use his fists instead of his words, or to use off-putting words like "Shut up, you idiot" instead of good preschool words like "I didn't like it when you took my block." I wanted to show his mother what I meant, so I said, "Hey, Robert, can you run real fast around the kitchen?" He immediately decided to tell *me* how fast to run and in which direction to run. He knew what he wanted to do, and it sure wasn't what I had in mind. He didn't know anything about PlayTime, but he had the basic idea. He wanted to play at being in charge of *me*, not practice some self-regulation game I wanted to teach him. I knew what to do. I ran fast when he told me to run fast, walked slow when he told me to walk slow, and generally built up a strong bond of trust in that first meeting by following his lead.

A few months later, I heard from Robert's mother right before our session that he had had a terrible day in preschool, ending with several other children telling him they didn't want to play with him. These children told Robert's mother at pick-up time that he had been bad. In our session he was very excited to see me and eager to play. I had a plan for the session, something I don't usually do. I was going to say, "Let's pretend that I want to be friends with you and you don't want to be friends with me." A classic role reversal. I was very proud of it and ready to roll. Before I could get the words out, he said, "You chase me, and I'll tell you how fast to run." I had forgotten that game we played in our first session, but obviously he hadn't. Every few minutes I would try to shift things to *my* idea, but I never got out more than "Let's . . ." or "I've got an idea. . . ." Each time he interrupted me with a command for me to do something, and each time I went along.

As part of the chase game there were many doors, some of which he would shut in my face. When I tried to open them, he would say that I couldn't come in that way, that I had to go around. By the time I went around, he'd be through the door and on the other side. I knocked on the door and begged to be let in. He shouted, "No! You can't come in. I don't like you, you're stinky." Aha! Here we were, just where I was hoping to get, playing a game where he reversed the roles and he could be the one who didn't want to be friends with me. I got to play one of my favorite games, begging and pleading to be allowed in the room, to be his friend. But the play came around to this key theme only because I followed him, rather than because he followed me.

Robert would never have sat still for a lecture on how you can't make friends very well by kicking them and telling them they're stupid, but through this game I was able to exaggerate that approach in a playful way, so he could giggle about it. I threatened to kick him if he didn't let me in.

I promised to be his best friend and then said in a stage whisper that I would steal all his toys as soon as he let me in his room. Laughing about this topic—which had previously been only a source of tears and frustration and denial ("I don't know why they don't like me, they're just mean")—led to real changes in Robert's ability to make and maintain friendships. And it could make positive changes in your children's lives, too—if you just let yourself follow their lead.

CHAPTER 10

TAKE CHARGE (WHEN NECESSARY)

". . . not-quite-permissive [play] . . . begins when you notice
where a child can't function . . . where a child can't play
rough or can't accept affection or can't be tender or can't take
certain risks like being very far away from [mom or dad]. . . .
You want children to know that you're willing to design play
that invites them to try [new things] in their own ways . . .
providing challenges that are tailored specifically to their
needs."

—PATTY WIPFLER[1]

In the last chapter, I described a game of freeze tag with my daughter during which I tried to take over the game instead of following her lead. I had forgotten one of my basic rules, which is to follow at least until you have a pretty good reason to jump in and lead. Sometimes, though, following a child's lead isn't enough, or doesn't work. At those times, the Playful Parent takes charge of the play, at least for a moment, redirecting it in order to help a child get unstuck. If the child is locked in the towers of powerlessness and isolation, she needs a helping hand to get out. Sometimes all the child needs is a gentle push, and then a return to following her lead. Other times, we need to insist on making a connection. Some other common ways of taking charge are to provide a challenge to the child, introduce important themes, and make things fun that seem boring.

—OFFER A GENTLE PUSH—

The key to taking charge is to have a light touch, to introduce a theme or an idea or some contact and then see what children do with it. One of my favorite gentle pushes is to ask a simple question, or make a comment. If I feel as if we're not connected enough for the play to go well, I might say, "The next thing we need to do is connect; how do you think we ought to do it?" Children who aren't used to being asked this question may need some ideas or suggestions about how to reconnect, such as hugging, looking in each other's eyes, shaking hands, wrestling, giving a high-five, etc. Children who have been asked a few times generally have very clear ideas about how they want to connect (or else they say, "No way!" and run away laughing, and then a new game begins).

A gentle push might be as simple as saying, "Let's play," instead of waiting for them to say it to you. Or "Let's play soccer," if they usually like to sit inside and watch television. Just about any of the principles of Playful Parenting described in previous chapters can be the basis for a gentle push. Suggest a wrestling match to a child who seems to be feeling powerless, reverse the roles after an upsetting incident, empower girls, or connect with boys. With a boy who wants to spend the entire therapy session playing a video game alone, I might give a variety of gentle pushes to try to get some interaction going. A not-so-gentle push might be to unplug the set.

Greenspan describes a gentle push as "making every encounter into a two-way exchange . . . rather than engaging in parallel activities."[2] For example, if the child is building a tower and ignoring you, don't just build your own tower off to the side. Take all the blocks, so she has to ask you for the ones she needs. Pick up blocks and ask her how to build something. Then do everything wrong so she'll give you instructions on how to do it right. Or fight—gently and humorously—over a block you both need.

Another style of gentle push is to join in with whatever the child is doing, and then change it a little bit. If he is repetitively jumping up and down without any laughs or giggles, you can start jumping, too, then introduce a song or slowly add variations in the rhythm. If a young child flits from toy to toy, picking one up and then dropping it, you aren't going to get very far with a lecture on increasing attention span. Instead, try following behind him, collecting each thing he drops. At the end, offer the pile to him to start over.

Is the child sitting like a lump? Say, "You're asleep; I'll be your blanket," and lie on top of him, singing a lullaby. Or my personal favorite: Sit on top of him, pretending not to notice, and say, "This couch sure is lumpy." Of course, I am not suggesting nonstop entertainment and interaction with your child. That would be exhausting—for both of you—and intrusive. I am talking about once in a while during the day, or during times when you've put aside your work and your worries for some concentrated PlayTime.

—INSIST ON CONNECTION—

Pamela Haines wrote an article that made a deep impact on me.[3] It was about how newborns and infants reach out to us, taking the lead in establishing a profound connection. It's no accident that most parents bond so powerfully with their babies, or that the inability to bond—whether it comes from the parent or the baby—is instantly recognizable. Babies are experts at sending out signals of cuteness and/or neediness so that we will be compelled to smooch them up and to take care of them. As they get older, they aren't nearly so obvious about what they need, especially when they need to connect with us. Haines goes on to say that at this point it becomes *our* job to take the lead in connecting. In fact, our job is to insist on connection, to assume that children want more contact and more affection underneath their rejecting or obnoxious behavior. Not that they want to cuddle with us every minute—they also need to spread their wings and fly. But joyfully exploring the world, knowing that we are cheering them on, is vastly different from feeling sullen, withdrawn, depressed, or lonely.

Sometimes children like to play with that tension between distance and closeness, between expressing their need for connection and wanting us to make the first move. My sister Diane used to teach preschool, and she made a home visit at the end of the summer to a girl named Roxanne, who had been very attached to her the previous year. Roxanne's mother let her in and shouted to Roxanne that Diane was there. The two adults went into the next room, where Roxanne was sitting on the floor, coloring intently. Without looking up, she said slyly, "Who *was* Diane?" After a little playful banter, they made a great reconnection. Hearing this story, I loved how that one teasing question expressed so much: *I missed you, I wasn't sure if you were coming back, I'm not sure if I should get close to you again because then I'll miss you again, I'm going to yank your chain a little bit to get back at you.* That's a lot of meaning for three words.

Oddly, even though children demand so much attention from us, they often tune us out when we finally put everything else aside and get on the floor to play with them. This can be confusing and even annoying, but it actually makes perfect sense. They are feeling locked away in the tower of isolation. And they are a bit mad at us for that. When we give them our full attention, they show us what's going on in their hearts. They don't say it in words, they say it in play, by pretending we don't exist or don't matter. When we were busy, they felt as if they didn't matter to us. So don't give up or walk away; be persistent. Our job is to take the initiative and push (gently) for a connection.

If a light touch in making a connection does not work, we may need to step in more vigorously. These more intensive techniques often involve children's release of very painful emotions, through crying, throwing tantrums, or kicking and screaming. This release leaves children free to reestablish a deep connection with their parent. These emotions also clear the way for a restoration of children's confidence. We may have to insist that they—with our help—take some time to work on a problem that they would rather avoid. We may have to insist on connection to break through a thick wall of isolation.

For example, a boy I see in therapy is afraid of dogs, but he never wants to talk about it or think about it. That makes it hard to get over the fear, so occasionally I will insist on our taking a walk during the session. When we pass by a dog, I try to help him through the fear, by walking with him slowly, closer and closer. Once we are near the dog, he is the boss again, and I follow his lead about how fast or slow to approach it. But in order to get there, I have to direct the session, since he would never have said, "Let's go find a dog so I can work on my fear today."

With this kind of fear, there is usually a specific distance from the dog that I call the edge. This edge is where the healing work of overcoming fears takes place. Sitting in my office talking about Nintendo is too far away, but getting jumped on by a barking dog is too close. Somewhere in between is just right. Finding that edge usually requires an adult stepping in to direct the play. You can usually tell when you are at the exact edge, because the child may tremble or shake with fear, or cry, or laugh. *Stay right there.* When that wave of emotion subsides, take a step closer. These emotions come pouring out of the child because he notices two things at the same time: I am with a dog, and I am safe. That's why the edge is so important, because it is the exact spot where both of these are true. Another common response at the edge is for the child to talk nonstop about every experience he has ever had with dogs. Or he may talk himself through the fear, saying out loud, "It's a nice doggy. It's on a leash; it's not going to bite me." If you have a fearful child, try seeing if you can find this edge with him; you can't just send him outside to find it himself. He needs you with him so he can feel the safety and security as well as the fear. We can't simply lecture him about how ridiculous his fears are, or how safe the dog is. He has to figure this out by doing the emotional work at the edge of the fear, with us nearby.

Sometimes the fearful thing that the child avoids is not a dog or a swimming pool but making a close connection. In that case, it is again up to us to push it a little, because children won't put a sign outside of their tower that says, "Please help me out of this isolation." Martha Welch wrote a book called *Holding Time*,[4] about a special technique for holding children to help them overcome their resistance to making contact. Her book has been quite controversial, because of concerns that her techniques can be coercive or even harmful if used inappropriately or incorrectly. The basic ideas in the book, however, are very useful. Based on her work with a wide range of children, especially those with autistic and attachment disorders, Welch argues that *children need adults to persist in connection until there is a breakthrough.* The adult physically holds on through children's struggles to resist the contact, and does not settle for less than a profound human connection.

The idea that I have found most useful in Welch's work is that adults usually settle for a superficial level of connection with children. Our expectations are low. We may not even notice when we don't have a deep bond, or we may think there is nothing we can do about it. Welch claims, I think correctly, that if we are willing to put in the time and effort, then there is plenty we can do about it. We can reclaim that extremely warm, close, deep connection that most of us thought was no longer possible. Finding this level of connection often requires a period of calmly holding children very close while they struggle and fight and cry to break free.

This technique is not for everyone. Some people swear by it, but it gives other parents the willies. Even if you don't hold your child as she fights and struggles to get away—the way Welch suggests—her idea of insisting on a deep connection is a useful guide for Playful Parenting. I usually use a variation of Holding Time with children, which I call feelings time. In feelings time, I will start by holding children close, either to prevent myself from getting hurt or to comfort them. Perhaps our PlayTime has released a pile of aggressive feelings, and they can't stop trying to hurt me or another child. Perhaps they race around breaking things, refusing to make any kind of eye contact or other contact. Or they hurt themselves a little and come to my lap for comfort. No matter how the holding starts, at some point they will start to pull away or insist on being put down. Welch describes this step very accurately. Usually I will try to hold them just a little longer and see what happens. If they tell me to let them go, I usually do. If they go right back to hitting me, I go right back to holding them. If they retreat to a corner or a locked room, I give them a little space and approach more tentatively. If they are ready to make a connection, then we shift to playing.

In other words, I keep insisting on connection, but I want it to be on the child's terms as much as possible. When in doubt, I don't hold children against their will, unless it is necessary for safety. In the same way, I won't try to force children to make eye contact with me, but I will invite them to look at my eyes. And I will keep inviting them, instead of giving up after the first rejection. If I do hold children while they kick and scream—and, yes, sometimes it is the only thing to do—I always ask them about it later: "What did you think of that holding stuff? You were screaming for me to stop, but when I stopped, you kept on hitting me." "You look like you feel much better; do you think the feelings time helped?"

Holding is, of course, the hallmark of Welch's holding time, but it is also a technique suggested by other experts as well, when free play becomes impossible because of aggression, withdrawal, or some other sign of overwhelming emotions in the child. Patty Wipfler, for example, sees insistence on connection as a way of helping children release their pent-up emotions. For example, if children won't stop hitting or biting, gently but firmly stop them from doing it. That often is enough to bring a healing flood of tears. This emotional release is typically followed by a new level of closeness and cooperativeness.[5] Stanley Greenspan recommends the use of firm holding to calm children down if they get violent or agitated; the contact and the firm pressure and the safety help children to organize their sensations and their impulses.[6]

In all of these variations of close physical holding, it is important to remember that the goal is not to punish children or assert your control because you are bigger, but to let them release the painful emotions that interfere with their connecting to others. Therefore, it is best not to hold children when you are feeling angry or out of control yourself. In those situations, take a time-out from each other and come back when you can be calm and loving.

In the previous chapter I stressed the importance of just saying yes to children, at least some of the time. I don't want to be confusing or contradictory, but there are also times when we need to say no. One such time is when children want something very badly, and they get it, and then a moment later they want something different just as much, and then they get it, and then the same thing happens again. Or they keep trying to do something dangerous or destructive or hurtful. A firm no here may help them release all of the backed-up feelings that are keeping them from enjoying what they do have. In a way, the no acts like the holding in Holding Time: It provides a resistance that children then use to let out their excess feelings of fear and anger and frustration. They may respond to the no with a temper tantrum, a bout of tears, or a raging fit. They aren't being brats; they are "playing," even though it isn't the kind of fun time we usually associate with play. They are choosing some little thing to have a fit over, because they don't have the words or maturity to talk directly about their feelings. Don't be too judgmental about this; most adults do the same thing. Think of the last argument you had with your spouse or partner or friend. Did you pick a fight over some little thing because you couldn't figure out how to really express yourself?

—CHALLENGE—

Challenges lie somewhere between following children's lead and taking charge. Stanley Greenspan calls this being *playfully obstructive*, while Patty Wipfler calls it *not-quite-permissive play*. For example, if a child's attention is entirely on a toy, and you want to make some contact, you can start by picking up another toy and having your toy interact with her toy. If that fails, and she tries to wander off, you can block the door with your toy. If you still can't make a connection, you may try grabbing her toy and making a run for it. If that is too scary or annoying for the child, maybe just reach for her toy and miss, falling over on your face instead.

Now, why would you want to be so obnoxious? To make a connection. To draw children out of the tower of isolation. To push them to try something new that they have been too timid to try. Instead of just being aggravated by their staring at the TV, you might stand in front of it and block their view, or climb under the covers with them instead of nagging them to get out of bed. With one client, who isn't big on contact, I will frequently stick my hand out and say, "I challenge you to a thumb wrestle." Sometimes he says yes, and we thumb wrestle. Sometimes he says no, and I pretend to beg and plead. Sometimes he says, "Next week," and I say, "Okay."

Those examples of challenges are mostly about breaking through children's isolation. Other children need more of a hand with powerlessness. Instead of doing anything the child wants, you might use PlayTime to set him a challenge, such as climbing a tree, riding a bike, doing an extra-hard math problem, calling a friend (if he is shy), and so on. The sky's the limit. Brave parents may also offer the child a chance to give *them* a challenge!

I was walking on the levee along the Mississippi River in New Orleans one day when two boys, around nine or ten years old, came down nearby on their bikes. It was a pretty steep hill, especially for a city that's mostly below sea level. At the bottom they fell off their bikes, half on purpose, laughing and shouting. One boy said, "Were you scared?" The other said, "Nah, I wasn't scared." The first one said, "You must not have been going as fast as me then, because *I* was *scared*." I love that story, because it says so much about boys and competition and about boys and feelings. I also love it because these boys had raced down the hill clearly to give themselves a physical challenge. As children get older, play may mean choosing to do something a little scary to overcome their fear.

Physical challenges give children a chance to test themselves, find their own limits, see how much strength they have. I think one reason teenagers seek out thrills and dangerous activities is to create these types of experiences for themselves. It's much better to join them and structure these scary-but-safe adventures, so that we can provide both safety and emotional support, rather than try to forbid them. They may prefer to do this with other adults, such as on an Outward Bound course, rather than with us. We might prefer that, too, since as they get older and stronger, we might feel as if we are getting older and creakier.

—INTRODUCE IMPORTANT THEMES—

As we have seen, children at play often bring up the themes important to them. Most of the time, this happens spontaneously and automatically. In fact, you may not be able to stop a theme, even if you are tired of it, like bathroom humor or aggression or romance. At other times, though, an important theme may be avoided or neglected, and an adult can jump-start the play by introducing it. As with every time you take the lead in play, remember to have a light touch. If a theme that you introduce doesn't go anywhere, drop it. This idea is similar to the way therapists say, "You haven't mentioned your mother lately. . . ."

With children, it is even easier. After seeing him for several months, I learned that my ten-year-old client Ramon was having a hard time sleeping in his own bed. He certainly had never brought it up. We were playing with pillows, so I made up a game where I said I had to have the pillows in order to feel safe and go to sleep. He grabbed the pillows from me, and I pretended to cry. He loved that game. A preschooler, Nancy, didn't want ever to talk about her problems with toilet training. So whenever we played house, I always had my characters search for bathrooms or have accidents. I was playing with a six-year-old girl and her mother at an afternoon family-play workshop. It seemed to me as if the mother was hovering a bit over her daughter, worried about her getting hurt. The daughter wanted to do her own thing but also wanted to please her mother. This tension made it hard for her to play.

I started following the girl around the room, saying "Oh no! You aren't going to *walk*, are you, that's so dangerous! You aren't going to put on roller skates, oh no, I'm so worried, I can't look." I was personifying and exaggerating the worry. Both the mother and the daughter laughed at this gentle caricature of the mother. The daughter began to play with more and more confidence, being brave and daring but not at all reckless, as I kept up my mock horror. If I stopped for a minute, she would say, "Hey, Larry, look, I'm going to jump off this chair onto the mat," which would be my cue to beg her not to do it, while she laughed and jumped. I could have just suggested to the mom to back off and not hover so much, but that may well have left them both more tense. I don't think the girl would have been able to be as adventurous, or as safe.

My sister Jeanie told me a story about a mother she knew whose child was having severe separation anxiety at preschool. The boy would cry for the whole morning, not just for a few minutes after his mom left. Jeanie recommended that they play school at home. They built a Lego house to be the school, and the mom and her son pretended to be the teachers and students. This play was relaxed and fun and didn't stir up any feelings, but the boy still cried when he went to the real school. Then the mother thought of adding a crucial element to the game, having a little car pull up to drop off the little Lego guy at school. The boy would make his character say, "Don't leave, Mama." The mom would have her Lego mama cuddle the scared boy. After just a few games of this, the situation at school changed dramatically, and he made a good adjustment to being there. What happened? At first he avoided any tough emotions in the play, but the mother was tuned in enough to know what themes to introduce. The play became highly emotionally charged, and the mother was soothing in her dual role as mother and teacher. The child was then able to carry this soothing presence with him into the real school, because they had played out the scene in fantasy at home.

Sometimes a child will play out the same theme over and over. In that case, try broadening the range of themes in the play. If his fantasy games are always about aggressive dinosaurs, be a dinosaur that gets hurt and ask the child's dinosaur for help. Even if he refuses, you are at least starting a dialogue about dependency and empathy, not just about aggression. Rule-breaking is a good theme to introduce for most children. I love to make up wacky rules and then pretend to be upset when children break them, or have them make up rules for me—with appropriate punishments.

One theme that is loaded with difficulty is exclusion and inclusion. Like adults, children have a natural inclination toward wanting to be included by the group, but they are all too willing to exclude others. We can't just order children to be nice and then walk away. We have to stick around and help children figure out the actual nuts and bolts of including and what to do when children exclude or feel like excluding.[7] Having the child's dolls or stuffed animals act out exclusion and rejection is my favorite way to introduce this theme.

Some themes are just as difficult for adults as they are for children, so it can be a challenge to introduce them into play. Some schools and neighborhoods are segregated by race and class; others are integrated. Some are in between. Whatever your child's situation, they live with the fact of these similarities and differences, and the fact that race and class matter tremendously in our society. Yet we don't talk about it very much. Generally, children either play out the same old terrible stereotypes that they hear and see around them, or are afraid to bring up the topic at all. If children can't play out a theme or feeling that is important to them, they can't really figure it out. Multiculturalism has made impressive strides (remember flesh-colored crayons?), but racism still pervades our society and affects all of our children. I consulted at a school where every girl in the second grade was in Girl Scouts, except for three girls whose families had recently immigrated from Asia. Only a couple of white parents noticed or cared. Other differences, such as physical or mental disabilities, are also taboo subjects. I will never forget visiting a preschool class taught by my sister Diane, where all the students lovingly included a girl with cerebral palsy into every aspect of their play. As parents, we have to get over our own fears, embarrassments, and prejudices in order to help our children deal with these topics.

Recently, a colleague asked me if I had any suggestions for a difficult problem he was facing. His daughter was in a diverse preschool and seemed to get along with everyone, but when it came time to invite people to her birthday party, she wanted to invite only her white friends. My first suggestion was that parents should be in charge of birthday party guest lists at that age (and beyond), because many young children tend to be "casually cruel," publicly excluding and including people without regard for the emotional consequences and hurt feelings. Birthday party lists are *not* a time to empower children; they are a time to guide them, especially when it comes to exclusion based on race or class, or exclusion of a scapegoat or outcast.

Children also need to be pushed to overcome their resistance to differences of any kind. It is a myth that young children are blissfully "colorblind"; they are as aware of race as the rest of us. An even more important suggestion for these parents goes by the fancy name of intergenerational socializing, which simply means that if you want your child to be friends with someone, the parents should invite their whole family over. Finally, the Playful Parenting approach applies just as well to thorny problems like racism as it does to having problems at school or getting a shot at the doctor's. The parent can pick up a doll and have it say to a frog Beanie Baby, "You're green. I don't want to play with you." The idea is to get the child giggling about the whole issue rather than to give a thinly disguised lecture. It may seem funny, but those giggles actually help the child think better about the topic.

—MAKE IT FUN—

Taking the lead in play also means having an attitude that anything can be fun. Chores, errands, cleanup, drudgery—why shouldn't these be as fun-filled as playing? In his autobiography, Patch Adams, the hero of the recent film, talks about his commitment to making *everything* fun. "The file room of the Navy Federal Credit Union in Anacostia might seem like an unlikely place to thrive. The people who worked there spent half their waking hours doing something they hated. Filing was considered particularly horrible work: joyless, boring, and dull. I decided to change all that. My fellow file clerk was Louis Fulwiler, who remains my oldest friend. . . . From the very first day we decided to make the files a 'happening'—it was, remember, the mid-1960s—and egged each other on. . . . We interacted with other people in the office by singing file information. . . . Louis was my partner in fun and we gave each other the courage to be goofy in public. When we went back to visit ten or fifteen years later, everybody still remembered us. We had opened whole new vistas in the filing shtick."[8]

Patch Adams goes on to say, "Waiting in line becomes a great opportunity to meet people, daydream, or play. Washing dishes—too often seen as drudgery—becomes a ballet performed in gratitude to the cook." My friend Andy, who was in a fathers' group with me when our children were two and three, once said, "I used to get upset at long lines and stuff, but now Seth and I can have a great time in line at the supermarket, or whatever we are doing." Back when my daughter was a baby, I remember realizing how much I separated the world into diaper duty versus playtime. Heaven forbid we get these mixed up.

So now, when my daughter and I go grocery shopping, we sometimes play a game in which she tries to sneak things into my cart that I would never buy, and I have to spot them before we get to the checkout. Sometimes we have more fun during cleanup time than we did playing. I think parents often resort to bribes when children revolt against unpleasant tasks such as getting a haircut or going to the doctor—the legendary spoonful of sugar that helps the medicine go down—and I know I've certainly done it myself. But bribes are not the same as actually figuring out how to make it fun. In fact, bribes backfire, making it even less likely that children will want to do something on their own initiative, whether it is getting up in the morning, or studying in school, or doing chores.[9] Unlike bribes, making everything fun fosters closeness, confidence, and cooperation.

—LEADING THE WAY—

At the end of the last chapter I introduced a boy named Robert as an example of following a child's lead in play. He is also a great example of the leading end, and of points in between.

Robert is a five-year-old boy whose mother called me after he was sent home repeatedly from his preschool (and later, sent home from camp). He tended to be aggressive when he was frustrated, and he was beginning to be rejected by the other children for being bad. Robert is an incredibly bright child, but he's socially unskilled and hard to settle down. In the first few sessions, we just played whatever he wanted to play. Once we had a good relationship, there were several times when I wanted to direct the play to help him past a spot where he had difficulty.

For example, one time I tried the close physical holding technique I described earlier because he kept hitting and kicking me, and my other attempts to get him to stop all failed. When I held him so I wouldn't get hurt, he screamed that he hated me. This type of play (*play?*) is exactly the type of situation that I think calls for close holding and insisting on connection. I asked his mom to hold him close while he struggled to get away. He screamed at her to let him go and for me to leave. She told him she would let go when he calmed down. I suggested that she say instead, "I'll let you go when we are connected again. When we can look at each other in the eye and really see each other." She did, and the holding changed. He was less agitated and confused. He still avoided eye contact, but it was no longer a power struggle between the two of them over settling down. Instead, it was a joint effort to reconnect.

As he wound down a bit, I asked her what she thought these feelings were all about. Clearly, underneath the aggression, there was a little boy who was scared and hurting. Some of his teachers realized this, but they were still at a loss as to how to keep him from hurting others and digging himself deeper into a hole—the role of a bully and bad kid. As his mom told me about some scary things that had happened to Robert when he was younger, she began to cry; Robert relaxed in her arms, looking at her. She told me how bad she felt about how scared he was, and how little he was, and how he had to be brave and strong. I asked her to talk to him,

instead of to me. She did, and they looked deeply at each other, no struggling now, just being gentle together.

Our previous sessions had created a strong rapport between the two
of us but had not produced much in the way of results at school or at
camp. This session, however, with his mother holding him, made a dramatic difference. That weekend, they spent a lot of time talking as a
family about how Robert felt when he hit people, and for the first time he
admitted that he felt scared and worried, instead of just saying that other
people had been mean or stupid. Mom and Dad helped him think about
ways to feel safe. To their surprise, he announced that he thought that hitting people really didn't make him any safer, because they just stopped
liking him. Since then, his camp and school experiences have been better.
I think it was the mother's new level of awareness that made the difference, at least as much as Robert having the holding time. But if she hadn't
held him through those tears and screams, she probably would never have
felt close enough to him to talk about the deeper issues of fear and safety.
Certainly he wouldn't have sat still to listen to it. Since then, he has had a
few more of these holding sessions, but mostly we play. I should also say
that at the end of each of these holding sessions, he was very eager to have
me come back and play with him the next week, so I knew that his yelling
at me to go away forever was just his way of saying that he was dealing
with some heavy-duty emotions.

Another time Robert was mad at me; I forget what I had done
wrong. He closed the door to the kitchen in my face and said, "I am going
to have popcorn, and you can't have any."

I burst in with a big frown, "Waaah!"

He said, "Okay, you can have one kernel."

"One kernel, yippee, what a generous guy, I am so happy. Hey, wait a
minute, what flavor is it?"

"Oh, butter."

"Well, that's okay then, because I hate buttered popcorn."

"Tricked you, it's plain!"

"Waaah!"

"Mom, where's the popcorn?"

"I'm not sure you should have any if you don't share."

I told Mom, "It's okay, it's part of the game." Then I said to Robert, "Do you have any peanut-butter-caramel-soy-sauce-flavored popcorn? That's my favorite!"

"No!"

"Waaah!"

He sat eating his popcorn, and he handed me one kernel. I said, "Hey, is this peanut-butter-caramel-soy-sauce flavored?"

"Yep."

I ate it. "This is butter flavored; you tricked me."

He laughed.

"Maybe that piece just didn't have any peanut-butter sauce on it. Try this one," he suggested.

"I'm not sure if I trust you. Are you *sure* this is peanut-butter-caramel-soy-sauce flavored?"

"I'm sure it is; try it."

"If it isn't, should I make a mad face?" I wanted to help him be able to handle other people being mad at him, and I thought this could be a playful way to introduce this idea. But I wanted to ask him first, so I didn't really scare him.

"No!" He said no very emphatically—he wasn't ready for me to make a mad face at him.

"What should I do if this *somehow* turns out not to be peanut-butter-caramel-soy-sauce flavored?"

"Make a sad face."

I ate the popcorn, made a *very* sad face, and he laughed and laughed. We repeated that a few times. In one sense, I was following along in this game with the popcorn. But in another sense, I was leading, by introducing themes like disappointment, anger, and power.

One time Robert and I were on the couch, and he bopped me with a pillow. We could have launched into a pillow fight, but I decided to try something else instead. I said, "Oh hi! Welcome to Dr. Cohen's School of Pillow Management. You must be our new student. I'm very glad to meet you." I shook his hand to get some contact. By responding playfully to his whack on my head with the pillow, I was following his lead. But by creating a game about school, I was stepping in as a guide. This game—Dr. Cohen's School of Pillow Management—was something I was making up as I went along, not some fancy therapy thing. I was just looking for a way to introduce the themes of school, rules, and self-control, themes he usually tried hard to avoid.

I continued, "You are just in time for the first lesson—*No bopping!*" I fully expected him to break this rule. I started talking at double speed: "Now, put this pillow here and that pillow there and then switch the two pillows like this and then spin around and stack these two pillows. . . ." I made the instructions very confusing but funny, to be kind of like school but not quite. Mainly I was setting him up to bop me with the pillow, so I could pretend to be all upset and chase him around while he giggled about getting one over on me.

"Oh, and remember, there is only one rule, no bopping!" (Sorry to interrupt again, but with some children, you have to whisper to them, "It's *really* okay to bop me, I don't mind; I'm just saying it's a rule for the game." With Robert that was hardly a problem—he was itching for a chance to wallop me with the pillow.) Robert picked up the pillows, started to move them around the couch, and then when I wasn't looking, he bopped me. I screamed a funny scream, and he ran away, saying, "You have to chase me now." Naturally I went chasing after him. Whenever possible, I switch back to following children's lead once things get going. I caught him and carried him back to the couch, and I said, "Now, that was very good except for one small thing. *No bopping!* Are you ready to try it again, with no bopping? Okay." I repeated the instructions, and we had a replay of this game, about ten or twenty times, with a great deal of giggling from everyone (including Robert's mom, who was in the kitchen watching this goofiness).

At the end, when it was nearly time for me to go, Robert asked if we could play it one more time. I said sure, and he proceeded to follow the very complicated instructions about the pillows, and he didn't bop me. He had a huge smile of accomplishment on his face. I said, "That was amazing. I think you get to move on to the next level of pillow management." He beamed. "This level is called advanced bopping." He really beamed now. "In advanced bopping, you can bop me on the head, but you have to stand on one foot and sing." He did that, and we all laughed.

Let me explain this last bit of the game. Since he had done so well with playing at breaking rules, I thought I'd introduce a new twist. This time, I took what he wanted to do, bop me on the head with the pillow, and instead of making that *against* the rules, I made it the thing he was *supposed* to do. This is a little twist that helps many children develop skills in being more cooperative, as I explain more fully in the next chapter on learning to love the games you hate.

"Okay," I imagine you asking, "that explains the invitation to bop you, but what was that bit about having him stand on one foot and sing?" That is an attempt to help Robert with emotional regulation. Everyone has aggression, just as we all have many types of impulses. The key is to regulate these—to have a dimmer switch instead of only an on-off switch. One thing I knew about Robert and aggression was that he had no dimmer; if you were lucky, you could help him turn the fury off, but he didn't have much skill at toning it down to manageable levels. So I took the aggressive action—hitting me with a pillow—and I did two things with it. First, I invited it, which has a profound impact on aggressive impulses. The invitation makes the pillow bop a playful act instead of a hostile act. The invitation also makes it an interaction *between* us, instead of something he does *to* me. Second, I had him do it on one foot, while singing. It could have been anything; that's just the first thing that came to my mind. The idea was to change the action in some small way so he could begin to get some control over it. If you can stand on one foot and sing while you bop someone, you can possibly stop yourself from shoving a kid who steps on your foot in line.

Here's another example of transforming behavior by first joining, then leading. Betty teaches an art class for nine children, ranging in age from three to twelve. One day, they were having a hard time focusing and concentrating. She took them to the Mount Auburn Cemetery, where she had hoped they would calm down. They didn't.

Near the tower, which is a structure with a skinny spiral staircase, Betty had them put down their sketch pads and materials. She was speaking slowly and deliberately, and they were surely thinking that she was expecting them to settle down and work. All of a sudden, she shouted, "Last one up the tower is a rotten egg," and she led the way running up the tower. At the top, she said, "Now we have to run down," and she started down, the rest following boisterously. As she went down, she slowed the pace gradually, until near the end they were going *very* slowly. She started saying, "Feel the gravity pull your foot down as you take a step. . . ." By the bottom, they were calm, focused, and ready to draw. By first joining the children where they were (boisterous and wild), Betty was then able to lead them to a new place (settled and grounded). She said it was the best class ever.

CHAPTER 11

LEARN TO LOVE THE GAMES YOU HATE

"Those who'll play with cats must expect to get scratched."
—MIGUEL DE CERVANTES

So far, we have assumed that adults *want* to go to the world where children live, at least to visit. But what about when we don't? What about when that world disturbs or aggravates or scares us? What about when we just want to get them to stop what they are doing, and never do it again, and we don't want to be playful or lighthearted about it?

In the chapter on connection (chapter three), I referred to Max, the hero of Maurice Sendak's *Where the Wild Things Are*, who returns from his fantasy world to the real world because he wants to be where someone loves him best of all. But before that, he unleashes the wild energy that parents find so destructive and unsettling. He imagines taming a bunch of wild creatures, who make him the king of all wild things. " 'And now,' cried Max, 'let the wild rumpus start!' " The wild rumpus is Sendak's fanciful shorthand for all the things children do that make adults uncomfortable, or horrified, or furious. In psychological terms, there are three key themes lurking underneath every wild rumpus: *dependence-independence, aggression, and sex.*

—DEPENDENCE ("I CAN'T!") AND INDEPENDENCE ("I'D RATHER DO IT MYSELF!")—

Babies are born completely dependent on us, and yet they are already separate beings, with their own needs, desires, and preferences. Throughout their lives, they experience powerful drives to be both dependent and independent. Both drives can be confusing to adults. Think about children who cling to their parents or their teacher, or have a hard time trying new things, or who seem to regress to a younger stage whenever they are under stress. Their motto is "I can't."

On the other hand, children can exasperate us by running out into the street, by breaking rules, by insulting us and pushing us away, by getting into trouble, by ignoring our superior wisdom and guidance. The motto this time is "I'd rather do it myself." Some children seem to flip-flop back and forth between dependence and independence, and we simply can't keep up. One minute they want to go to the store alone; the next minute, they want to ride in the baby's carriage.

I have described disconnection and powerlessness as locked towers. Children may literally lock themselves in their rooms, or hide underneath headphones, or maintain an emotional distance that lets no one in. When the tower door slams, we can almost feel the wall that separates us. Other children confuse us by looking as if they are *too connected*. They cling; they cry if someone new picks them up; they hang on to mama's skirts; they call home every day from college; they never move away from home. But is this really a matter of too much connection? Actually, the problem is a different version of disconnection. They can't connect with anyone but mom, or with anyone new, or with their peers.

The teacher's lap, mom's skirt, the endless hours plugged into the computer—these become the fortresses of isolation. Even when other people are around, the overly dependent child does not connect with them. The child clinging to her mother's lap is not looking happily out at the world, just waiting for a good moment to plunge in. Instead, she has her face buried in a shoulder. As parents, we may like the coziness of this burrowing in, or we may feel smothered and irritable: "Why do you have to follow me around? . . . Are you physically attached to me or something? . . . Go play in your room."

One Playful Parenting approach to clinginess is to push your child an inch or two away from you. Don't send him completely away, just put a 'tiny distance between you. Try making eye contact and see what happens. Often the result is a big burst of tears or a tantrum, as the child tries to retreat back to that buried spot of safety. Yet we need to coax him out so he can see that the world outside is safe as well, or at least that its dangers are worth risking. When he is burrowed into your shirt like that, he isn't really connecting with you, he is hiding. Gently push him to come out and join you, and then help him notice the wide world. This strategy may not seem like play, but it is a way of physically playing out the child's mixed feelings about dependence and independence.

My friend Carla called me for help with her daughter, Isadora, who, at eleven months, had an extreme case of separation anxiety. She screamed at the very thought of being left with anyone other than her mom, including her father or her grandmother, both of whom she loved. She would cry the whole time her mom was gone, not just for a few minutes. I told Carla I'd come over and give them a hand. She had someone take her older boy for a while, and we sat talking for a few minutes while Isadora sat on the floor, eyeing me warily.

I talked to Carla about all the stuff I've been saying in this chapter, and suggested that we see what happened if I tried to hold Isadora. As if she could understand me, Isadora started fussing and asking to be held by her mom. I nodded to Carla to pick her up, and Isadora clung very tightly, giving me a dirty look. I reached out and touched Isadora's shirt, very gently, just barely touching it. Isadora started to cry, and she cried hard for the next half hour or more, with her head buried in Carla's shoulder. Every once in a while she would look out and see me still touching her shirt, and she would cry some more. She seemed to be pushing her mom away with one hand and clinging to her with the other, a very common pattern.

I suggested to Carla that she keep trying to make eye contact with Isadora, and keep talking to her gently. Carla said that Isadora never cried like this with her, and this must be what it was like when she left. I said, "Not quite. This time she gets to have you and not have you at the same time, which is very different from being with you or being left by you."

You see, most of the time Isadora was either with her mom, and every-thing was fine, or she was not with her mom, and everything was awful. She couldn't notice other people, even people she was very close to, if her mom wasn't around. All she could see was *not-mom*. With anyone else, she didn't cuddle in to cry, releasing the painful feelings; instead she re-sisted all comfort and screamed. When I very gently tugged her away from her mom, Isadora could still have her mother, while releasing the fear of being separated from her.

Toward the end of all this crying, I asked Carla what she thought these tears were about. She told me about having to hand over Isadora at the hospital for a medical procedure when she was first born. Carla started to cry telling this story, and Isadora stopped crying to watch her mom cry, another common pattern. Carla held Isadora tight, telling her how much she loved her, how afraid she had been at the hospital, and how hard it was to have to give her to someone else to hold. After both had finished crying, they held each other in a very relaxed way, looking deeply into each other's eyes. Isadora even looked at me with affection, though she still wouldn't come over to me. When I touched her shirt again, she just laid her head on mom's shoulder and gave me a dreamy look. On later visits though, and ever since, she has been very cuddly and affectionate with me. Afterward, Isadora's separation anxiety was reduced significantly, and she no longer howled when left with her dad or her grandmother.

Now, this hour of tears certainly wasn't play in the sense of fun and games. Yet, in a way, it was play. I was *playing* at pulling her away from her mom, instead of *really* taking her away. Perhaps an adult example will make this clearer. I saw a man in therapy who couldn't stand it when the hour was up, and he found a dozen ways to try to keep my attention in-stead of leaving. He didn't care that I had people waiting. He couldn't take a hint, or even a direct statement that he had to leave. I tried a few typical therapy ploys to change this behavior, with no success. He refused to be-lieve that he had any deep psychological reason for wanting to stay. Each time he insisted that he just needed to talk to me about "one more thing."

Then one day I decided to make it into a game. I said, "At about halfway through the session, I am going to say 'the time is up.' You can argue, complain, beg, plead, whatever you want, for as long as you want, until the hour really is up, and then it will really be time to leave." He said, "That's stupid; that will never work. I'll know that it isn't really time to go, and it won't bother me." I finally convinced him to try it, and it worked perfectly. I said, "Our time is up," and he said, "What do you mean? I just got here. I need your help; I don't care how many people you have waiting. . . ." Instead of being annoyed and eager to rush him out— as I usually was when he pulled this at the end of our sessions—I just kept saying, "Gee, sorry, our time is up." Instead of acting as if he just needed to talk about one more thing, he was finally able to admit to being needy and dependent. At the real end of the hour, I said, "Hey, look, the time is really up." He started to argue, and then gave a big smile and said, "See you next week." And left. That was it. No more hanging on for dear life at the end of the sessions. The therapy sessions themselves became more productive, too, as neither of us spent them dreading the ending anymore.

A very different Playful Parenting approach to excess dependency is to reverse the roles so that you grab on to children and cling to *them* for dear life. Children who cling are used to being sent away, and they dread it. We may like being clung to at first, but eventually we get tired of it, usually before their neediness runs out. Thus, every time they come close, they are already tense about the impending separation. They hate separations so much that they forget to enjoy the times they are actually together. When we are the ones who cling, letting them be the ones eventually to squirm away from us, they can notice the connection instead of focusing on the separation. This doesn't take as long as you might think, especially if we are really silly about how much we love them and how we are never going to let them go. Once the tables are turned, they don't need to cling, so they let go pretty quickly.

I discovered this idea by accident, when I was having trouble putting my daughter to bed when she was very little. She wanted me to lay down with her until she was asleep, but as soon as I got up she would wake up and want me to stay. It was nerve-racking. Finally, I figured out that she could never relax because she knew that as soon as she fell asleep I would leave. No matter how long I waited after she fell asleep, she still woke up and caught me leaving. So I started getting up *sooner*, before she was all the way asleep, saying that I was going to go put on my pajamas, and then I'd come back and check on her. I told her that if she was still awake when I came back, I would lie down with her again. Otherwise I'd kiss her good night and tuck her in. She was almost always asleep before I was even out of the room. On the rare times she was still awake when I came back to check on her, all I had to do was give her a kiss, and she'd roll over and fall right asleep—she could relax, I came *back*. Instead of bracing herself for the separation, now she knew that the next thing that would happen was that I'd be back, so she could relax and drift off to sleep. Thinking about this solution to the sleep problem, I realized that clingy children are always waiting anxiously for the dreaded separation. But if we cling to them, *they* can be in charge of when to separate.

Many family conflicts happen when children won't do something independently that we think they should be able to do (like dress themselves, do their chores without being nagged, finish their homework). Because they *can* do it by themselves, we think they *should*. But at these moments, when children have taken a step toward independence, they may need *more* contact with us rather than less. They need to balance all their new accomplishments with some extra closeness. That replenishes their supply of confidence so they can move on to the next step. Therefore, any increase in expectations or responsibility should be accompanied by an increase in playtime together.

When children regress—acting younger and less mature than they are—parents often get extremely annoyed. This regression happens most often when there is a new sibling or when children are under stress. Of course, these are already difficult times for parents. Yet regression can't be eradicated by punishing it or disapproving of it, because it represents a deep need in children to go back to being a little dependent for a while. Then they can regroup and move out toward independence again. If you fight it, they will want to do it all the time, but if you enjoy it and make it a game, they will get over it quickly. If your four-year-old climbs into the baby carriage when the toddler climbs out, say in a delighted voice, "What a marvelously enormous baby! I've never seen anything like it. Goo-goo-goo baby." When the child talks, exclaim how amazing it is that a tiny baby can talk. Soon he'll get out of the carriage and show how he can run, jump, etc. His cup gets filled by the brief excursion into babyhood. To an older sibling, it looks as though all a baby has to do is lie there in order to be loved and appreciated by adults. After the refill, he can go off running with a new boost of enthusiasm for being four. Other regression games are quieter, like just letting older children cuddle in your lap long after they have given that up, without teasing them about it.

At the other extreme, children exasperate adults by being too independent. They want to be away from adult supervision and adult rules. This is hard. We have to protect them, but we also have to let them spread their wings a little. Sometimes all we need to do is relax and not hover so much, trusting that they will be safe enough, even if we can't guarantee 100 percent safety. Other times we just need to find safe ways for them to practice their independence. We can hold their hands while they practice cutting with a sharp knife, we can follow a block behind while they go "alone" to the store, we can go to a park where there is nothing breakable and they can go wild.

We can also loosen up about things like mess, noise, and bathroom humor, if those things bother us. Power struggles disappear if we don't fight over them. And we can let them make more of their own decisions. When my daughter was around two or three, she wanted to play with Band-Aids. In fact, she wanted to cover herself head to toe with them. I found myself saying sternly, "No, these are for when you get a cut," as if play and first aid are worlds that dare not intersect. I did the same thing with tape: "That's not a toy!" But, of course, tape and bandages *are* toys (and fashion accessories). Children don't make these distinctions. It turns out that my "need" to keep Band-Aids hoarded away for medical emergencies was a pretty dumb rule.

Children are into rules—making them, discussing them, breaking them, negotiating them, arguing about them, enforcing them, finding loopholes, turning other children in. Most children love games that let them make and break silly rules. So invent a rule—like no giggling or no blinking—and then make a big pretend fuss when they break the rule. This gives them a chance to giggle about an area of their life that is very challenging. Sometimes children will want to use their PlayTime to be completely in charge of the rules. They may want you to follow the rules exactly, or they may want you to break the rules and be punished. Adult involvement is crucial here, because other children will never allow your child to have so much power. When children try to control the rules with one another, it doesn't usually go over very well. Parents don't really like being bossed around either, but I have noticed that parenting goes much smoother if we cheerfully obey orders during PlayTime. It helps them cheerfully follow our rules at other times. Well, maybe not cheerfully, but would you settle for cooperatively?

My daughter made up a game that she calls Emma's Rules Monopoly. We had played Monopoly a few times and it was starting to get a little boring, so one time she asked me if she could make up some rules. I said sure, thinking she would make the game more interesting in some way. Instead, she made it ridiculously lopsided—in her favor. She got big wads of money no matter who landed on what. I'd buy something and she'd take it away from me, and so on. We both howled with laughter all the way through the game, with me pretending to be surprised that each new rule made her richer. We were no longer playing Monopoly, but a new game— perhaps it could be called Life Is Unfair.

Some parents fear that letting their children play this way will leave them unprepared for the cold, cruel world of their peers. Other children, after all, would never let them get away with such selfishness. On the contrary, being in charge of the play and the rules fills children's cup—and that refill then leaves them more able to play happily on a level playing field with their peers. It also helps them play out their tensions and upsets about the confusing world of games, rules, and competition. We can help this process along by exaggerating (in a funny way) the thrill of victory and the agony of defeat.

Just to make it more confusing, sometimes children have their cup filled by *not* being given a special break. Sometimes they like to be treated as one of the big kids or one of the grown-ups, and to have to play their hardest to keep up. My friend Susan told me about her nine-year-old son Mark. At home, he insists on winning every game. So she was very surprised to find him at the gym one day, playing basketball with a bunch of teenage boys. They were not giving him any special breaks, and he was playing extremely hard, but he was still the weakest player on the court. He loved it. The "being in charge" and "letting me win" play gives children roots; the all-out play with no special advantages lets them test their wings.

—AGGRESSION—

Many adults are disturbed by aggressive play: teasing, play fighting, being superheroes, using pretend guns or toy guns, engaging in rough-and-tumble play, and having battles for dominance and power on the playground. As with dependence and independence, if we can understand where aggressive play comes from and what purposes it serves, then we can perhaps hate it less and join in more.

We've all seen pictures of bear cubs or lion cubs play fighting. Animals tease each other, too. Frans de Waal, a primatologist, described a study of Bonobo chimpanzees at the San Diego Zoo.[1] They are extremely playful and active, and a favorite game involves climbing down a chain into the dry moat around their enclosure. One male, Kalind, often pulled the chain up after another chimp had climbed down. He especially liked doing this to the dominant male chimp, Vernon. "Kalind would look at Vernon with a play face and teasingly slap the side of the moat. On several occasions Loretta [the dominant female] rushed to the scene to 'rescue' her mate by dropping the chain back down."

Play fighting and real fighting can be hard to tell apart. Here are some clues I use: Is there any eye contact? Are they looking at the other person for a response, or are they blind with rage? Is there laughter? Is anyone getting hurt? Anthony Pellegrini,[2] a psychologist who writes about rough-and-tumble play, describes playful aggression as running, chasing, and wrestling, accompanied by smiling and laughing. When play fighting ends, children keep playing together happily. The stronger ones will hold back their full strength in order to keep things roughly even (like Paul the baboon in chapter six).

In contrast, real fighting involves hitting with fists, shoving, pushing, and kicking. At least one child is usually frowning or scowling, and another may be crying. Real fighting generally ends with the children unhappily going their separate ways. The stronger child does not hold back, and injuries are much more common. Bullies often mix rough-and-tumble play with real aggression. That is, they escalate playful fighting into real aggression, or they disguise their violence as playful rough and tumble.

When we see aggressive play, we need to stay calm and relaxed, and possibly insert some connection (as in the love gun, page 50) or help children build confidence (as in the power room, page 60). When we see real aggression, we need to help children cool down. That means either holding them or giving them breathing room. Good aggressive play actually helps children control their aggressive impulses and helps them deal with the aggression they see around them on TV or in real life. Destructive aggressive play is simply violence, and if unstopped it promotes more violence.

I was playing with a girl named Ellen once. She was playing at hitting me, and I was jumping out of the way. She was switching back and forth between looking playful and looking angry. One time, when she just missed hitting me, she caught the edge of the table and whacked her hand. When I went over to make sure she was okay, she pushed me away and said it was my fault. I said it was a case of the chickens coming home to roost. She thought that was a very funny expression but didn't know what it meant. I explained that she was the one being aggressive, and then she ended up getting hurt. Later in the game, I pretended to fall just before I caught her, and I hammed up a tragic scene of agony as I lay on the floor. Ellen laughed and said, "The chickens have come home to see the roosters!"

Another type of play does not involve actual aggression but symbolic aggression—superheroes, Power Rangers, action figures, pretend guns, and so on. Some parents ban this type of play because it disturbs them, or because they fear it will numb their children to the effects of real violence. Banning this type of play does not work. It is almost always better to join in with the play and transform it rather than to ban it. If children have a desire to play these games, then that means the aggressive impulses and the scenarios of violent destruction are already in their heads. You can't force this stuff out of their heads by not allowing them to play. You can only do it by playing *with* them. I know this will be very hard for some parents, but give it a try and see how it goes.

Some people say fantasy gunplay promotes real violence; others say it actually makes children less aggressive by letting them get it out of their system. In fact, it can go either way. Are they getting lost in the violence, or are they having fun? Are they playing out scenes of aggression in order to master their aggressive feelings, or are they getting sadistic pleasure out of fantasizing about hurting people? Many parents forget to make an important distinction between toy guns and pretend guns. Toy guns, especially realistic ones, are more likely to promote destructive types of play because they limit creativity. What else can you do with a gun besides shoot people? Pretend weapons, on the other hand, grow out of children's own themes and needs and concerns and can be endlessly creative.

Child psychologists are also quite divided on the issue of whether it helps angry children to have them bash on pillows or rocks or trees. Some argue that this is a healthy release of aggression; others say that it just reinforces the aggression and teaches violence. I think both can be true, and it depends on whether or not there is any human connection. A teacher in an after-school program told me about a very successful intervention he did with an eleven-year-old boy who was ready to explode with anger. The teacher put his hand on the boy's arm and led him outside, saying, "Let's go whack some trees." They found some sticks and let off steam together, hitting tree trunks and making loud noises. The effect was very calming for the child, because a close connection with the teacher was at the heart of it. An example at the other end of the spectrum is a client of mine who once spent an hour destroying everything in his parents' garage. No adults were around, just another boy who alternated between egging him on and trying to get him to stop. This destructiveness was not therapeutic and just left the boy with more of an appetite for violence, because he was trapped in a locked tower of isolation.

In good play fighting, children can experiment with their physical strength. With action figures, they experiment with the idea of power by fantasizing about fighting, weapons, and superpowers. Again, try to help children keep the play creative and lighthearted, instead of purely destructive. I like to play bad guys or monsters who are just a little bit scary, but also kind of funny, bumbling, and incompetent, so children can use the play to overcome their fears. If the bad guys or monsters are too scary, the play just increases children's fear.

In another area of aggression—children being mean to one another and jockeying for dominance—parents often get very confused. Most children can be cruel or mean sometimes.[3] Here's a spot where children are experimenting with something very complex, so it's no surprise that feelings and bodies can get hurt. Children need to experiment with social power without too much adult interference, but we also need to be available to protect children who are more vulnerable.

Two mothers in a parenting class told the following story. Their sons, ages seven and eight, were at the playground with a mixed-age group of kids that plays together often. The usual games of tag were escalating into name-calling and wood-chip-throwing. One of their boys hit a girl in the neck with a belt, raising a large welt. This boy is quite active and energetic and somewhat impulsive, but this behavior was uncharacteristically violent. The belt belonged to the other boy whose mom was in my class. Both mothers were horrified by what their sons had done or participated in. It later came out that an older boy, new to the group, had told them to do it. The parents were even more upset by this explanation—that their sons had followed the lead of a bully. The mothers did not understand how this could possibly have happened.

They seemed to see their sons' behavior as monstrous, a sign of serious disconnection from the human community. I agreed that it was a terrible thing, for the boys as well as for the girl, but I also felt that there was a lot more going on than just boys being wild, reckless, and violent. In fact, I think they were engaging in social experiments: *What happens if I ally myself with a stronger peer? Will I be more powerful in the group? Can I get away with telling Mom it was someone else's idea?* The instigator—the new boy who gave the two younger boys the idea—was doing his own experiments: *Can I get someone else to act out my aggressive impulses for me? Who will get in trouble if they do, me or them? I'm new here; how much power do I have because I am big? Can I make a place for myself in this group by being the biggest and toughest?*

I would describe both behaviors—the boy who tries to hand over his aggression to a younger peer, and the boys who eagerly try out an alliance with a stronger peer—as misguided attempts to figure out a difficult problem. Of course, there are dangers, above and beyond the injury to the girl who was hit with the belt. The older boy could come to enjoy the cruelty and become sadistic; the younger ones could begin to be entranced by the power of the alliance and become his henchmen. At the same time, we need to understand that the boys were trying to figure out what to do with their aggressive feelings. They were experimenting with the complexities of social interaction—making alliances, betraying friends, giving orders, following orders, ganging up, etc. Their attempts worked out badly, but they weren't monsters. Just as toddlers will pull a cat's tail to see what happens, school-age boys will yell out "Everybody get Mickey" just to see what happens. Girls are more likely to whisper such a thing ("Everybody wear a dress tomorrow, but don't tell Susie.").

The way to prevent these experiments from going too far astray is to spend more time actually playing with children so that we can protect them, and also so that we can model how to express aggressive feelings in a safe way. Maybe we can spot trouble before it boils over, instead of waiting until something bad happens and then yelling. You might let them gang up on you instead of against a smaller child. Call frequent breaks so things don't get out of hand. Fall over and get everybody giggling.

—SEXUAL FEELINGS AND EXPRESSIONS—

This chapter is as good a place as any to tackle the difficult issue of childhood sexuality. I know this topic makes many parents uncomfortable, even a hundred years after Freud shocked the world with the news that children have sexual feelings. We don't really know much about healthy or normal sexual development in children, because young boys and girls are exposed to so much misinformation and so much sexually explicit or suggestive material before they are prepared to handle it. They get it from their peers and especially from popular culture. Take a random ad and look at the message to boys: If you drink a certain kind of beer, you will be surrounded by gorgeous babes. And this is the kind of girl you're supposed to find most attractive. The message to girls is even worse: This is how you're supposed to look, and this is the most you can aspire to—to be the prize for some guy who bought the right kind of beer.

Parents get very confused by children's discovery of sexual play and masturbation. Sexual play between peers is generally nothing to worry about if it is occasional, playful, and exploratory. Consider getting a professional opinion if it is coercive, habitual, or goes too far. Make sure all children have access to accurate information that is the right level for their age. Above all, avoid punishing or humiliating the child. From the earliest days of psychotherapy, therapists have been trying to help their patients overcome the problems caused by being punished or humiliated for masturbating or playing doctor when they were children. When children make their dolls do sexual things, there is no cause for alarm. But if that's the only game they want to play, or if you suspect that they are playing out an experience of sexual abuse, then by all means get a professional opinion.

On the other hand, while sexual exploration and sexual play are perfectly normal for children at all ages, some sexual play is children's way of dealing with things that are confusing or scary or too much for them. They have been exposed to more than they can handle, and they are trying their best to deal with it. The way they deal with it, of course, is by playing, usually in secret, with another child. Then that child may have something confusing or exciting to play out. In this case, the best response is to have conversations about sex, answering their questions simply and honestly, and to reduce their exposure to provocative movies, television, or nudity at home. Some children have no trouble with mild nudity or sexual material; others are disturbed by it.

I consulted with a family where the parents were worried about their six-year-old daughter's frequent masturbation. I thought they were handling it very well. They didn't freak out or punish her or forbid it. They asked her to do it in her room and not when other people were around. Usually that's all that parents need to do. But these parents started to worry because she seemed to do it most after she had asked one of her parents to play with her and they had been too busy. This suggested to them, and I agreed, that she might be substituting the sexual self-stimulation for other forms of connection, or as a way to deal with feeling lonely or bored (the same reasons many adults masturbate). Masturbation is so intensely pleasurable that it overwhelms the original need for connection and becomes a habit.

This girl's parents also noticed that she would masturbate while watching videos—not pornographic videos, but just regular kids' videos—and they worried that it couldn't be good for her to associate sexual pleasure with zoning out in front of the television. I agreed with that, too. When I asked more questions about the behavior, I discovered that she always masturbated using a particular stuffed animal to rub up against. I recommended that they use Playful Parenting to interject a little human connection into this "play." I suggested that they play a game during a time when she wasn't involved in the sexual activity. The game was to pretend to have that animal beg and plead with their daughter to be her new favorite toy. "Please take me to school. Can I sit with you while you eat your dinner? Please, please, please, please!" They made this animal plot and scheme—in a humorous way—to overthrow her favorite stuffed animal, the one she always slept with and took on trips. She laughed heartily at this game, and the response was immediate and dramatic. The masturbation stopped, but without any guilt or negative feelings about sex or sexuality.

Apparently, all she needed was a way to playfully deal with the feelings that had become attached to the intense physical stimulation and had taken on a sexual meaning. At the same time, the parents figured out how to spend more time together as a family and to figure out alternatives to saying, "Go away; I'm too busy." One thing they did that was very successful was to say, "I don't have time right now; let's have a big hug and play in fifteen minutes." Like serving a snack after school to tide a child over until dinner, that extra contact helped her manage the wait until she could get some attention from her parents.

Preteens and teenagers face extreme pressures to be cool. Part of this coolness is pretending to know much more about sex than they really do, and pretending to have it all together about dating and romance. We need to lose our dignity a bit in this area, so that our children then don't have to play it so cool. We want them to know that it's okay to be curious, to not know something, to be scared and confused. A playful way to convey that message is to play the role of what Patty Wipfler calls *the happy dense person.* "Let's go outside in our underwear and run around in the woods like in that commercial." "Hey, you keep calling each other fag and homo. What does that mean?" "Oh my gosh, those people are kissing. Did you see that?" "What on earth is that dog doing to that guy's leg?"

Remember the game for toddlers where we stumble and fall right before we catch them in a game of chase, so they can feel competent and confident? The preteen equivalent is for us to stumble a bit in this area of sex and romance that is so loaded for them. As I like to say, it takes a village idiot to raise a child. So I do totally uncool things, like ask them if I can have the gum they've been chewing, or sing very corny love songs. I say that I have a crush on Barney the purple dinosaur, or on Barbie.

Some children will start to take their clothes off or writhe around in your lap at any opportunity. Adults are rightly worried when children's play strays this far into sexual territory. No one wants to be seen as a pedophile or child molester. But it's a paradox. In order to develop a healthy sexuality, children need to play out the sexual themes that concern them. But we can't help them play out their sexual feelings and confusions directly, the way we can play at school if they are having trouble at school. We need to find safer ground. First, we need to provide plenty of healthy, close contact that isn't abusive, exploitative, or sexual. Any kind of physical play, from playing sports to wrestling to running around outside, can help children dissipate their excess sexual energy. Most children need much more of this healthy physical contact and physical play than they get. Another good play activity is the sock game, which I described earlier, where each person tries to take off the socks of the other players while keeping his or her own on. This is a safe way to address children's feelings about having their clothes on and off, and it's also lots of fun. For some people this game won't have anything to do with sex; for others, it will be a symbolic way of playing out an important sexual theme in a way that no one gets hurt or freaked out.

With married couples in therapy, I have them play a similar game. I tell one of them to ask the other, "Can I put my finger in your ear?" The other one usually says "Eww, gross," or something like that. I have the first person beg and plead, and soon both are laughing wildly. In a safe and symbolic way, they are playing with the topic I call who puts what where. An area fraught with tension becomes a playground for silly giggles, which often translates into a better physical relationship.

—INVITE THE BEHAVIOR YOU HATE—

Sometime when things are going smoothly, and you have slightly more attention to spare than usual, invite your child to do the things you can't stand. If your children are driving you nuts with their sibling rivalry, for example, ask them: "Could you guys please have a fight?" (Or tease each other, or take things from each other, or fight over who gets your attention, or complain about who got a bigger piece of tofu, or whatever drives you crazy.) "Would you do that for me? I'll watch and take notes." Usually they won't actually do what you ask, but if they do, just pretend to be a news reporter. Watch with great interest, ask questions, ask them to do it again so you can study it.

The idea of inviting behavior that you hate is that it gives the difficult situation a playful twist. This twist usually lets the adult think better about how actually to handle the situation, and it catches children off their guard. "Instead of taking the garbage out tonight, could you sit like a lump in front of the TV for a few hours?" "I'm in the mood for a big argument about what time bedtime is tonight; what about you?" The invitation is a way of following children, since you are responding to their usual behavior, but it is also a way of leading, because you are turning the whole family dynamic upside down. After all, getting on the floor means joining in with play that we would rather ignore or eliminate, not just with play we enjoy. Inviting the behavior we hate simply takes this idea a step further.

The other day my daughter had six girls over. I had to take them to the park because of the noise level. On the way back I said, "Last chance for shrieking." They screamed those piercing nine-year-old-girl screams a few times, and everybody laughed. One girl asked if she could have a solo. Not only did inviting the screeching get it out of their systems, but it meant that I could get away with asking them not to scream later.

If children start being obnoxious before you have a chance to invite it, you can still play this game. "Hey, I see you guys are fighting! Can I watch? I find it so interesting the way older siblings are so bossy, and the way younger siblings are so sneaky." You can provide a running commentary, a play-by-play, about whatever it is they are doing. "Wow! Ladies and gentlemen, did you see that? He's lying there on the couch; he's been there for three hours; he's not moving. It may be a new world's record; no, he flicked his eyes a little; he may actually be preparing to move."

The play-by-play narration can also be a good way to express what we are thinking and feeling in a playful way. So often we either hold everything in or we scream it all out. Neither of those is very satisfying— or very effective. Try expressing yourself playfully instead: "I'm looking at the unfolded laundry. I am turning to the child who was supposed to fold it four hours ago. I am looking back at the laundry. I am starting to feel a screaming fit coming on. No, wait; I'm calming down."

Just about every behavior we can possibly hate can be transformed into a game or type of play that we can enjoy. If a child has trouble following the rules in games, and it bothers you, play a game like I doubt it,[4] where cheating is part of the fun of the game. If they lie, make up whoppers together. You'll be surprised how joining the behavior, and making it something fun that you do *together*, makes the problem disappear.

A friend of mine complained to me that her children had atrocious manners, and that she was not sure what to do about it. I offered to take them out to the park so she could get a break. They are great kids, ages five and ten. I decided to try this Playful Parenting approach of making a game out of the problem behavior. One of the children asked me which park we were going to, and I said, "What horrible manners, I can't believe you asked me that!" They both laughed. I said, "Next thing you're probably going to ask me what my pocket number is!" I have no idea what a pocket number is; I was just making something up. You won't be surprised that they spent the next hour asking me what my pocket number is, and I played along, begging them not to say such impolite things, warning them not to mention pocket numbers at the playground. (They shouted out, "Hey, everybody, ask Larry what his pocket number is!") A lecture about bad manners would have had no chance at all. This way, they got to laugh about an issue that had previously been a source of great tension in the family. Another benefit of this kind of invitation is that it helps you out of power struggles. At dinner, instead of saying "Use your fork," and getting into a no-win power struggle, you can say "Okay, everybody, there is to be no talking about pocket numbers; it is not polite."

While they rattle on and on about pocket numbers to play the game out, they are using their forks and napkins and not fighting you about table manners.

These techniques often bring a laugh. Inviting the behavior we can't stand can change a problem behavior in a nearly miraculous way. Of course, not every joining-in or invitation changes the behavior in question. Sometimes it has a more subtle effect, improving our own outlook on that behavior and our ability to handle it in the future. In other words, joining in or inviting children's play that we hate sometimes changes the play, and other times it changes how we feel about it. Either one is fine, as long as we no longer hate what they are doing. After all, hating their favorite games is invalidating to them, and hard on us.

CHAPTER 12

ACCEPT STRONG FEELINGS (THEIRS AND YOURS)

"Suddenly it's fun again."
—RUTH, AGE 4, AFTER A LONG CRY
OVER A MINOR PLAYTIME INJURY

Playful Parenting involves expecting and accepting strong feelings, from little frustrations and embarrassments to heavy fears and deep-seated grief. These emotions are at the root of most of the so-called behavior problems that so exasperate parents. Children's play also includes happier emotions of joy and excitement and exuberance as well, and these can be just as difficult for adults to handle as the "negative" ones. Just think of the times you have said "Settle down" when children have just been laughing and having fun.

Before I talk about the relationship between feelings and children's play, I need to back up and say some things about emotion. Everyone has emotions, all sorts of them. We can experience pure joy and contentment, for example, or we can feel bad in a variety of ways—hurt, afraid, embarrassed, frustrated, sad, angry, anxious, jealous. When we have a feeling, if we're in luck, we can express it freely, showing our zestful exuberance if we are feeling joy, crying if we're sad, trembling and shaking with fear or anger, laughing and blushing with embarrassment, having a temper tantrum if we are frustrated or outraged. Unfortunately, we have all been inhibited from this free expression of emotion: "What are you laughing at?" "Never let them see you sweat." "Don't you dare talk to me that way." "It's not ladylike to shout." "Go to your room until you can be in a good mood." "You're fine; you're not hurt." "Crybaby!" "You're so cute when you're angry." And the infamous "Big boys don't cry" or "I'll give you something to cry about."

If emotions are not expressed freely, either the emotion is locked away, creating all kinds of problems as children grow up, or the emotion leaks out in indirect ways. Children may bottle up everything and then explode when their younger sibling touches their toys. Children going through the pain of a parental divorce or the loss of a grandparent are well known for not talking about it, then turning around and hitting other children, being surly and mean, or refusing to do homework or chores. Children say "I hate you" because it feels too vulnerable to say "I'm scared and I need you." Anxious about not being prepared for a test, children might say they are feeling sick and can't go to school. Older children begin to find stronger ways to keep emotions buried away, such as with alcohol, drugs, and casual sex.

Playful Parenting helps bring children back to the free expression of emotion and out of the pitfalls of burying those emotions inside or having them come out sideways. These unexpressed or indirectly expressed emotions are a sign that children are trapped in the towers of powerlessness and isolation. Children who are feeling confident and connected are either able to play happily, or are able to let us know how they are feeling. They let us know in words, or through the direct release of emotions, or through the themes in their play.

—CONTAINING FEELINGS
VERSUS RELEASING THEM—

I was baby-sitting my niece once when she was around two years old. She had a hard time saying good-bye to her mom and dad and started to cry when they finally left. I went to hold her and comfort her, but she hid under the table and told me to go away. I asked her if I could come under the table with her, and she said no, I should leave the house. I said I couldn't do that, but I would move farther away. I stepped back a few feet and sat on the floor and asked if that was far enough. She said yes. In between our conversation she was crying quietly. After a few minutes she came out from under the table and sat on my lap. She said, "The tears just popped out."

"They certainly did," I said, and we both smiled.

"Let's watch *Cinderella*," she said. "That wicked stepmother is really really mean." If I had left the room, she would have been all alone with her sadness. If I had moved in too close, she would have been mad at me for crowding her. What happened instead was that she was able to cry in a way that released the pain of separation, which made it possible for her to make the transition to enjoying herself with me. Many adults say that it hurts to cry. I think that's because a part of us is always fighting against releasing those tears. When my niece talked about her tears just popping out, she was expressing how easily tears can flow if you aren't trying to shove them back in.

Most of us use up lots of mental energy holding our emotions back and trying to get children to hold theirs back. But emotions have a drive to be released, no matter how much we try to hold them in. The result is a tug-of-war, an inner battle between releasing and containing emotions. Contain them too much, and you get explosions or symptoms of too much pressure building up inside—stress, anxiety, violence, depression. When the emotions erupt, it may look as if the problem is *too much* emotional expression, but really the problem was *not enough* expression, which led to the eventual eruption.

For many children, emotional release is most likely to come when they are unable to keep the lid on anymore. That's why children are more emotionally expressive late at night, or when they have a fever. Their guard is down, so the emotions escape. They scrape their knee and cry for an hour: *I might as well cry about everything stored up, now that I've started.* One strong emotion, too powerful to hold in, can result in a flood of other emotions, which have just been waiting for an opportunity to come out. So a torrent of giggles can shift instantly to a flood of tears, or vice versa. That's also why angry outbursts often include a long list of things that happened long before, or that don't have anything to do with the person being yelled at: *As long as I'm yelling, there are a few other things I'm mad about.* Once the feelings start to come out, there's no stopping them, which is why some children reject all of our efforts to make them feel better.

Since men are especially pressured to hold all those vulnerable emotions in, it's no wonder that they have a hard time with crying babies and emotional children. A study of college men found that they reacted to a tape of a baby crying as though it were more painful than a fire alarm. Given the chance to drink alcohol, they drank more than students listening to other loud noises.[1] It's not surprising that so much child abuse against young children happens when they are crying. When I worked with men who battered their wives and children, they often described the unbearable feelings of agitation and "jumping out of their skin" that they experienced when they were faced with a woman or child who wouldn't stop crying. Of course, the man's escalating aggression just increased the crying and the fear, which then intensified his need to stop the crying, no matter what it took. That isn't the only scenario of battering and child abuse, but it is a common one. In nonviolent homes, tears and tantrums are still a powerful force, and they have the power to stop people in their tracks. Many people will do *anything* to get the crying to stop: bribe, threaten, tease, plead, scold, send the child away, give in to unreasonable demands. If we just accept the feelings and let them flow, they don't cause half as much fuss. And after the tears are really done, everyone feels better.

—TAKING TIME OUT FOR FEELINGS—

If giggles are the engine of play, tears are the lubrication that keeps the engine running smoothly. While playing with her cousins, four-year-old Ruth hurt her hand. I held her while she cried hard for several minutes. Looking at her hand, I was reassured that no medical attention was needed, just comfort. After crying a while, Ruth told me the story of what happened, and then she immediately began crying again. After a few minutes more, she held tightly to me while the cousins returned to playing around us. They had been watching closely. I think they were impressed by her lung power and by my allowing her to cry without the usual distractions, bribes, or threats.

Then, while deliberately looking away from me, Ruth started to squirm away. I gently pulled her back, reminding her, "That really hurt." She cried a few minutes more and told the whole story over again. At that point, she looked right at me with very bright eyes, then looked at her cousins, and back at me, laughing now. "Suddenly it's fun again," she said, and climbed down to play. I know most people would have let Ruth go the first time, then figured the episode was finished. I held on to her a little longer in order to promote emotional healing, instead of telling her to get over it. After crying a little more, she was really over it.

Most children learn from us to short-circuit the healing process, to cut off feelings as quickly as possible. But they do this without finishing the important job of releasing their emotions first. That makes it likely that when they return to play, they will be fearful, or reckless, or nothing will be right, or they will hurt themselves again right away. More and more young athletes are becoming permanently injured from playing on after they've been hurt. Therefore, we have to help them finish the emotional task of releasing their backed-up reservoir of tears or other feelings. They will never get every last drop of feeling out—there is always more—but we need to help children express enough of it so that they can go on to function well and find the room to be happy. In order to do that, most children need to be reminded that crying is okay, that being afraid or angry is okay. That's hard for us parents, who want our children to be happy (and quiet!). Yet a happy side benefit of helping children release these feelings is that it fosters a deep connection between us.

When Ruth was sitting in my lap, she told me the story of what happened to her hand. Later, when I reminded her that it was okay to notice that it really hurt, she told me the story again. I think that those retellings of the story, in addition to releasing the tears, were what allowed her to go back to playing so happily. Some children won't tell the story on their own, so we need to ask them. Then, since the story is probably very short, we can ask them to tell it again. Most children love that; it signals that we really care about what happened to them. Also, when you repeat a story over and over, it loses its sting. If the child is too young to tell the story, or doesn't want to, you can try telling it to them. "You were having so much fun playing on the bench and then bang, you hit your head. That really hurt."

Another reason for telling the story is that it strengthens the relationship between you and your child. Healthy emotional expression requires a close connection. We can cry alone, but it is so much more healing to cry on someone's shoulder. That's why I recommend that parents not send their children to their rooms to cry alone, or leave them alone to cry themselves to sleep. It is more time-consuming to stay with them, to help them let out their feelings of loneliness and sadness, but those feelings don't just go away because we shut the door on them. In fact, I am starting to see eight-, nine-, and ten-year-olds in my practice whose parents followed the advice to "let them cry it out" when the children were babies. These infants were seen as manipulating parents into cuddling with them or lying down with them to sleep. These children now are having trouble sleeping through the night because of fears, nightmares, and worries. In my less mature moments, I feel like saying, "I told you so!"

—ADULTS' UNFELT FEELINGS—

When emotions are unexpressed, I call them unfelt feelings. They still affect us, even though we hope that denying them will make them go away. Because each of us has our own pile of unfelt feelings, being with children who are in the midst of a strong feeling either feels as if we're being tortured or as if we're torturing them. We feel as if we're being tortured because the release of their raw emotion is so intense that it's harder for us to keep all our own unfelt feelings buried inside. So we end up with a battle in our own heads between releasing feelings and holding them in. We feel as if we are torturing children when they cry because they are so extravagantly expressive of their deep feelings. Crying over a minor upset or a little injury, children seem to act as though they have just invented pain and suffering. Partly this is to make sure we will give them some comfort and loving attention, and partly it is because they don't have the inhibitions against pure emotional expression that we grown-ups have.

Given how hard it is to listen to children's emotions and express our own, it's no wonder that parents go to such great lengths to get children not to cry. These efforts range from friendly to abusive, from offering sweets and bribes to yelling at them to shut up. I used to see an eight-year-old boy at his house for play therapy. He always wanted a sweet snack as soon as I came over. I suggested that his mother hold off, since so many children use sweets to stuff their feelings back inside, and part of my play-therapy approach is to bring the feelings up and out. She agreed, but she was skeptical. One day she told me that I wouldn't be able to see her son for several weeks because of various scheduling conflicts. I said, "Oh, that's too bad." He looked right at me and said, "Mom, I want some Fruit Loops." I said, "I'm going to miss you, too; three weeks is a long time." He screamed, *"I want Fruit Loops now!"* She gave me a look that said, Oh, so this is what you meant about sweets and emotions.

Tears and tantrums aren't the only feelings that bother adults. We are often annoyed or aggravated when children are too excited or exuberant. Maybe it's too noisy for us, or we are worried they will break our precious knickknacks. Go outside with them if you need to, but try not to discourage their excitement and exuberance. Before you know it, you'll be nostalgic for that childhood energy once they are loafing around the house. Join in the fun. It will be good for you, for the children, and for your relationship with them.

Some adults are bothered even by the most delightful expression of childhood emotion. I have friends who live in a large apartment building, where some neighbors complained because their daughters were laughing as they walked down the hall. It wasn't the middle of the night, and the girls weren't yelling, but I guess these grown-ups didn't want to hear *anything* from children, not even happy laughter. Fortunately, when the neighbors complained to the management, they could not find any rules or regulations that prohibited children from being happy.

We all have some emotions that we find harder to handle than others. For example, when a beloved nanny or baby-sitter leaves, parents are often unable to help children grieve their loss. They may be jealous of the children's attachment to the caregiver, or preoccupied with finding new child-care arrangements. A friend of mine told me about moving across the country when she was eleven, leaving behind her grandparents and cousins. She only cried, however, when saying good-bye to her nanny, and her mother was furious at her. Instead of the compassion and comfort she needed for all of her losses, my friend was punished for not expressing the right feelings about the right people.

In a divorce, it is exceptionally hard for each parent to set aside his or her own anger and resentment and allow children to freely express whatever they are feeling. Parents can't help thinking, How could you miss that jerk? or How dare you be mad at *me*. Children end up with the idea that their feelings aren't welcome, on top of all the other pain of the situation. Of course, they still feel all that anger, betrayal, and loss, even if no one wants to hear about it. Unable to express the feelings freely, children may develop behavior problems, or become depressed and withdrawn. A similar thing happens when grandparents get sick or die. The parents are sometimes too overwhelmed with their own feelings of loss to be very helpful to the children. In both of these circumstances, it helps to have other adults available for children to talk to and play with—adults who aren't involved in the family emotions.

—HANDLING TANTRUMS AND FRUSTRATIONS—

I consulted with the Jorgensons, who were having trouble with their fourth child (out of four boys), who was five years old. He had been having huge tantrums for a couple of years, and they were getting worse instead of better. Whenever I hear about tantrums, I have a few questions I ask parents. I'll identify these in the following passages in italics. If your child throws tantrums, go ahead and answer the italicized questions yourself.

● *What do you think the child is trying to express through the tantrums?* In the Jorgensons' case, they weren't sure. They thought he was just being difficult or had gotten into a bad habit. When I pressed them to think in terms of translating the tantrum into a message, they thought that he was saying he was frustrated that he couldn't keep up with his brothers. That makes sense. It is so frustrating to *almost* be able to do things that you see other people doing effortlessly, but not have your body work the way you are trying to get it to work. That's why toddlers have so many tantrums. But the Jorgensons' son wasn't a toddler anymore; he was five. The advantage of that is they could ask him: "What are you trying to tell us?" Of course, a child this age may not be able to put it into words, but it's always worth asking.

● *After a tantrum, is your child happier, more relaxed, confident, connected, cooperative, or engaged?* Most parents forget to ask themselves this question. They have decided in advance that tantrums are a problem, probably because they are so unpleasant (not to mention the dirty looks from other adults at the grocery store!). But often children are back to

being themselves after a good temper tantrum, the same way we feel better after we get something off our chests. Tantrums are children's way of
expressing and releasing frustration. Once they've expressed it, they can
move on. Sometimes a tantrum that comes in the middle of a difficult
task—such as homework or an art project or mastering a computer
game—is followed by a breakthrough, a burst of understanding or creativity or accomplishment. It's as if the tantrum has stormed down the
door of the tower of powerlessness. If they can't express their frustration,
or if they are punished for having a tantrum, it continues to interfere with
their happiness, their ability to cooperate, or their achievements.

In her book on toddlers—who, after all, are the tantrum professionals—
Alicia Lieberman says, "When . . . the child finds his will thwarted by
higher powers, he may have no choice other than a temper tantrum. What
else could a toddler do? His language skills are not developed enough to
articulate his case persuasively. His access to the family resources is minimal, so he cannot get his way by threatening to withhold an allowance or
take the car keys away. . . . The temper tantrum—throwing oneself on the
floor with a mixture of heartrending crying and angry screaming—is a
wonderfully eloquent if seldom appreciated expression of the toddler's
inner experience."[2]

When older children are stuck in a pattern of tantrums, or they feel
worse instead of better after a tantrum, then they are probably not getting
rid of their frustration. Though they tantrum a lot, they may never feel
that they have fully expressed themselves, because no one is ever listening.
The family goes into overdrive to stop the tantrum, and so the next time
they feel they have to start from scratch. Or they are sent away, isolated,
during their tantrum, and they miss out on sharing these deep feelings
with someone and reconnecting afterward. Believe it or not, sometimes
all we need to do is let one or two tantrums run their natural course, all
the way to completion, with no attempts to interrupt it. Then the children
may stop throwing tantrums because they finally feel as if they have really
been heard.

To let a tantrum run its course, all you need to do is just ride it out,
staying near the child instead of sending him away or leaving him alone
or pestering him with questions and solutions. "If the parents can remain

emotionally available even while firm in their position of denying something, tantrums can also teach a child that he will not be left alone in his 'dark night of the soul.' "[3]

● *What is the family's usual reaction or response to the tantrum?* Most families have a habit of either caving in to tantrums or of never budging an inch, not wanting to reward what they see as negative behavior. Ironically, both of these responses generally lead to children having more tantrums instead of ending them.

In the first instance—that of caving in—the problem may be not the tantrum but our habit of saying no because it is more convenient. And when children start to whine and fuss, we suddenly find it more convenient to say yes. The lesson to the child here is that our no doesn't mean much, and the result is more tantrums, because she believes she can get her way. Be firm and don't cave in if your no was well thought out and you still stand by it, and try not to say no if you aren't willing to stand by it just because of a tantrum.

On the other hand, tantrums may help us realize that we didn't have a very good reason for saying no. But we may feel stuck; we don't want to give in to the tantrum. We need to be willing to change our minds if our no was unreasonable. Our children can tell the difference between caving in to their screaming versus reconsidering our position based on thinking about it some more. If we never budge once we've made a pronouncement, we aren't really being consistent. We're just refusing to consider points of view that differ from our own, refusing to acknowledge that we were wrong or hasty in our decision. Those are hardly the behaviors we want to model for our children.

Many children are sent away to their room or to time-out when they have a temper tantrum. Or worse, they are teased and taunted. We are embarrassed by tantrums that happen in public, and we feel helpless when they happen at home. Children in the midst of a tantrum are flooded with feelings, and they feel out of control. They need a loving human being near them—maybe not within kicking range(!), but close by. We may need to step outside and take a break first, to cool off, but then we need to show them that their having strong feelings does not isolate them from the community of civilized people. We want children to learn that nothing inside of them is too awful to be shared with us, not even overwhelming feelings of frustration.

If we don't, and they have to be all alone with these feelings, there are two likely outcomes. First, children may be stuck in a cycle of tantrums, hoping against hope that *next time* someone will listen to them or stick with them. Instead, all that happens is the family gets more and more annoyed and hostile. The other alternative is even more disastrous: Children learn the lesson that they're all alone in this life, it truly is a cold cruel world, and you can't count on anyone when the going gets rough. They retreat into a completely sealed-off tower of isolation. So stay engaged with children, even when they are full of tough feelings.

In the Jorgenson family, the boy's brothers ignored him or teased him when he had a tantrum. That was really painful for him, since all he wanted was for them to recognize him as one of the guys, to wait for him, to give him a little slack in his efforts to keep up with them. Understandable goals, but big brothers are not the likeliest bunch to give comfort and support to a tantruming little brother.

● *What have you tried to do to end the tantrums?* This is the therapist's trick question. We never want to suggest something that's already been tried and hasn't worked. Yet this question lets parents see that they do have strategies, some of which actually help. It also helps parents see that they often keep doing the same thing over and over, even though it never helps. The Jorgensons had set aside time to play with each of their sons one-on-one, and had even set aside PlayTime for the five-year-old to have with both parents. That's something I recommend for large families, even though I know it can be nearly impossible to arrange. While the tantrums decreased, they didn't disappear.

After listening to what else the Jorgensons had tried, I made a few suggestions. In addition to PlayTimes that focused on doing whatever he wanted to do, I recommended PlayTimes during which the parents set up games that directly addressed his difficulties with frustration. For example, follow the leader could give him a chance to be leader for a change, and give him a chance to follow someone who wasn't trying to leave him behind (like his big brothers often did). Another idea was to have PlayTimes with this boy and just one of his brothers, who might be more inclined to match the younger child's pace one-on-one than in a group.

Since most of the tantrums happened on family outings, such as trips to the playground, I suggested that they ask him before they left the house, "How do you want this to go today?" You need to be sure to have a casual, pleasant tone of voice with this question, not to be sarcastic or cutting. "Shall we have a fight?" I think it helps to call it a fight instead of a fit, since then you are making it a family problem and not just blaming him. "How do you want it to go when I say it's time to leave?" "What should we do if the big kids want to do something, and you can't keep up?" A boy of five might not be able to answer all these questions, but at least he'll know you are thinking about the situation and trying to include him in solutions.

My favorite tantrum preventer involves jumping in playfully when you see things beginning to get out of hand. I'll say things like, "One of us needs to scream. Shall I, or do you want to?" Or, "Everyone's starting to get a little frustrated, let's have a giggle-fest." A giggle-fest is when everyone pretends to laugh until they are really laughing. Or, "I challenge you to a thumb-wrestling match to determine the championship of the world." These types of silly comments take the edge off the frustration and can restore a playful mood.

● *Is there a pattern to the tantrums?* Often, if we stop to notice, difficult times follow a pattern. Usually we are so absorbed by the outburst that we miss the buildup. For example, when my daughter was a baby, she hated having her face wiped off after meals. She would whine and fuss and I would get irritated and exasperated. It didn't happen all the time, so finally one day I decided to see if there was any pattern to it. There was. There usually is, if you look hard enough. When Emma and I were "talking" and looking at each other, and I showed her the washcloth and waited for her to stick her face out in that cute way one-year-olds do, everything went fine. If I was preoccupied and ready to get the meal over with, and I grabbed a cloth and started wiping her face without any connection, she made a fuss. Once I figured that out, it was a very easy problem to solve. Just make sure to connect first.

Tantrums are surprisingly common in families where children almost always get their own way. What's that all about? I think children use limits as a chance to unleash their stored-up frustration. When they almost never hear no, they store up their frustration for long periods, and it comes barreling out when a limit finally confronts them. The solution is actually pretty simple. During PlayTimes, make up funny nos and let children play with these pretend limits. With a young girl named Johanna, I make up silly rules constantly. No giggling! No standing on both feet! No breathing! When she breaks the rule, I pretend to be so mad I can't see straight, so, of course, I fall over trying to catch her.

—HANDLING EXPRESSIONS OF ANGER—

For many families, expressions of anger are even harder to handle than tantrums. With children's anger, we always have to decide whether we can help them release their feelings in a playful way, or if we need to tread more gently. Either way, the important thing is to *stay connected.* "You need to help your child stay in the relationship even when anger overwhelms him. You can do this by making him feel safe."[4] Acknowledge the anger, talk soothingly, stay calm. Be firm about basic safety limits, but don't go away or send children away, unless *you* need a break in order to stay calm. Don't force children to pull it together or go to their room until they can come out with a smile on their face. They need to recover in their own time, which is usually longer than our patience. When the anger is milder, it can sometimes make for a playful encounter, provided that they do not feel teased or invalidated. To play with these minor angry feelings, I either reflect the angry face back to them in an exaggerated form, or I pretend to run shrieking from the room from the power of their glare. "Oh no, not the look!"

When the anger is stronger, with screams, curses, punches, and kicks, we naturally feel overwhelmed and even angry ourselves. We often strike back aggressively or with severe threats. We may scold or criticize or lecture. Have you noticed that these typical responses don't usually work too well? We usually keep trying them anyway, but when children are feeling intense anger, they are not able to reason or talk or listen very well. If it's safe, they just need room to storm and yell and stomp. If they are hurting someone else, or themselves, or breaking valuable things, then they need to be held, gently but firmly. That can be hard, especially since this kind of holding really works only if we are calm and soothing, not furious and vengeful. Talk gently. Try not to take their angry words or aggressive actions personally. They may be parroting back mean things that were said to them, or they may be indignant over some past injustice or mistreatment.

Most experts in childhood emotions agree that anger covers up other, more vulnerable feelings, such as pain and loss and fear. Children guard these feelings with a minefield of insults, curses, and violent attacks. This angry front is intended to keep the more tender feelings from being exposed. Instead, the anger usually drives away the very people who could help them with these painful feelings. As author Patty Wipfler says, "It's unfair and irrational, but it seems that when children have felt endangered and helpless, they direct their reaction—usually anger and mistrust—toward the people closest to them."[5] If we can remember the hurt children underneath the angry facades, and reach out calmly and persistently to them, we will be rewarded with a more direct expression of the buried feelings. Gently stopped from lashing out, children will release their scary or vulnerable feelings directly through tears, trembling, or talking. For example, if you stop violence with the most minimal, gentle intervention you can manage, instead of with more violence or with threats or screams, you'll usually get a burst of tears, followed by a clear discussion of what's really going on underneath the anger and aggression.

I am not suggesting this approach to anger is easy. We are much more inclined to yell or punish or scold or start to spank them—whatever was done to us when we were little and we got mad at our parents. We may need to talk with other parents about our own angry responses, as discussed in chapter fifteen, before we can really deal effectively with our children's anger.

—HANDLING FEAR AND ANXIETY—

We don't want our children to be afraid, so we say, "There's nothing to be afraid of; don't be such a baby." Or we say, "You don't have to go in the water if it's too scary." But fear is fine; it is a basic human emotion and even necessary for survival. The gazelle who calmly keeps napping when the rest of the herd starts to run will be eaten by the lion. We need to help children develop *courage*, not fearlessness. *Confidence*, not toughness. You have to feel fear in order to be brave, otherwise you're just reckless and thrill-seeking. You also have to push yourself to do what you're afraid to do; otherwise you will never try new things.

At the same time that we tell them not to be afraid, we scare children. We threaten them; we leave them alone; we expose them to terrifying movies (and the nightly news). Many children are hit or bullied, by adults or other children, or are exposed to other forms of violence in their lives. Some are scared to go to school because of a bad social situation or because they feel stupid. All in all, many children carry around a great deal of fear, but they don't have much chance to express it.

The result of all this confusion about fear is either recklessness, or anxiety, or shyness and inhibition. When children are reckless, they need someone to play with them, to climb trees with them, in order to provide a calming influence and a model of safe adventurousness. When children are shy and inhibited, they need to be drawn out of their shell, again through play. They may need us to go down the slide with them a few times before they feel comfortable joining up with the other children at the playground. Most shy children don't do very well with the typical sink-or-swim approach. But they are not well served by just letting them stay home or in the corner forever, either.

When people are anxious, they feel it in their throat or their chest or their gut. That's because anxiety is fear that is stuck halfway in and halfway out. They're afraid, but the fear can't be freely released. Anxiety is a compromise. It isn't the full-blown expression of pure terror, but it isn't a sunny stroll in the park. The goal is to take that anxious feeling, that stuck fear, and get it the rest of the way out. Play, creativity, and fantasy are all great ways to help children do this. Some children relieve their anxiety by talking about their worries. More commonly, they get their anxieties out by playing. Perhaps they have a fantasy character who runs into trouble and is rescued, over and over. They may spend hours designing or building invincible spaceships, to symbolically protect themselves from harm. I remember a few years ago worry dolls from Central America were very popular in the United States. These are tiny dolls that a young person can whisper their worries to. Talking to a doll is a nice bridge between talking fears out and playing them out.

Artistic expression is one of the best ways to release anxiety or fear, whether it is by singing, drawing, dancing, sculpting, or writing. "Give that tight knot in your throat a voice. What would it say?" "If those butterflies in your stomach did a dance, what would it look like?" "Can you draw that scary monster from your nightmare?" Many children will bring fear and anxiety into their play without any push from us in order to master it. Others will need an invitation, such as, "Let's pretend we're going to the dentist," or "That was really scary last night; let's play a game about it."

Parents today are pretty shocked about how neglectful parents used to be in the olden days. Now some parents think their job is to protect children from every hurt and danger. But that is not possible, and not desirable. What we need to give them instead is the strength, the confidence, the skills, and the connection with others that allows them to cope with being hurt, and even grow from it. Of course, we provide basic safety and try to keep the big dangers away, though some things such as illness and injury are largely beyond our control. Why do we keep playgrounds open even though it's possible for children to break an arm or a leg? Because they have to play, even with the risk. The harsher realities of life—death, homelessness, war, poverty, injustice, violence—are scary to children, but we can't keep them sheltered indefinitely. Don't be surprised if these themes show up in your children's play.

—HANDLING CHILDREN'S TEARS—

Tears are good. When we release grief and loss and sadness through crying, we generally feel much better, think more clearly, and recover. These benefits are especially true when we cry with someone who is caring and empathic. I have spent years trying to help adults in therapy, especially men, to cry so they could effectively heal from their traumas. Then I became a parent and I was surrounded by people trying desperately to get babies *not* to cry. Very few adults seem to realize that crying is the only way for babies to forcefully command our attention and express themselves. In addition, people seem to think that if you stop babies from crying you've actually stopped them from being sad or hurt. On the contrary, you've stopped their natural healing process, and the hurt just builds up inside. I like to think of crying as getting "un-sad." I know it ruins the metaphor, but a good cry actually *fills* children's cups, especially if they are being held and comforted.

Crying is babies' first form of communication, followed by gazing into our eyes, then smiling, then other sounds. The original cry stands for every single thing babies want to say, before it separates into a hunger cry, an angry cry, a wet cry, and so on. Therefore, stopping them from crying is the same as telling them to shut up. Of course, if they are crying because they are hungry or wet or tired, you feed them or change them or put them to bed. They will stop crying because they are happy now. But often babies cry just to express themselves, or to release their pent-up frustrations and tensions from the drama of all their new experiences.

The questions that I ask parents about tantrums work pretty well for tears, too. "What do you think the child is trying to express? Are they happier and more connected with you after a cry? Do you go into gyrations to get them to stop: begging, pleading, threatening, bribing, sending them away? If so, what happens then? Is there a pattern in your family of teasing people or humiliating them for crying? Have they ever seen you cry? Have you tried staying with them, physically and emotionally, listening to them cry for as long as it takes to express themselves fully?" I also ask parents to recall their own history of crying as a child. "Did you have to cry alone in your pillow, or not cry at all, or were you lucky enough to have a friend or parent or caregiver who offered a shoulder?"

If I limit myself to one piece of advice to adults about children's crying, it is this: Please do not send them off alone to cry. Tears can be a tremendous opportunity for strengthening a connection between any two people, but especially between parent and child. There is nothing as satisfying as the feeling of a baby falling comfortably asleep on your chest after a big fuss. If you always cut the tears short, or hand the baby over to someone else when she cries, you never have this wonderful experience.

One sign that tears are related to connection is what I call peeking out. Someone who has been crying hard, or having a tantrum, or digging their face into your shoulder to avoid eye contact, will occasionally peek out. It's a wonderful thing to see. If children have been crying hard for a while, they will often peek out, make eye contact, and then, seeing a loving, relaxed adult, will go right back to the tears. They aren't sad to see you, but they *are* reassured that they are safe, which means it is okay to cry. Eventually they don't just peek out, but look deeply into your eyes. If they don't peek out, they may need some additional contact from us. Talk to them in a soothing voice, call their name, snuggle in closer, peek in at them. If you rush to stop the crying, you will never experience this.

Peeking out is not to be confused with something that children do when they are fake crying. They will look out to see what effect the crying is having on the adult. *Is it working to get me what I want?* Fake crying is a mystery to most parents, if not downright infuriating. Some children fake cry because they have learned from adults that tears get a powerful reaction. But more children who fake cry have a river of unshed *real* tears inside but don't feel safe enough or close enough to anyone to let them out. They are testing the waters to see what kind of reception their real tears might get. That's an unfortunate strategy, since most adults react to fake tears with anger and rejection. Children assume—rightly or wrongly—that their real tears will meet the same reception. Actually, the best response to fake tears is playfulness. "Hey, I think you're faking it. That makes me so sad, waaah!" "I'm not fooled by those fake tears, but I'll play a game with you if you want." If children have a reservoir of real tears locked inside, then fun playtime and extra closeness may make it possible for her to spill them out eventually.

The term *crybaby* is an awful slur. It reinforces a very destructive idea that crying is bad, weak, and immature. However, some children actually do cry a lot, for no apparent reason. Just because we don't know the reason, though, doesn't mean they don't have a good one. Emotions don't come from nowhere. It is presumptuous for us to decide which tears to be compassionate about and which ones to dismiss. Since we usually stop tears before they are done, some children get stuck in an endless loop of trying to express their feelings through tears, only to be stopped midway. Every time they cry, they are shushed up. They never get to finish, and therefore they keep starting. To their parents or their peers, they seem like crybabies. From their own perspective, they never get to finish a cry. Have you ever tried to have a conversation with someone who kept interrupting you? You either give up on whatever you have to say, or you keep making false starts.

Children are often full of deep feelings that they can't get out. The real emotion is just too intense to handle. So they pick some little thing to get upset about, a pretext. I was trying to describe this idea of pretexts to my friend Alice. I wasn't explaining it very well, partly because I was also dealing with my daughter, who wanted ice cream. She was three at the time. We were at a restaurant, and I had seen a sign that said blue ice cream. Emma wanted some of that. I had been telling Alice that I thought Emma was frustrated and sad that her mother was away at work so much, even though she acted as if it didn't bother her. Emma said emphatically, "No, I'm not!" The ice cream came, and it certainly was blue. Emma immediately burst into tears. I asked her what was the matter and she said she thought it was going to be a different shade of blue. She climbed into my lap and sobbed. I turned to Alice, who said, "Oh, I get it—pretext." These were not tears about blue ice cream but about missing her mom.

—PUTTING THE BRAKES ON WHINING—

I was hiking with my daughter and another seven-year-old a couple of years ago, and we were getting close to the top of the mountain we were climbing. My wife and daughter were up ahead, and I was staying back with the other boy and his mother. He was flopping over and begging his mother to carry him and whining that he couldn't go another step. I'm sure you know the voice I mean. It seemed to me to be just feelings, not real fatigue, so I started encouraging him. What I wanted to do was yell at him to stop that awful whining. I kind of knew that wouldn't help much, though. I also knew that the way he was talking and flopping his body was making it harder for him to keep going, not easier. But how to get him to do something else without being the big adult authority trying to *make* him stop whining? As you can tell, I am a big fan of letting kids have their feelings rather than shutting them up. On the other hand, I also believe that whining isn't a true expression of feelings, but a spinning of wheels when children can't quite get the feelings out, but can't be happy, either.

So I tried something new. I said, "You know, that kind of voice is like brakes, like putting on the brakes of a car. It actually makes you go slower and makes it harder to climb. There's another kind of talking that's like putting on the gas." And I proceeded to use my cheeriest voice, saying "I can do it; no big old rocks are going to stop me. I don't care how tired I am." He stopped whining and started climbing. Whenever he started to mutter and complain, I said, "Wait! Don't hit the brakes, we're almost there. Step on the gas." I'd talk in my gas-pedal voice and get him to talk in that voice, too. He'd get another burst of energy. At one point he wanted to stop again. For the first time he said it in a relaxed, nonwhiny voice: "I need a break." I said, "Oh, a refueling stop! Great. Let's have some water and raisins. This is a gas break, not a brake break." We made it all the way to the top, and he was very proud. So was I. I was glad to find a new way to talk to people about why moaning and complaining doesn't really help much, and why using a powerful or cheerful voice does help, even if it may feel like pretending. In fact, though, it isn't pretending. It's *choosing* to be positive and upbeat instead of miserable, even if you *feel* like whining.

One thing I hate about whining (besides the obvious) is that it is neither hot nor cold, neither fish nor fowl. It isn't the healing release of painful emotion, and it isn't carefree happiness. Because we have inhibited children's straightforward emotional expressions, most of them can't freely express raw emotions like deep grief or pure terror or intense rage. But they can't hold it all in, either. So it comes trickling out—in whining, in jealousy, in boredom and loneliness, in destructive behavior, in stomachaches and other physical symptoms. Our job as parents is to help our children let these feelings out more directly, especially through playfulness and our close relationship with them.

When the feelings don't come out a little at a time, they can come out in huge bursts, often when least expected. My colleague Sam Roth and I were consulting with the staff of an after-school program. They described a girl who had a huge tantrum, the biggest they had ever seen. It lasted an hour and a half. She was inconsolable during that time. The teachers were especially surprised by this tantrum, because she was Child of the Week that week. Sam explained that being flooded with so much attention left the girl unable to use her usual strategies to keep her feelings under wraps. When we have buried emotions, we need to keep a certain distance from people, or else the closeness will tug at those emotions. Being Child of the Week broke through that wall, and the dam burst.

Many parents are familiar with this same scenario from children who fall apart at their birthday party or at the end of a perfect day. Receiving all that happiness and warmth makes it hard to hold all those tears in any longer. It's awfully confusing to adults.

—EXPERIENCING THE "BIG CRY"—

My last point about tears has to do with a certain kind of "big cry" that combines what I have been saying about tantrums, fears, and tears. Whenever a child is learning something, especially something they really want to master, they inevitably experience frustration. They've almost got the hang of that jump shot, but not quite. Everyone else seems to understand the math homework, but they don't. They have an idea in their mind of what they want to draw, but they can't get it down on paper. Sometimes they are so motivated that they keep trying in spite of the frustration, or a gifted teacher helps them make the leap to "getting it." More often, they give up, or stop putting all their effort into it. This outcome is a big loss for children. What they need here is a chance to express their emotions, their frustration, sadness, and fear, so they can get back to the challenging task at hand. That usually just takes persistent encouragement: "I know you can do it. Don't give up. You are a great artist; give it one more try. I'm confident you'll get it." But don't expect them to say "Thanks, Dad," and go back to it. Instead, they are likely to say "I'm stupid; I'm terrible at this. I'll never understand it." They may well burst into tears or try to tear up their artwork. Just sit close and let them vent. Keep being calmly confident, without exerting any pressure. If they are able to finish expressing all the emotions blocking their way—and be prepared for that to take a while—they will often go back to their activity with renewed enthusiasm, creativity, skill, and pride.

—ENCOURAGING EMOTIONAL LITERACY THROUGH PLAY—

This chapter has focused on strong emotions, and maybe you're wondering where play comes in. Everybody's talking these days about emotional intelligence, emotional literacy, emotional competence. In a way, that's what Playful Parenting is all about, since play is children's way of expressing themselves and their emotions.

> The child's world is a world of great emotional intensity . . . that
> can only be fully expressed through children's spontaneously
> generated play. . . . The process of play provides healing for
> hurts, releases emotions, [and] dissolves tension. . . . Play is one
> of the most important ways in which children learn that they
> can safely express their feelings. . . .[6]

Emotional competence means that we have a dimmer switch, instead of just an on-off button, on our feelings. We want children to be able to express strong feelings in a modulated way, safely and respectfully, but directly. We don't want them to have a switch that is stuck on *off*, or that can't be shut off at all. We can help by being direct and open about our own feelings. In fantasy play, we can introduce characters with rich emotional lives. We can teach them how to identify the bodily sensations that go with different emotions. I've had many adult clients, mostly men, who didn't know that sweaty palms and a pounding heart were signals of fear, or that the burning sensation in their eyes was tears that were trying unsuccessfully to come out.

Emotional competence means that children have developed from the stage of acting out their emotions, to expressing them through play, and ultimately to verbalizing them. Without words or play to express themselves, children can let their feelings lead directly to impulsive behaviors, like slamming doors or hitting or screaming. We can help children along in this development by asking them what they are feeling, asking what they think other people might be feeling, or asking about their doll's emotions.

As parents, we would like children to hurry up and be at that final stage, *right now*, where they can say it in words. But development takes its own time. Besides, I think we rely too much on this insistence that children "say it in words." Children may be highly verbal but emotionally immature. And many feelings are simply too strong for mere words to carry. Just because children can say "I'm mad" or "I'm sad" does not mean that they have fully expressed themselves. They need to cry or storm around, too. I also find that many adults misunderstand the concept of children acting out their emotions. They think it's a kind of misbehavior that should be punished. They don't realize that acting out is the best children can do at the moment to express their emotion, and that you can't just stop the acting out without finding some better outlet for that feeling.

Before children can learn to talk about their emotions instead of hitting someone or collapsing in a puddle of tears, they need to learn how to play out the feelings. That crucial middle step is often overlooked. To help children take that step, we can ask them to draw their feeling, or make up a story about it, or do a dance that expresses it. Play therapists are fond of saying, "Show me with these two puppets what happened and how you felt." Another playful way to build emotional competence is to pretend to have a feeling that children are having trouble expressing. You can model the safe release of that feeling: "I am so mad! I am going to punch this pillow." You can exaggerate an emotion they are denying they have: "Waaah . . . I'm so scared I'm going to faint. . . . Grrrr, I am so mad I could spit." When one child hits another, or says something mean, I often say, "Ouch, that hurt," because the children are acting too tough to notice any pain.

There's a "game" that children play that I call *emotional hot potato*. The one rule is you try to pass unwanted feelings on to someone else. Adults do it all the time, too. We're upset, so we pick a fight or put someone down. Then the other person gets upset, and, like magic, we feel better. I was playing with a seven-year-old boy, and he fell and hurt his leg. He was lying on the floor holding his leg. He was a kid who hurt himself a lot, because he played quite wildly and recklessly. I went over and talked to him about how he got hurt and tried to get him to say "ouch" a few times (as usual, he was grimacing in pain but saying he was fine). When he didn't want to say ouch anymore, I said it, which made him laugh. Suddenly he started hitting me, even though his leg still hurt.

His father, who had up to then been only watching, came over and told his son angrily to quit hitting me. I said to the dad that I thought what was happening was that his son had gotten hurt, and he didn't really want to feel how badly it felt, so he was trying to hurt me so that *I* would hurt instead. The boy nodded his head vigorously in agreement, with a giant grin on his face, all through this explanation. He even stopped pummeling me for a minute to listen. He seemed to think that what I was describing was a perfectly natural and reasonable thing to do. And in a way, it is. If you don't have the resources to handle a feeling, you would do well to eliminate it. One of the best ways to eliminate it is to pass it on, like a hot potato. As playful parents, we can give them more workable ways of handling their feelings.

CHAPTER 13

RETHINK THE WAY WE DISCIPLINE

"There are many terrible things in this world.
But the worst is when a child is afraid of
his father, mother or teacher. He fears
them, instead of loving and trusting them."

JANUSZ KORCZAK[1]

Playful Parenting is based on an attitude of respect toward children and an attitude of wonder toward their world. If children are happy and we are, too, that respectfulness is pretty easy. It's harder when they're miserable or making us miserable. Something must be done when children yank the cat's tail or hit their friend on the head or don't do their homework or come home drunk. I am as opposed to letting things like this slide as I am to harsh punishment. Something indeed must be done, but punishment and threats are not it. When punishment falls short—and it always does—there are a variety of alternatives that work better. Taking a fresh look at discipline and children's behavior, we can see that closeness, playfulness, and emotional understanding are better bets than punishment, behavior modification, and too much permissiveness.

—COOL OFF—

Effective discipline rarely happens in the heat of the moment. Before you try to deal with a problem, count to ten, take a break, wait a few hours for things to settle down, call a friend. Of course, we have outbursts of emotion when we get kicked in the shin, or our favorite lamp gets broken, or the big sister is teasing the baby—again. But these outbursts do not need to be the basis for our response to the child. *Cool off.*

A FRESH LOOK AT DISCIPLINE

- Cool off
- Make a connection
- Choose a "Meeting on the Couch" over a "Time-out"
- Play!
- Instill good judgment
- Look underneath the surface, at the child's feelings and needs
- Prevent instead of punish
- Know your child
- Set clear limits

Talking to other parents is one of the best ways to cool off. They understand how mad we get, how exasperated and frustrated. We're not the only ones who ever wanted to shake children, or slap them. Other parents may offer a reality check—"They are just being kids, don't sweat it"—or they may offer support—"I'll be right over to take the kids so you can take a walk or a nap." Other parents understand the hopes, dreams, fears, and worries we have for our children. Just talking to other parents can unload our feelings of frustration and anger, which makes discipline a whole lot easier. If you don't have anyone you can call, and you feel that things are getting out of hand, Parents Anonymous (www.parentsanonymous-natl. org) is a great organization that can help.

I can't quite believe we've reached the twenty-first century and people still hit their children, but it's true. Some parents hit only when they are overwhelmed, and they feel terrible afterward. Others think corporal punishment is necessary for discipline, while a few think it is actually good for children. Some adults insist that a good wallop never did them any harm, but the actual research suggests the opposite. Other people have written whole books on this topic, so I will just summarize: Hitting children makes them more aggressive, more antisocial, and more likely to end up in prison or with serious emotional problems.[2] There are other kinds of punishment just as harsh as hitting. Humiliation, name-calling, sarcasm, or threats can leave emotional scars that last much longer than bruises. Even if we don't ever hit children, we may still need to cool off before we decide how to handle a problem.

—MAKE A CONNECTION—

I think it is obvious by now that I see most "misbehavior" as really just a matter of disconnection. Children who feel connected also feel inclined to be cooperative and thoughtful. So instead of punishment, which tends to create an even bigger disconnection between parent and child, try thinking about how to reestablish a connection. When was the last time you had PlayTime together, or a cuddle, or just hung out together? When you look your children in the eye, is there anybody home? Is their cup empty; is that why they're acting up? Is yours empty? What do they need for a fill-up? How about you? Reconnecting might require a hug, some quiet time together, wrestling or running around outside, a snack, or a talk. For more serious disruptions, I recommend what I call the meeting on the couch. Most punishments involve exerting power over a child, which just increases his or her sense of isolation and powerlessness. Meetings on the couch build connection and empower children. At the same time, they give us an effective way to provide real discipline: the teaching of our values and principles.

—CHOOSE A "MEETING ON THE COUCH" OVER A "TIME-OUT"—

Whenever there is any problem, either a parent or a child can call a meeting on the couch. It could be anywhere, but we use the couch at my house. The goal is to get reconnected. I always assume that whatever the problem is, disconnection either caused it or made it worse or made it harder to solve. The rule is that if someone calls a meeting on the couch, the other person has to show up for the meeting. Once you are both at the couch, anything may happen.

You might talk seriously about what has been going on, or you may not even talk about it, just take the chance to reconnect. Children may let loose a big volley of tears about something that's been bothering them, that they've been holding in. You may rant and rave a little about your frustrations—the living room is a mess, the homework isn't done, the noise level is deafening—and then give them a chance to talk. You might repeat your insistence on basic rules and values—everybody does their share of cleanup, for example, or no teasing the baby. Sometimes just changing the scene and making reconnection the top priority can create a dramatic difference, and the tension is gone as soon as you get to the couch, so you might end up just goofing around and being silly together. The anger and frustration are forgotten and connection is reestablished. Try to stay on the couch until both of you are ready to go back and do things differently from before.

I hope it's clear how this technique differs from a time-out. There's no power struggle about how many minutes are left, no dragging children kicking and screaming to their room. Best of all, it is something that parent and child do together—unlike punishments, which are things that adults do *to* children. One thing I like about meetings on the couch is that they are not just for misbehavior. You can call a meeting if you notice your child is sad or blue, or if you have both been irritable lately, or if you haven't had a chance to connect for a while, or if you need to decide what to do over school vacation. The other thing I like about these meetings is that, unlike punishment, usually everyone leaves feeling better.

In Playful Parenting, discipline is a chance to improve your connection with your children instead of forming another wall that separates you. The best way to make discipline more connecting is to think *We* have a problem instead of *My kid* is misbehaving. When discipline is presented to children as a joint problem requiring a joint solution, things go much better. There is less lying ("I didn't do it!") and less sneaking (figuring out how not to get caught, instead of choosing to do the right thing) if parents are not in the role of policeman, judge, and jury. If we are all in this together, the result is always more cooperation. That's why I say "We need a meeting on the couch," instead of "You go to your room."

When I talk to parents about punishment, they are often shocked when I say that I am also opposed to time-outs. But with the emphasis in Playful Parenting on connecting, it really shouldn't be a surprise. Time-outs were supposed to be a humane alternative to whacking children, but they have somehow become the ultimate "positive parenting" tool. The main problem with time-outs is that they enforce isolation on children who are probably already feeling isolated and disconnected.

A few years ago I was sitting in my car while I waited for my friend Lena to come out of her apartment. I was listening to a show on the radio, a call-in show about handling children's behavior problems. The "expert" on the radio was saying that young children who want to come into their parents' room at night should be locked out, and kept out no matter how much they cry, even if it means they eventually fall asleep curled up outside the door. Lena got in the car, hearing just the end of this advice. She said, "Oh, is this that show about dogs?" No. Most dog experts are more understanding of the animal's need for comfort and contact when they are feeling sad and lonely.

In most homes and schools, time-out is used as a punishment or as a way to control children's behavior. But look at how the term is used in sports. You take a time-out for *yourself* or your own team. You don't *give* a time-out to the other team. This type of time-out, a break for everyone, is an excellent idea. At my daughter's preschool, Susan Engels, the head teacher, would say, "Time-out! Break in the action!" Everyone would freeze, and she could step in to redirect the play, get close to someone who was about to explode, stop a conflict before it got out of hand, or tone down the activity level. This type of time-out is nonpunishing and non-isolating. In fact, it is a way of joining in children's play and making a connection. Another way time-outs can work in a positive way is if children have a cozy place where they can go to calm down or feel comforted when they choose to go, not when we choose to send them.

Given everything I have said about the importance of connection and paying attention to children, you might guess that I hate the phrase, "He was just looking for attention." For years, the standard advice has been to ignore such behavior. I don't get that. We don't say, "He keeps asking for food, but just ignore him; he's only saying that because he's hungry." We don't say, "Your cup is empty, so I'll make sure you don't get a refill." If someone is looking for attention that bad, I figure *they must need some attention*! If we give them enough of the good kind, they won't be so desperate that they'll settle for the bad kind.

For most children, I think time-out is just a nuisance. For a few, it may even help them settle down or think about what they are doing before they do it. For certain children, though, it's a torture. These children want and need contact, they are afraid of separation, and they see time-outs, or being sent to their room, as banishment. They will create more trouble resisting time-out than they were causing in the first place. They will make pathetic promises to be better, to behave, to do anything you ask, but they will not be able to keep these promises. They were made out of fear, and the behaviors may not actually be under these children's control. For these children especially, a meeting on the couch is a much better bet.

I said above that most punishments disrupt the connection between parent and child. That's true, but sometimes punishment *does* get the child's attention. Perhaps it goes without saying, but in order to connect with someone, you have to have their attention first. With all the obstacles to connection, and especially with all the distractions available today, that can be hard. Children may need to hear a louder tone in our voice, or to feel a hand on their shoulder, or to see us look right in their eyes, in order to tune in to us. Remember, the goal is to get their attention in order to make a connection, not to scare them or show them who's boss. If we focus on getting their attention, we can probably think of more effective ways than yelling or threatening or hurting them. Sometimes we go too far, and after we get their attention, we lose it again by going overboard. When children are sitting resentfully in their rooms after being hit or grounded, we'd like them to be thinking about what they've done. Instead, they are more likely to be plotting how to make our life miserable in revenge, or how to make sure they don't get caught next time. Once you have their attention, and you use it as the basis for a real connection, you will get real cooperation, not resentful (and temporary) obedience.

Like every therapist, I've heard countless bitter stories from adults—especially men—about the effects of being harshly punished and relentlessly criticized, when all they wanted as children was to be cherished and accepted. The saddest stories were from groups that I led for men who battered their wives and girlfriends. Many of them also hit their children, and virtually all of them had been beaten when they were boys. They passed on the violence that was done to them, and some of them even defended it: "My daddy hit me with a belt, and there's nothing wrong with me." When they were able to break through their defensiveness and really talk about what it was like for them growing up, many of them said that the worst part wasn't the violence, but the lack of any tenderness from anybody.

These men were not terribly lovable, but I'm sure they were regular little babies once, just like you and me. When they started heading down the wrong path, not one of them got any love or gentle guidance, only more harsh discipline. We are often reluctant to give out love to people who have been bad, even when it's what they need. I have always liked the poem by Edwin Markham, which A. S. Neill quotes in the beginning of his book *Freedom—Not License!*:

> He drew a circle that shut me out—
> Heretic, rebel, a thing to flout.
> But Love and I had the wit to win:
> We drew a circle that took him in!

—PLAY!—

A lot of parents can't imagine being playful as a form of discipline. Discipline is supposed to be deadly serious. Don't believe it—play! My friend Roger told me a story about being with his children at a historic site when it started to pour. His family and a few other families were trapped in an old barn with nothing to do. Several of the other children quickly got bored and started trying to chip chunks of plaster off the wall. Their parents yelled at them, threatened them, fumed at them. Roger realized that with no TV or activities or store-bought toys to entertain them, all these children knew how to do was complain and then act up. All the parents knew how to do was yell and threaten and punish. Roger suggested to his children that they play an animal guessing game, like twenty questions, and invited the other children to join in. Soon everyone was perfectly happy as they settled into a game. All they needed to do was play.

Are you having battles with your children over bedtime? Play bedtime. Having battles over dessert? Play dinnertime. It doesn't really matter if you play a mean mother who says no dessert, or if you play an absurdly nice mother who says "We're having ice cream for dinner tonight." Whatever makes them laugh. Having trouble with back talk? Pick up two dolls, and have one talk back to the other. You'll have fun imitating children's obnoxious behavior and making up snappy comebacks. Children will think it's a riot. If you're having trouble with rules, make up a rule you don't really care about, and play at making, breaking, and punishing that rule. Instead of one more round of "You have to get dressed, right now," try saying "There's only one rule: You can't wear one red shoe and one black shoe!" See what happens. I guarantee this will not train them to break real rules, but will instead help them to be more cooperative.

Often children don't even need a specific game—they just need to play more. A huge number of so-called behavior problems would be solved overnight if all children had a safe, fun place in which to run around until they were tired. One of the things I have never understood about school is the way that kids—especially boys—get punished by having recess taken away. If they can't sit still or behave *with* recess, I don't know how they are going to do it without that chance to let off some steam.

A playful tone goes a long way toward keeping discipline from being harsh. Again, this is especially true for boys, who are more likely to be targets of that kind of discipline.[3] I saw a father and son in the grocery store the other day. The boy was into everything, and the father was getting a little frustrated. At the checkout line, the boy tried to sneak a candy bar. The father said, with a hint of severity in his voice, "Put that back; you can't have that." The boy hung his head and sullenly put the candy back. The father softened his voice, "Nice try, though." The boy gave his father a big smile. "Hey, Danny, want to carry my change," asked the father, and the boy suddenly lit up.

Not only did this father backtrack from his initial impulse—to fuss at the child—but he then did something much more effective. He joined playfully with the child, congratulating him on his attempt to get one over on his dad. Then, he recognized that what the boy needed and wanted was some autonomy, something of his own to hang on to. The dad gave him a job, carrying the change, which made him feel big and valuable. He left the store feeling six feet tall. If the episode had ended with his being scolded for trying to get the candy bar, the boy might have left the store feeling small and misunderstood, feeling guilty that he wanted something forbidden, or resentful that he couldn't have it.

That scene at the grocery reminded me of my favorite playful approach to discipline. I say things that sound like threats but are kind of goofy. "If you do that again I'm going to have to sing the 'Star-Spangled Banner.'" A similar strategy to ease tensions is to *pretend* to be upset, which helps us unload some of our feelings without dumping them onto our children in a hurtful way. In fact, if you review all of the principles of Playful Parenting, you'll see how appropriate they are for preventing and dealing with family struggles. Join with them, connect with them, roughhouse, follow their lead, tune in to them, have fun. Do something totally different from your usual response: "You spilled the milk again? I'll have to do my milk-spilling dance."

In the rush to punish children, we forget that the essence of discipline is to *teach*. Remember how dropping the food off the side of the high chair is a one-year-old's way to learn about gravity? We shouldn't be punishing their first science experiments! Children a little older love to do experiments about the difference between knocking something over (or hitting someone) on purpose or by accident. They probably don't even know that they are being philosophers and scientists, trying to figure out free will versus determinism, cause and effect. Do things just happen, or do I make them happen? If I push Murray into Carole, was it me who knocked her over, or was it Murray? Like everything else, children learn about this through play. I like to help this along by taking a child's hand and making her (gently) whack someone else. "Stop hitting him," I say. "That's not nice." When they are just learning these complicated concepts, they think that's hysterically funny. On the other hand, when we punish children for doing something on purpose, before they really grasp that concept, we haven't helped them learn it. I have seen so many children who think the phrases "It was an accident; I didn't mean it; I'm sorry" are magic words that will ward off punishment. Adults treat these like magic words, too. Yet if one child constantly knocks other children over, even if each time is an accident, you still have a problem. What's worse: to do something on purpose and feel bad about it, and sincerely apologize, or to do something by accident and not care?

I think parents avoid playfulness in difficult paren[t] cause they are afraid of rewarding bad behavior. *I have t[o] angry and cold so he'll know he did wrong.* But being pla[y] rewards or punishments, it is about restoring the missi[ng] connection—that caused the problems in the first plac[e] of being playful. You will do a much better job of teachi.. your values and getting cooperation with your rules by being playful than by being stern.

—INSTILL GOOD JUDGMENT—

Instead of trying to get children to be obedient, I recommend that we strive for them to have good judgment. Obedience lasts only as long as we are in the room with them. It does not help a child know what to do in a brand-new situation. I think every parent has had this experience: Children do something so wild that we never thought of making a rule about it. We usually punish them anyway, because they "should have known better." But we can't expect them to have the flexible intelligence to figure out what is right or wrong in a new situation if we have taught them to obey only by enforcing rules. Our world is so complex that children need to have intelligence and good judgment, not just rules.

The goal of most punishment is obedience. Good judgment, on the other hand, comes from talking with children, brainstorming about how they might handle different situations, and discussing moral dilemmas. We have to be on the same wavelength with our children before we can have these types of conversations, so connect first. Connecting with children after they've done something wrong, listening to how they feel about it, and telling them calmly how we feel, all do much more to instill good judgment than punishment does.

Children develop into thoughtful, considerate, honest, and kind adults because of love and affection, because of high moral standards, and because of a close relationship with someone who models those values. I have never seen anyone punished into being good. Bribes don't work either. Promises, threats, rewards, and punishments have been called "the most primitive way of dealing with human beings."[4] Since humans can think and reason, and because close connections are so important to us, it makes more sense to use loving and talking as the basis for our discipline.

Behavior-modification programs try to bypass thought and go directly to our response of rewards and punishments. That might be why they don't work that well. In a common misunderstanding of behavior modification, my friend Lucy rewards her son Alexander when he stops being whiny and obnoxious and demanding. Do those behaviors disappear? No, he *increases* them, so he can be rewarded for stopping! Another mistake is trying to stop a behavior, through rewards and punishment, that children actually have no control over. A newborn, for example, is in big trouble if his parents can't stand his crying. No matter how badly he may be punished for it, he can't make himself stop. I've seen older children punished for not learning to read fast enough, for getting a math problem wrong, for being fidgety, for focusing so intently on a book or a game that they don't hear their mom call them for dinner. These are all examples of things that children may not be able to change, not even for a million dollars or to avoid a beating. Most parents just keep searching for a more effective punishment instead of reconsidering the whole idea of punishment.

Recent work on the brain suggests that punishment has a different impact on different children. The surprising thing is that *punishment has the least impact on the very children who are most likely to be punished.*[5] That is, certain children are more impulsive, have a harder time developing a conscience, and have trouble making connections with people or feeling as if they are part of a community. These traits make them more likely to get into trouble. These same traits make them less able to make changes in their behavior because of punishment or fear of punishment. With these children, punishments escalate, getting more and more severe, but they continue to be ineffective. Those children who have strong consciences and who hate the idea of getting into trouble, meanwhile, don't need punishment. These same traits make it possible for them to behave just by telling them what we expect.

What misbehaving children need instead of punishment is help in organizing themselves. That doesn't mean having a tidy room. It means having the ability to process incoming information and organize an effective response. Most punishments disorganize children further. To help them organize, provide a quiet space, with fuzzy toys, blankets, and pillows. Rock them in a rocking chair, go to the swings, hug them and hold them close. Older children also benefit from these activities, even though they may seem geared to younger children. Disorganized behavior is partly the result of not getting enough of those kinds of comforts or rhythms in their life when they were infants and toddlers. For older children, a structured schedule, art projects, and safe roughhousing can be additional tools in fostering this type of cognitive organization.

—LOOK UNDERNEATH THE SURFACE, AT CHILDREN'S FEELINGS AND NEEDS—

If we take children's needs and feelings as our starting point, our whole approach to discipline changes. Imagine that your children's behavior is a coded message. (Actually, children's behavior *is* a coded message.) To break the code, translate what they are doing into a sentence that starts with "I need_____" or "I feel_____." Fill in the blank, and then respond to that need or that feeling, not to their behavior. So if a toddler starts pulling everything off the counter, he may be saying, "I need something to do, and I want somebody to do it with." If an eighth-grader starts forgetting to do her homework, she may be saying, "I'm scared of high school coming up; I'm not sure if I'm ready." You may not always be right about your translation, but it always helps to try to find the need or the feeling underneath every behavior that bugs you. It can also be fun, which is a nice change from frustrating and infuriating.

Here Are Some Common Translations That Fit Many Problem Situations:

- You're bored? You must be feeling lonely. Let's play a game, or we can invite someone over.
- I can see you're starting to get discouraged, so I am going to give you encouragement.
- You and I haven't had much time together, so maybe that's why you've been so annoying. Let's do something special.
- You seem sad, so I am going to comfort you.
- You need more room to run around and get some energy off. Let's go outside.
- You seem mad, so I am going to hold a big pillow so you can whack it.
- You've been trying to get my attention all day, in all kinds of

ways, so I'm going to put down my book for ten minutes and give you my undivided attention.

- You seem too fidgety to sit still. Let's dance!
- You seem overwhelmed. I am going to help you calm down. Let's take three deep breaths together.
- You've been really nasty toward your brother lately. What's the matter? I'd like to hear about what's bothering you.
- You seem cranky and irritable. Let's have a snack and see if that helps.

Note how none of these translations lead logically to a punishment. It doesn't make much sense to say: You are feeling bad, so I am going to yell at you. You are lonely, so I am going to send you to your room. You are feeling disconnected from other people, so I am going to hit you. You're hungry, but I'm going to take your toys away instead of feeding you. Absurd! Punishment enters into the scene because of our own feelings: I am mad, so I am going to yell at you. I am frustrated, so I am going to have a temper tantrum. I am scared, so I am going to scare you. I've had a hard day, so I'm going to take it out on you.

When children have been "bad," it's hard for parents to remember that children need comfort rather than punishment. If you focus on the underlying need and feeling instead of reacting to the surface behavior, it is less confusing. No one ever died of a punishment deficiency, but babies do die or get sick from not being loved. Giving children what they need is always the best way to change their behavior. At the most basic level, we are usually so exasperated with our children that we forget to ask the truly important questions: Are these children unhappy? If so, why are they unhappy?

As long as we are looking under the surface of our children's behavior, we may as well take a closer look underneath our own behavior. When our children misbehave, or worry us, or give us grief, we naturally get angry and upset. When we try to discipline children while we are feeling this way, we are much more likely to punish and yell. In fact, if we really look honestly, I think we'll find that a lot of our discipline is just acting out *our* feelings!

We act out feelings of revenge when children annoy us or hurt our pride. We act out feelings of anger when they don't live up to our expectations. We act out feelings of frustration when we've had a rough day and our children's noise level provides the last straw. We get irritable when we hear their tears or fears or tantrums. Young children run out in the street and we spank them, because we're scared and we feel guilty about not stopping them. Teenage boys get an ear pierced and we blow our stack, instead of calmly reflecting on the fact that they're getting older. Instead of acting out these feelings (by yelling at our children or punishing them harshly), talk about them. Maybe we need a giant preschool teacher following us around reminding us to "Say it in words."

—PREVENT INSTEAD OF PUNISH—

One reason punishments are so ineffective is that they are after the fact. To really have an impact on behavior, we have to prevent it, or interrupt it, not react afterward. My sister Diane was consulting at a day-care center, which had a problem with a boy who punched other children. They had "tried everything," meaning every form of punishment allowable by law. Diane was sitting talking to a teacher, who said, "Now look, there he is; he's getting ready to punch that girl." The teacher could see it coming, but she was just going to let him do it, and then try to come up with a punishment that would work! Diane said, "Oh no, he's not," and went over to grab his arm in midswing. The boy was mad and boiled with anger as Diane told him gently she wasn't going to let him hit the girl. At first, he was afraid she was going to hit him—you won't be surprised to learn that this boy was hit at home—but when she just held his arm gently, he burst into tears. For the first time ever, he talked about feeling as if no one at school liked him. The teachers had not been able to think in terms of prevention or feelings, because they were so stuck on punishment. Interrupting a destructive behavior isn't punishment. It is a limit. Limits help children gain control, express their feelings, and think about what they're doing. Hearing about this boy's frustration and loneliness, his teachers then could make a plan to help him develop better friendships.

All the punishments the school had tried with that boy just made him shut adults out of his life more and more. But effective discipline—the interruption of the behavior pattern—led him to bare his true feelings. Effective discipline leads to conversation and connection; ineffective discipline to shame and separation. Our job, then, is to stay engaged with children even while we're setting limits. That's hard, because often we're angry or annoyed when we have to impose limits or interrupt a problem behavior. But harshness and coldness from us just leads to isolation and powerlessness from them. So make eye contact, talk softly, hold them as gently as possible, take a breather if you're too hot under the collar.

It should go without saying, but I'll say it anyway: Playful Parenting is the best way I know to prevent problems before you even have to think about discipline. The more playtime you have with your children, especially play where they get to be in charge and you help them maintain their closeness and confidence, the less you will need any of these alternatives to punishment.

—KNOW YOUR CHILD—

When I see what people punish their children for, it often looks to me as if the child was doing something perfectly normal and ordinary for their age. Toddlers throw a tantrum or won't share. Preschoolers can't sit still. Eight-year-olds run down the hall. Preteens say "I hate you." We punish children for being messy, for being noisy, for being selfish, for being cranky when they're tired, for being impulsive—in short, for being children. Children cannot be punished into maturing faster, or scolded into somehow skipping a step of child development. Of course, we need to manage these behaviors, to help them move to that next stage of development when they can share, or walk calmly down a hall, or be polite. But punishment does not rush development. If anything, it slows down development.

We also punish children just for being different from us. We like to rush; they like to dawdle. We sit quietly; they fidget. They like their room messy; we like it neat. We like it quiet; they like it loud. We like it calm; they like it wild. But punishment can't change a child's temperament any more than it can speed up development. We are just different, but guess who gets punished? Because we're bigger, we can get away with acting out our annoyance. With children, we punish the things that bother us most.

When children get too old for time-outs, parents usually turn to strategies such as grounding, taking away telephone or television privileges, restricting time on the computer, threatening to take away toys. These punishments don't usually work very well. They just cause resentment and strife without helping children develop a stronger sense of morality. Of course, you may well find that children can't handle having their own TV, can't get their homework done if they have access to the phone after school, can't control the time they spend online, and so on. Setting limits in these areas is not punishment, it's parenting. It's a matter of knowing our children. There is a big difference between imposing a sentence on children *after* they mess up (punishment), versus sitting down together and figuring out a workable solution for the future (parenting).

Knowing our children also means knowing how they respond to different types of discipline. What works for my child may not work for yours. But all children are susceptible to being frightened by discipline that is too stern or severe. Janusz Korczak, who wrote the epigraph at the beginning of this chapter, was the director of an orphanage in Poland. He once gave a lecture entitled "The Heart of the Child" to a group of students who were studying to be teachers. Korczak brought along a four-year-old boy from the orphanage. The students could see that the boy's heart was beating wildly:

> He was frightened—so many strange people. . . . Speaking very softly, so as not to add to the child's fears . . . Korczak told us "Don't ever forget this sight. How wildly a child's heart beats when he is frightened and this it does even more so when reacting to an adult's anger with him, not to mention when he fears to be punished." Then heading for the door with the boy's hand in his, he added, "That is all for today!" We did not need to be told any more. Everybody will remember that lecture forever.[6]

—SET CLEAR LIMITS—

If many families rely too much on punishment and harsh discipline, other families go too far the other direction, into excess permissiveness. Children need limits, guidance, and structure. These need to be applied lovingly and in a relaxed manner, not in anger or revenge. Most of us think we have to choose between "tough love" and "anything goes." But we can set limits and have high expectations for children while still having empathy for their feelings and compassion for their needs.

First, we have to understand the difference between children's real needs and their unrealistic wish to be the complete center of the universe. Catering to children's every whim is not at all the same as meeting their legitimate needs. You can't spoil a baby by giving him food when he is hungry. You can't spoil an older child by giving her attention, love, or comfort. When children have a need, fill it. That's not the same as waiting on them hand and foot, especially as they get older, because they also have a need for independence, and a need to feel competent and mature. We have to meet those needs as well.

When we give something to children out of respect for their choices, that's not spoiling them. After all, we control just about all the resources in the family. They have to ask for things that we don't have to ask anybody for. On the other hand, if we give something to children because we're afraid of their emotional reaction, or because we feel guilty, we are on the road to excess permissiveness. The true cause of spoiling is giving in to children *against our better judgment*. Maybe we can't bear for them to experience or express any sadness, anger, or frustration. We may refuse to believe they could feel so bad, or perhaps we just don't want to listen to them fuss. Either way, we aren't giving *to* the children. We are giving *in*.

As society changes, many conservative critics are whining for a return to strictness and a rejection of the permissiveness of the Dr. Spock generation. I think they miss the point. The real problem is that neither repression nor permissiveness has provided children with the connectedness they need in order to be moral, responsible, and happy members of a community. The pendulum has swung from beating children to spoiling them, but both extremes are lacking in true connections between adults and children. The strict parent ignores children's ability to make their own decisions. The permissive parent ignores children's need to be a contributing part of the family.

The extremes that adults go to in order to stop tears and tantrums reveal a surprising similarity between abusive parents and overindulgent parents. Abusive parents often punish children harshly for tears or tantrums, because they can't stand to hear them. At the other end of the parenting spectrum, overly indulgent families often give children their own way in order to prevent them from crying or tantruming. Again, the adult can't stand the sound of it, but instead of lashing out they bend over backward to avoid an upset. That opens the door to emotional blackmail, and children can easily become manipulative and bratty.

Parents who are excessively permissive usually think that they are empowering their children. They might let their child lie or steal or not do chores or sulk all day without any consequences or limits. All children benefit from high expectations, especially the expectation to be a moral person and to pull their weight in the family. If children are not provided with firm, clear limits, they end up feeling either omnipotent or out of control. Neither of those is real confidence. Omnipotent children are outraged at any reminder that they are not in complete control of the universe. Out-of-control children look at their parents and think, "Uh-oh, if *they* aren't in charge, then who is?" The result is either fearfulness or bouncing off the walls, or both. If limits are given lovingly and respectfully, they provide structure and safety, and, hence, security. This helps children feel less anxious about their own impulses. Limits also help children feel safer about other dangers in the world: *Mom and Dad are powerful enough to keep me safe until I can leave the nest and fly on my own. But not so powerful that I'll never be able to test my wings.*

Patty Wipfler argues for a link between limits and listening: "Limit, then listen as her bad feelings come rolling off."[7] All too often, limits either aren't given at all or they are given in anger. We set the limit, and we don't want to hear another word about it. Or we don't set the limit at all, because we don't want to hear the reaction. Stay engaged, knowing that the limit will provide children with an opportunity to be sad or mad. If the limit was reasonable, don't give up the limit because of this emotional reaction. Just listen.

In my practice, I often hear from worried parents who are usually indulgent, but who occasionally blow up at their children when they can't take anymore. Then they feel terrible. This situation is very confusing for children. The only time they ever hear a no is when the parent is furious. In return, these children—who almost always get their way—have huge fits on the rare occasions when they don't. All children need to hear nos that are loving and gentle, not just angry or explosive.

In some families, frustrations come to a head with a tantrum or out-of-control behavior by children, followed by an explosion by the parents, then tears, reunion, apologies, hugs, ice cream. This cycle can become a habit. The parents may think they are giving a punishment (the yelling), but from the children's perspective, it is really a reward (the reconciliation after the yelling). If children don't know how to arrive at the reconciliation directly, they do it by setting off an explosion.

In indulgent families, limits are often a moving target. The parents may actually say no a lot, but they don't ever follow through (except as above, with a big explosion). We have to save our no for when we really mean it, and then follow through firmly. That might mean physically restraining children from hitting their younger sibling. It might mean sitting down with them and watching them finish their homework. It definitely means that we don't tell them what to do and then walk away and never notice if they did it or not.

Empty threats, which are not followed through on, can be especially anxiety-arousing for children. We may know we would never leave them in the grocery store, but children aren't sure. Saying, "Stop, stop, stop, please stop," in a timid voice, also conveys a confusing message to children. They aren't going to want to reward that behavior by stopping! They count on *us* to keep them in check until they can do it themselves, and that kind of weak pleading implies that we can't provide this safety net for them. Some families bounce back and forth between indulgence and punishment. The result is random and unpredictable. The limit might be stated twenty times, for example, with no effect and no weight behind it. Suddenly the parent is furiously screaming: "I told you twenty times it was time to go!" Yes, but the first nineteen didn't count, and the child knew it.

Punishment, ineffective discipline, and too much indulgence send children to the towers of isolation and powerlessness. Playful Parenting and the discipline alternatives that flow from it lead children out of these towers. The single most important thing to remember is that everyone needs a full cup of closeness and connection. Everyone. This last story is an example of this.

—AN UNEXPECTED HERO—

I was sitting on the veranda of a restaurant in Isla Mujeres, a little island off the coast of the Yucatán in Mexico, when a drama unfolded at the tables around me. At one table was a group of three young men, laughing and drinking and having a merry time. At another table sat two other young men, looking morose and not speaking to each other as they drank their beers. If you painted this scene, you would make the first group glow with light, while the second pair would be shrouded in shadow. After a while, one of the miserable pair walked away, without either of them saying a word of farewell.

The man who was left alone, a heavyset guy in poorly fitting clothes, stared straight ahead into space, making a point of not looking over toward the men at the other table. Suddenly, he turned to them and said something in a deep voice. Then he turned back and stared into space again. From my minimal understanding of Spanish, I recognized it as a rather foul obscenity. The three men at the other table were surprised and angry. They looked over at the man, glared at him, turned back to their beers, and shrugged at one another. The man sitting alone began a regular, dull drone. Every twenty or thirty seconds, in a monotone, he would repeat the word.

The men at the other table went through a wide range of responses to this. They ignored him, insulted him back, yelled at him, threatened him, cajoled him, tried to argue with him, told him to get lost, begged him to stop. None of these approaches changed the pitch or the frequency of this obscene metronome in the tiniest bit. Nothing they said even made a dent. Finally, one of the three guys, my unexpected hero, said something like "Hey, come over here." The big guy seemed to think this was an invitation to fight but wasn't sure. If it was, he didn't know what to do about it. The young man asked him again to come over. The heavyset man got up slowly and deliberately and came shuffling over, eyes staring down at the floor. I tensed up a bit, not wanting to get caught in a cross-fire of fists.

Nothing like that happened. The man at the happy table said, "No, no, bring your drink, come sit down with us." No one seemed stunned by this (aside from me, that is). The other man shuffled over, got his beer, and shuffled back, standing a step away from the table. My hero leaned back and twisted an empty chair around from my table, pulling it over very close to himself. He made a little gesture indicative of wiping it off for the newcomer. The big guy sat down. I could almost hear his muscles snapping as he forced his body to bend. He looked lost and confused, but the group made him genuinely welcome. There was no recrimination or teasing about the cursing. The issue was resolved.

After a lot of fumbling, one of the men had stumbled over the elegant solution. They all went back to laughing and talking. The man who had given the invitation kept his hand on the big guy's back or shoulder all the time, guiding him through the conversation. When there was a pause, he gently urged his new friend into the opening, asking him a question. The big guy would speak, then look quickly at his sponsor for feedback, ready to drop it fast. When he was done, he would sink back into his seat with a sigh. His sponsor would quote him, carrying on the conversation. And all was well.

I sat there stunned. I promised myself I would always remember that people just want to be close, no matter what crazy stupid ways they might show it. And still, like most everybody else, I forget.

CHAPTER 14

PLAY YOUR WAY THROUGH SIBLING RIVALRY

One day, hearing the anguished cries of children in the street,
one of Abraham Lincoln's neighbors in Springfield, Illinois,
rushed out of his house in alarm. There he found Lincoln
with two of his sons, both of whom were sobbing bitterly.
"Whatever is the matter with the boys, Mr. Lincoln?" he asked.
"Just what's the matter with the whole world," replied Lincoln
resignedly. "I've got three walnuts, and each wants two."[1]

Few things upset parents so much as trouble between their children. Parents get aggravated by the conflict—it's loud, time-consuming, and emotionally draining—and they worry that the siblings won't be close when they grow up. As you might expect, I like to think in terms of playing with these feelings and behaviors instead of attempting to eradicate them. Playful Parenting with siblings introduces the added dimension of playing with more than one child and the complexity of family dynamics. To make it even more complicated, I will also try to explain why *all* children, not just siblings, have what is called sibling rivalry.

—PLAYING WITH MORE THAN ONE CHILD—

Some aspects of Playful Parenting are very different with more than one child, other aspects are modified a bit, and some are exactly the same. With two, three, or a dozen children, we still follow the giggles, build connections, foster self-confidence, and try to love the games we used to hate. We also face the same basic decision about when to step in and when to stand back.

When one child is suffering badly at the hands of another child, or is an outcast of a group, we have to step in and help. If a younger sibling is being beaten up, or the smallest child in the neighborhood is left out of every game, these children need our assistance. Many adults in therapy complain bitterly about having been overpowered by siblings or scape-goated by the neighborhood group when they were young, while their parents let the children work it out for themselves. On the other hand, if children actually are able to work things out, then don't try to fix what doesn't need fixing.

How much suffering is enough to warrant stepping in? As Jeffrey Trawick-Smith puts it, "Children need to get into arguments to learn how to resolve them; they must be excluded from groups to learn play group entry skills. They must play with disagreeable peers and bullies to broaden their repertoire of social strategies. They must have play ideas re-jected so they can learn to become persuasive. When adults intervene too quickly in conflict, these opportunities are lost."[2]

Jean Piaget, the first great observer of children's play, noticed that children learn about morality by arguing about rules. They actually *need* those conflicts about whose turn it is, about whether the ball was in or out, about what's allowed and what isn't. We tend to jump in to settle dis-putes and spell out the rules because we can't stand the conflict, but con-flict may be the very heart of the game. One of the main achievements of childhood play is figuring out how to deal effectively with conflict. They have to have *some* conflict in order to figure that out. But you don't really learn about conflict by being terribly bullied either. I think Piaget would be shocked that children's games are now almost entirely adult-organized and adult-led. On the other hand, he might have liked the recent Poké-mon craze; it involves such complicated rules that children can argue about them endlessly.

I try to walk a fine line between stepping in and standing back, but it's hard sometimes. There are persuasive arguments for both. My basic rule is: *Stand back, but with your eyes open.* Just because we step back doesn't mean we have to turn away and leave children entirely alone. *Step in, but with a light touch,* not a hammer. When we decide to jump in, we usually get carried away and interfere too much. I believe we can prevent the worst problems without taking over. We can stay engaged, while still letting the children be mostly in charge. We can offer a little help and then back off to see if that was enough for them to figure out the rest on their own.

A step-by-step approach works best for me. I like just to watch at first, then point out to children what I see. If they need more help than that, I ask them what they think might help the situation. Finally, I step in more forcefully, if necessary. I might start by just being a little more visible on the playground. "I'm over here if you need me." "I bet you guys can figure it out, but call me if you need help." When children come to us to be referees, or judge and jury, it's tempting to dispense our wisdom. Try instead just to listen to both children, without actually saying anything. Ask them questions, but let them propose the solutions. Be interested, but not overly worried. More often than not, they'll both walk away happy, thinking that you were as wise as Solomon.

If a little more adult input is needed, I will often go up to children who seem to be having trouble and say hello in a very friendly way, even if I don't know them. Sometimes that simple adult contact is enough. If they were shy, that hello might help them get up the courage to join in a game. If they were being bossy or mean, the hello might help them play more agreeably. I try not to convey the message that Big Brother is watching, but just that help is available if anyone needs it.

Other times I'll say a little more: "What's going on here?" "Yikes, that looked like it hurt." If one person is being picked on, I might say, "It doesn't look like he is enjoying that game as much as you are." I will also state my insistence on basic values: "Everyone needs to get a turn." "That kind of name-calling is not okay with me." "We can't do this if you all can't be safe." I try to just state the general principle, then let them work out the details.

If these subtle approaches don't work, we can always lay down the law. We can separate the bully from the victim (whichever one our child happens to be). We can join in the game ourselves, which usually changes the situation instantly. If one child was getting clobbered, the others will usually gang up and try to clobber the adult instead. If no one could figure out what to play, they will usually come up with something good that takes advantage of our offer to play with them.

Two aspects of Playful Parenting—tuning in and roughhousing—are especially complicated with more than one child. First of all, there is more to tune in to, not just what is going on with each child but what is going on between the children and within the group as a whole. We'll never be able to notice *everything*, but we can be alert for key themes: Is anyone being excluded, or ganged up on? Does one child use emotional blackmail (whining and fussing if he doesn't get his way)? Do the others give in? Do some children cheat at games? Do others make themselves the police officer, enforcing all the rules? Do bigger or stronger children know how to hold back so that they can play more equally with smaller or weaker children? Do younger ones have any skills that help them keep up with older ones?

The hardest part of Playful Parenting with more than one child is when you tune in and you find that everyone is on a different wavelength. This situation is most common with wrestling, roughhousing, and competitive games. I was playing with a group of boys at a neighbor's house. There were two brothers, age three and seven, and a twelve-year-old from down the block. The middle one wanted to wrestle, and he was using all his strength, so I had to really focus on no one getting hurt—especially me. The youngest, thinking he needed to protect his big brother, cried out "Stop hurting him!" and started punching me. Meanwhile, the oldest boy was encouraging the seven-year-old to beat the hell out of me and kept asking when he'd get a turn to wrestle me. There was a lot to keep track of! I had to reassure the younger boy that his brother was not getting hurt; I had to keep the actual wrestling from getting out of hand; and I had to tone down the oldest one's killer instincts.

A similar thing happens with competition, where one child wants to go full throttle and another child wants to be allowed to win. Or a child who isn't really able to keep up or play the game properly still wants to be included. At these times, children need us to be more actively involved in the play so that each child can get at least some of what he needs. We may need to level the playing field so that younger children are not at such a disadvantage. We can join their team, or suggest a change in the rules. We may also need to coax the younger one away to another game so the older ones don't have to hold back all the time.

As soon as there are two children, there is fighting—over a toy, the remote control, or who got the bigger piece of pie. My favorite response to this kind of conflict, whether it is between siblings or playmates, is to grab the toy and run. The two children then bond together to try to get it away from me. I don't do that all the time, since they also need to figure out how to negotiate with each other. But making myself the target always helps things get unstuck when children are locked in conflict. If they are hitting each other, I'll say, "Bet you can't hit *me*," and then run out of the room, pretending to be scared. If they struggle over fairness, I'll pretend to be crumpled into tears because I didn't get a turn. Or I'll grab a fork and say, "I'm not sharing this fork with anybody." If one or all of the siblings are fearful, I will be the cowardly lion, afraid of everything, and let them make fun of me instead of one another. These comments are like bait; sometimes children bite and sometimes they don't. If they do, they will quickly show you which sibling themes they want to play with.

Whenever there are three or more children, there are issues of inclusion and exclusion. We don't want to put too much of a damper on their games or their own choices about friendship, but we do need to make sure that no one is completely excluded, scapegoated, or attacked. My friend Tina takes the active approach. At the basketball court, she tells the medium-size kids that she will help them not get kicked off by the bigger kids if they will include the littler kids. Our job isn't to make everything completely fair, but to compensate for any big power imbalances. We also hold out a high standard for inclusion (no one gets left out or left behind), knowing very well that children will exclude, but providing a guideline to strive for.

The best kind of play is open to everyone. It bridges differences of age, race, gender, or social class. In an article on diversity and play, psychologist Patricia Ramsey[3] notes that "when children are engaged in true play—nonliteral, open-ended, and spontaneous play—they are creating their own world, which can potentially accommodate everyone." Our job as adults is to help achieve that promise of inclusion. She explains how the best types of play are universal and inclusive. Play based on TV shows or computer games is much less inclusive. She tells a wonderful story about her six-year-old son Daniel, adopted as an infant from Chile, and her three-year-old adopted son Andres, also from Chile, who had been with the family for only forty-eight hours. Daniel tried several times to get his new brother to play Power Rangers with him. Andres did not respond, and Daniel became increasingly frustrated and resentful.

"An hour later both boys are in the bathtub. They are blowing bubbles and pouring water over each other and laughing gleefully. Andres sticks his head in the water and comes up with wet hair. Daniel follows suit, and they both shriek with delight." What's the difference between these two scenes? The water play in the tub—a universal way to play—bridged the cultural divide. The Power Rangers game depended entirely on having watched the show (or having spent hours on the playground with boys who have watched it). One type of play brought them together, the other pulled them apart.

—EVERY CHILD HAS SIBLING RIVALRY (EVEN IF THEY DON'T HAVE SIBLINGS)—

The feelings, thoughts, and behaviors commonly associated with the term *sibling rivalry* are actually a part of *every* child's development, including only children. With siblings, parents are often annoyed or worried by the conflict. Meanwhile, parents of only children are often taken aback by their child's "sibling rivalry" feelings and behaviors.

My friend called me for help a few years ago because her five-year-old son Bobby was being mean to his little sister Tanya. He would be rough with her, take her things, complain about any attention she received, and have a fit if she so much as looked at any of his toys. At other times, he was loving, gentle, and protective. My daughter and I came over to play with them and give them a hand. Emma was five at the time, also. Usually when the three of them played together, my daughter—an only child—would take advantage of having a temporary little sister and dress Tanya up in doll clothes. While Emma played junior mom, the big brother would get very frustrated that his sister was monopolizing the attention of "his" friend.

I took the two older ones upstairs to the attic, the designated space for physical play and loud noise. I asked the mom to keep Tanya downstairs. I wanted both older children to be able to play through their feelings—whatever they might be—without inflicting them on the little one. So we were jumping on old mattresses and running around in the attic having a good time. I grabbed a doll and said, "Look, it's the new baby, how cute," and I cuddled it. The two five-year-olds looked at each other, looked at me, looked back at each other, ran screaming and giggling toward me, and grabbed the doll. The big brother said, "Oops, she fell into the hot lava from the volcano. I'll rescue her." My daughter (the only child and the "junior mom," remember) knocked the doll out of his hands and said, "Bad baby, you fell in the water, and a shark is going to eat you." The play went on in this vein for a half hour or so. It was a great game, though I was very glad the little sister was not there to watch it. Afterward, the three of them all played together very well, and the older one's aggression toned down a bit. Later I had the chance to spend time alone with Tanya, the sister. We played games that let her be the more powerful one, such as chasing her but never quite catching her, or wrestling and letting her knock me over easily and noisily.

The point of this story is that all children have the feelings that are called sibling rivalry, whether they have siblings or not. Children would much rather work out these feelings through play than by actually hurting anyone. They resort to aggression only when adults don't have the time or energy or know-how to use play to help them work it through. Often parents of siblings are burned out, while parents of only children don't realize that they have to deal with sibling rivalry, too.

At the heart of sibling rivalry is a set of profound and universal questions: Am I loved? Truly, absolutely loved? Am I wanted? Am I special? Am I powerful? Will my parents stop loving me if they start to love that other kid? Can I make the world bend to my will? Why can't I do what I see that person doing? Why can't I get what I see that person getting? There are certain ways these feelings affect younger siblings, older siblings, and only children, at different ages. For everyone, though, the goal is the same: to release and play through the feelings in order to be able to have close, loving relationships.

Siblings have thousands of opportunities daily for working on these issues (not always effectively, of course). Only children have to seek out opportunities to play out their rivalry feelings. For months, whenever my daughter would get in a car with her best friend and her friend's little sister, the three of them would argue about who got to sit in the middle of the backseat. They could easily have argued about this for hours (except, of course, none of the parents could ever stand it for more than a couple of minutes!). The interesting thing was that the sisters never argued about it any other time, and Emma never argued about this with anyone else. It was only when those three got together, and only in the car. Somehow this situation became the playground for this older sibling, younger sibling, and only child to play the rivalry game.

With siblings, the danger is not that sibling issues will be overlooked, but that children will struggle with these issues constantly without any effective resolution. Some siblings manage fine, of course, but in other families the older ones beat up the younger ones, while the parents assume that they are working things out on their own. In other families, the younger ones figure out indirect power sources, such as manipulation or sneakiness, and the older one gets in trouble all the time. Neither of these scenarios actually helps children to work through the daily frustrations of sibling life.

—SIBLINGS AND REFILLING THE EMPTY CUP—

The image of the empty cup (see page 43) is useful to keep in mind when thinking about siblings. The most typical manifestation of sibling rivalry is competition for those refills. Older siblings watch the baby get perpetual fill-ups, just for burping and farting and looking cute. Meanwhile, they look at their own cup and it seems as if the level is always on low. Even worse, nobody seems to care, except to scold them or punish them, which empties their cup even more. Later on, the younger one may feel as if the older one gets all the refills—a later bedtime, more privileges, a real bike. In fact, much sibling conflict can be seen as trying to steal a refill from the other child's cup—by stealing a toy, making her cry, winning a competition, being smarter, getting him in trouble, and so on. Children are natural Darwinians and Malthusians (life is a fight over scarce resources, and only the fittest survive). In other words, when an older sibling says, "You can't come with us, you're too little," he is saying, I'm off to get a refill and you're stuck here running on empty. When the younger sibling says, "Mom, she's being mean to me," she is saying, Please make up for the inequality in our size by giving me more.

Clearly, we need to be more involved in providing ample refills so our children don't have to steal them or fight over them. With siblings or playmates, we fill those cups the same way as we do it one-on-one: with attention, love, affection, listening, and (of course!) snacks. With one child, refills provide energy and enthusiasm. With two or more children, refills also help resolve conflicts, increase cooperation and inclusion, and promote creative ideas for playing together. It's hard to get a good refill, though, when you are always comparing your cup's level with everyone else's. And it's hard to give out refills when there is so much jostling and fighting for each drop. When children are pushy and obnoxious about getting more than their share, we may not feel like filling anyone's cup. When siblings fight because their cups are too low, often they get punished instead of replenished. Their cups just get lower and lower.

Caretaking responsibilities, such as when an older sibling takes care of a younger one, can either fill a child's cup or empty it, depending on the child and the duties. If the older child feels valuable to the family, and the younger child feels well cared for, then everyone's cup can remain full. But sometimes the older child feels angry, resenting the loss of playtime and freedom. Or the older child can simply be an inadequate caretaker, leaving the younger child's needs unmet.

I saw two boys, around ages seven and three, coming out of the public library by themselves holding hands. It was a very sweet picture of big brother protection and little brother adoration. As they headed to the car, where their mother was waiting, the older one apparently got nervous about the responsibility of crossing the parking lot with his brother. He started shouting at him to go faster and to stay closer to him. The younger one was crushed and scared, which made him go slower, and the older one got angrier and angrier. Their cups, which started out brimming over, ended up empty. If we are going to put children in the care of other children, we need to teach them emotional skills and playing skills as well as basic safety. For example, we can show older siblings how to let younger siblings be in charge of the play sometimes. This role reversal gives everyone an alternative to acting out the rivalry. The older one can feel important and competent, and at the same time can symbolically work through the key issues by "pretending" to be weaker or slower than the younger child.

My friend Jacob's son, Leonard, is an only child and a master of "fill my cup first." One time Jacob offered the Leonard and one of his friends ice cream, only to discover that there was just a little left. "That's okay," Leonard said, "just fill mine up first, really full. She can have whatever is left." Leonard also taught me why children immediately want something just because someone else wants it. We were over at their house one day and my daughter asked if she could borrow a sweater. Jacob asked Leonard to get Emma his red sweater. "That's my favorite sweater; she can't have that. She can have anything but that." He threw himself on the floor in a major fit. "But Leonard," his father said, "you haven't worn that in months. I don't think it even fits you anymore." "I don't care!" Suddenly this was Leonard's prize possession. Before that minute, the sweater was just a discarded piece of clothing. As soon as another child wanted it, the sweater became a cup-filler. And there was no way he was going to let *her* get a refill from *his* sweater. With siblings and only children, every drop in that cup is precious: I may not be low now, but you never know about tomorrow.

My friend Terry was five when his mother was pregnant with her fourth child. He and his four-year-old sister were excited about the idea of a new baby. Their older sister, though, at age seven, was wise beyond her years, from having suffered the arrival of two new siblings already. She called a meeting of the three kids. "Look," she said, "I don't want to see either of you being happy about this. There already isn't enough love to go around, and when that new baby comes, it's just going to get worse."

This story says to me that, as parents, we need to let children know that there really *is* enough love for everyone to get a refill, even if a new sibling or some other big event slows down the flow a bit. We also have to understand that many children fear that their siblings' refills will come out of their cup.

Most children seem to share this idea that refills are a scarce resource. In fact, most of us adults feel the same way. No one is knocking on our door offering us free refills. If we don't have enough ourselves to give our children what they need, we have to get support from other parents, relatives, friends, or therapists. What follows are suggestions for the various types of resources that we can offer to siblings and playmates to fill their cups. These are things they need from us when they are together. I hope you'll agree that these resources don't have to be that scarce. We should give them freely. You may be used to providing only one or two of them when your children are at each other's throats. In the future, try the others and see how they work.

● *Offer a solution.* We are the parents, and we know our children very well. Sometimes all we need to do is offer a solution to resolve the conflict. "Go outside . . . take a break from each other . . . let's invite a friend over for each of you . . . let's wrestle . . . let's have snack time." Let's say two siblings are fighting over who gets the last cup of juice. You could make the conflict disappear by mixing up a new batch. That's a simple and useful solution. Or you could tell them they have to split it, but that is less useful. If we're always solving these conflicts for them, they don't learn how to find their own solutions. One tip-off that we're offering too many solutions is when the children reject them all in a snit. Instead of trying harder to come up with a solution yourself, take that as a signal that they want to struggle through finding one for themselves. If worse comes to worse, you can always take the village idiot approach: "If you don't figure out how to share the juice, I'll have to pour it on my head!"

Because sibling conflicts are so emotionally loaded, we don't always come up with the best possible solutions. For example, some parents "solve" every problem by punishing the older child and siding with the younger one. Other parents will hear an older sibling beating up a younger one and solve the problem by saying, "Keep the noise down, boys." The solutions we impose also tend to lack creativity: "Split it . . . take turns . . . ten minutes each . . . you go first this time because she went first last time . . . say you're sorry."

Many parents think they have to choose between stepping in with a solution, or stepping out of the picture completely. There are actually a number of other resources we can offer children besides an adult-imposed solution.

● *Give encouragement and inspire their confidence.* In order for children to create their own effective solutions, we have to stick around and give encouragement and confidence. They will get frustrated, as you know, and they'll often revert to the most primitive method of dealing with problems—hitting, screaming, crying, tattling, whining. So we can't just say, "Work it out," and leave the room. Yet we also can't jump in too soon with the answer, because that undermines their confidence. We have to let them know that we truly believe *they* can figure out a solution that is right for everyone, instead of suggesting that we don't trust them to find a good answer themselves. While they figure it out, we have to stand by and offer encouragement, and stop them from hitting each other in frustration.

Encouraging children without butting in too much is a delicate balancing act. I will often say things like, "I'm sure you guys can work this out. Anyone have any ideas?" "I'm not sure what the right solution is, but I bet there is one. Let's all keep thinking about it." "Everyone has to be included. How are you going to manage that?" "We can't keep playing if you guys can't stop hurting each other. I have complete confidence that you can figure out a way to keep the game nonviolent." "This isn't working. Everyone is fighting over turns and nobody is getting to play. What can we do so everybody gets a turn?" Notice how these last few comments propose *half* of a solution—you have to include everyone, you have to be safe—but they leave the other half of the solution up to the children involved.

Another example of a half solution is to say, "Mark is really upset about this; what are you guys going to do to make it right?" instead of the more typical, "Say you're sorry," or "It was an accident; he didn't mean it." There is nothing that irritates me more than children's halfhearted, insincere apology just to get their mom or dad off their back. Yet I see parents falling for it all the time.

I have found that children are remarkably responsive to encouragement to figure things out on their own, as long as they can count on our support. They may end up with the same solutions we would have chosen, but it's different when *they* do it. Their solutions are more creative, their apologies are more sincere, and their compromises are more acceptable to everyone. Then they can truly cooperate instead of begrudgingly taking turns.

● *Flood children with love and affection.* Sometimes that's all we need to do. If we fill their cups in the most basic way—a hug, a cuddle, a story, a kind word, some special time together, their favorite foods—they will figure out the rest. As much as I talk about play and playfulness, there is also a time for just providing tenderness and comfort. When one child hurts another child, for example, physically or emotionally, you might want to listen to the tears first, before brainstorming solutions or stepping in with a playful idea. When we are giving out comfort, don't forget the one who threw the punch as well as the one who got punched. That child needs some attention from us, too, and I don't mean punishment.

When children are being mean, they are often sending us a signal that they are in need of more love and affection. Unfortunately, they may reject our love at those times. We have to be persistent and keep at it until they know they are loved. The problem is that we may not feel very inclined to offer much affection to children who have been mean, or sassy, or difficult. Perhaps that's why children feel as if love is a scarce commodity sometimes. If we get over our reluctance to give out love to children who have been "bad," then it won't be scarce anymore.

Children also have a need to *give* love and affection, not just receive it. In addition to loving us, they can play out this need with baby dolls, younger siblings, friends, or pets. Boys, unfortunately, are less likely to get much chance at this loving and nurturing, except, perhaps, with pets. With friends, since they can't hug or hold hands or say they love each other without being teased or beaten up, they tease and poke and pound and curse and put down each other. Boys do this to express both affection and hostility. They are refilling each other's cups and spilling each other's cups at the same time. This can be confusing to watch.

● *Protect.* Even though it can be hard to tell when children are hurting each other and when they are only playing, the next resource we can provide them is protection from undue harm. We can't protect our children from every bump and bruise and emotional injury, and we shouldn't try. But we must offer protection against the more deeply harmful hurts that children can inflict on one another. We can insist that a stronger child not beat up a weaker child, and we may need to supervise more closely if someone keeps getting hurt. We have to make sure children are not scapegoated or abused or terrorized.

Adequate protection, without too much intrusive meddling, does more than just keep children from serious harm. It also helps them feel safe. When children feel safe, they are able to get along much better with one another, and to play more happily and freely.

Children need to know that they can have some freedom, but not a license to hurt one another. In a program called Protective Behaviors, children are taught that they have the right to be safe; others have the right to be safe with them; there is nothing so terrible that you can't tell someone about it; and you can keep searching until someone listens.[4] I think that is a wonderful set of messages to give to children. Until they develop those internal abilities to keep themselves and others safe, they rely on us to make sure that they aren't abused or abandoned. Like every therapist, I have heard countless sad stories from adults who have been traumatized and brutalized by siblings, while the parents were oblivious or in denial.

● *Provide perspective.* As parents, it is easy for us to get wrapped up in the details of our children's conflicts: Who did what to whom, and who's going to pay? If we step back a bit, we can stay calm and reflect back to them what we see and hear. Sometimes, magically, all we have to do is point out each person's position in a relaxed tone of voice. "You want the ball because it's yours, and he wants it because he's never had a turn to play with it." Simply listening and reflecting may give them all they need. We can add a question at the end of our observation, nudging them to reflect a little bit as they consider their situation. "You want to play Lego, and you want to play basketball; what are you two going to do?" A light tone helps as well: "Hmm, this sounds like a bad case of it all started when she hit me back."

● *Promote win-win outcomes.* In the fields of negotiation and mediation, win-win means that it is possible for everyone to feel satisfied with the outcome. The alternative is called the zero sum game, in which someone has to lose for someone else to win. It may be impossible to achieve win-win every single time, but it can always be our goal. The key to win-win is listening carefully to each child's position and feelings. Often, underneath the irreconcilable differences, there is room for an elegant solution that makes everybody happy. At the very least, each child feels as if someone has listened to her and taken her feelings into account. Everyone gets her say, but not necessarily her way. When we jump in with solutions and compromises, we may actually interfere with win-win outcomes. For example, say that we jump into a sibling conflict by saying, "Stop arguing and take turns. Ten minutes each. Jody, you're first." They refuse that solution, or reluctantly agree and keep arguing anyway. Now consider if we said, "Okay girls, what's going on? What do *you* want, and what do *you* want?" Nan says she wants to have it first, because she thought of it, but she doesn't care if she has a long turn or a short turn. Jody says she wants a long turn, because she loves that toy, and she's afraid if Nan has it first she'll never have a chance. Simple: Nan gets a short turn first, then Jody gets a long turn. Everybody's happy, instead of nobody's happy.

Siblings need attention, time, and thought put into their relationship with each other. Relationships can have an empty cup, just like individuals. In a perfect world, all siblings would naturally have loving, cooperative, affectionate relationships. In the real world, for any relationship to work, it must be nurtured. Set aside time for the sibling relationship: "The next hour is going to be brother-sister time. We can do whatever you want." If they want to spend the hour arguing about what to do, that's fine. Don't jump in and solve it for them. If things have been especially hard, you may want to call attention to the need for reconnection: "I've noticed that you guys have been struggling with each other a lot, and I want to give you a hand with your relationship. It's important for me that you have a close connection."

After you have introduced the concept, sit back and follow their lead.

Maybe they'll take that as an invitation to complain about each other. If so, you can help them put their feelings into words and listen to each other respectfully. Maybe they'll start roughhousing, using your extra attention as a resource for playing out their struggle symbolically. Maybe they'll have some great suggestions that you never considered. Maybe they'll roll their eyes. That's okay, too.

● *Be playful.* Imagine if you took all the time you now spend fussing at siblings to stop fighting, and you spent it playing with them. What would happen? I bet they'd fight less, enjoy each other more, and you'd have fun, too. A great game for siblings is to grab the thing they are fighting over and run. A three-way pillow fight is good, too.

In an earlier chapter, I described the technique of providing a play-by-play commentary on the action in children's play. This idea works especially well with siblings. It combines several of the resources outlined above, but mainly it's fun. Imagine you're at a tennis match, moving your head back and forth, and you are narrating the scene:

(Stepping into the scene of a big blowup between two siblings) "What's going on?"

"He took my red crayon!"

"That's shocking!" (Head turn) "He says you took his red crayon."

"I needed it, and he wasn't using it."

(Head turn) "He says you weren't using it, and he needed it."

"I was about to use it, and it's mine."

(Head turn) "He says he was about to use it, and it's his."

In no time at all, they are laughing happily instead of fighting bitterly. Our tone of voice—relaxed and a little bit like the happy village idiot—helps shift things from conflict to giggles.

● *Give up the search for perfect equality.* Give each child what they need, rather than attempting to be equal. The demand for perfect equality is a setup for disappointment. Debbie just got new boots, so now Cathie wants a pair. She is on the verge of hysteria about it, in fact, but her boots are perfectly fine for another year. The confusing thing is that Cathie certainly needs *something*, and she's insisting that what she needs is a new pair of boots. What she *really* needs is to have her cup of love refilled. Seeing her sister so happy with her new boots, she figures that would be a good way to fill her cup. We know that won't really do the trick, but she doesn't. One option is to hold Cathie while she cries about the unfairness of it all, reminding her that our love goes deeper than a pair of boots. The other option is to find a way to effectively meet the real need for "enough" love and affection.

A second-grade teacher asked me for help with a set of twin boys in her class. She said that the parents tried desperately to make everything absolutely even, but their tantrums about fairness got worse and worse. I suggested that they forget about perfect equality, because it would never be equal enough. Focus instead on the feelings of not being loved enough. The teacher passed this on to the parents, who gave it a try. The next time the mother came back from a business trip, instead of bringing each of the kids the exact same treat as usual, she got one strawberry-flavored and one raspberry-flavored candy. She gave the raspberry one to Harvey, who had always been the twin most preoccupied with fairness. He had a big fit, saying, "It's not fair, it's not fair." She didn't try to make things even, as she would have done in the past, such as by giving them each half a raspberry and half a strawberry. That would have just made Joel, the other twin, scream about not getting what *he* wanted. Instead, the mother just held Harvey. She was empathic with him, saying gently, "I know, it's not fair." They repeated that exchange about four hundred times. At the end, Harvey looked up at his mother and said, "I like raspberry better," and hugged her. After that, things really turned around at home and at school.

—THE HIDDEN POWER OF YOUNGER SIBLINGS, AND OTHER MYSTERIES OF FAMILY DYNAMICS—

Because of our own histories, some of us are keen on protecting smaller and weaker children, even if it stifles the freedom of the play. Others are committed to protecting children's play from too much adult intervention, even if feelings might get hurt or bodies get bruised. I used to always side with younger children whenever I saw a conflict (guess who was the youngest child in my family!). But I am beginning to realize that it is more complicated than that. Families don't usually have simple villains or victims. Now, when I see an older sibling hit or yell at a younger one, I ask the "victim," "How do you get back at him for that?" Most of the time they just give me a little sweet smile with a twinkle in it, but sometimes they come right out and tell me: "I get him in trouble. . . . I sneak into her room and read her diary. . . . I mess up her stuff. . . . I practice how to annoy him."

My friends Louisa and Ross have a repeated scenario with their son Tommy, who is almost nine. Whenever the father and son play, Tommy ends up crying, sulking, and angry, yelling at his father about something he did wrong. Louisa then rushes over and yells at her husband, telling him that he's gone too far, that he doesn't know when to quit, that he's just a big kid himself. She accepts Tommy's presentation of the "facts," because he is the one crying and upset—and the youngest one of the two of them. Ross gets defensive, saying things like, "He was laughing about it before; I don't see what the big deal is." When Louisa tells the story, her husband is the one with the problem; Tommy is the helpless victim; and she is the helpless bystander caught in the crossfire. When Ross tells the story, Tommy is a bratty kid who always has to get his way; Louisa just makes things worse; and *he* is the innocent bystander.

As soon as they frame the problem this way, they are already stuck. Things are very unlikely to change. I proposed an alternative explanation to Ross and Louisa. I reminded them about what often happens between Tommy and his little sister Lucy. They will be playing together happily, Tommy will be too rough with her, and Lucy will scream and cry and get him in trouble. Mom runs over and yells at Tommy. Sound familiar? I think that Tommy is just playing a role-reversal game, playing out the scene between him and his sister all over again with him and his father. Except this time, someone else gets in trouble, while he gets to be the injured party. Mom yells at Dad instead of at him.

In fact, getting the older one in trouble is one of the tried-and-true power strategies of younger siblings. They have other strategies, too, and now that I see these I am not so quick to protect those helpless little innocent victims. I was playing Scrabble with Greg. His sister Barbara was sitting in the room reading. Generally, Greg is the bossy older brother, while Barbara is the sweet little sister. Barbara was fiddling with a cord, and whenever it touched him, Greg yelled at her. She didn't respond, but she didn't stop annoying him either. I asked Barbara what she does to get back at him when he yells. They both answered me at the same time: "Nothing!" A minute later Greg put down "peenut" on the board game and asked me if that's how to spell peanut. Barbara chimed in, in a superior tone of voice, "I really thought you'd know that, Greg. I knew that." "Aha," I said. "So that's how you get back at him, with little zingers like that." Barbara laughed. Greg just looked puzzled and shrugged his shoulders.

—PLAYFUL PARENTING WITH SIBLINGS—

The following story is based on what a mother in one of my parenting classes told me. (Note: I have collapsed several playtimes [and fighting times] into one story, in order to illustrate the basic principles of Playful Parenting with siblings.) Dave and Alice have been at each other's throats all afternoon. In fact, they've been at each other's throats for years; now, at ages seven and eight, it is worse than ever. Mom can hear an aggravating little voice in her head, the voice of her mother saying, "I told you not to have two so close together." She's about ready to scream. These children need refills (so does their mom). They also need play that repairs their sibling connection and play that helps them work through their feelings of wanting to rip each other apart. They need help finding the road back to exuberance and fun. Mom starts with offering refills for those empty cups: She gives them each a hug, offers each of them five minutes of "Mommy time" (undivided one-on-one attention), and suggests they break for a snack.

Taking a breather, Mom now thinks to herself: "How do I make sense out of what they are doing? It might be that they are not fighting only to drive me crazy. Maybe they have some needs they are trying to get met; maybe they are telling me they need more individual attention; maybe they are scared that I love the other one more; maybe the little one is frustrated that he can't do what the older one can, or the older one is afraid the younger one is catching up and she won't be special anymore." She tries to translate their behavior into the language of connection: "Dave and Alice want to be close—let's at least assume it even if it doesn't look like it—and there's only one small problem: Alice will play well with Dave if everything goes exactly her way. Dave will play well with Alice as long as no one tries to tell him what to do. No wonder they have trouble. When their cups are running low, Dave hits and Alice screams. That empties their cups more, and lowers mine, too."

In the parenting class, whenever we talked about Playful Parenting, this mother always said she didn't have time to get down on the floor and play. As she told us these stories about her children's sibling conflicts, and her ideas about them, we convinced her to try. I always suggest to parents that they add up all the time they spend punishing and fussing and being aggravated, and use that time to play. The class also reminded her that her children's strong negative feelings toward each other were pretty normal, and that underneath the anger and frustration they probably liked each other a lot. This was very supportive advice and seemed to help the mother. Afterward we all laughed, because we had just been talking about books on sibling rivalry, and we agreed that the main message of these books is: Sibling rivalry is completely normal; here's how to stop it.

Now comes the fun part. Using all that information and her new perspective, Mom decided to get down on the floor and play for a little while. But she wanted to make the most of it. She had tuned in to the themes of their fighting, which matched the themes she had seen in the two of them for years. Some of these themes were the following: each one feeling that the other sibling gets more; the older one feeling that the younger one is an intrusion; and the younger one feeling that the older one is bossy. The mom didn't have a definite plan when she dove into the play, but she was willing to try anything. In fact, diving in without a plan is an excellent Playful Parenting strategy.

She decided to go for maximum impact by starting with very close contact, so she grabbed both of them in the middle of their fighting over a toy and tumbled all three of them onto the couch in a torrent of shouts and giggles. She started hamming it up about getting a sword and dividing herself in half so they each could get half. Then she imitated the two of them fighting over her, "You got the liver, all I got was the spleen; that's not fair! I had her first!" Perhaps she had guessed wrong about the deep meaning of their squabbling, but at least she got their attention. Her usual technique of yelling at them to stop fighting never got their attention. She watched them closely to make sure they were laughing at this imitation of them and were not insulted. They were laughing, so she stuck with this theme for a few minutes, all the while enjoying cuddling with them both. She then let them have a tug-of-war over her. She shouted at them, "You love Sparky [the dog] more than you love me. Boo-hoo-hoo" (reversing the roles—making herself the one who is unloved). That didn't work so well, so she grabbed the toy they had been fighting over and said, "Aha! I have it now. Finally *I* get to play with this!" Then she ran out of the room. Dave and Alice chased her, a team now, united against a common enemy.

By this time, the children had recovered from their shock at seeing their mom act this way, and they were contributing ideas to the game, which made her job much easier. "Let's pretend we ran away from home, and you're the mom." So she pleaded with them, "Please don't run away; I'll let you fight with each other as much as you want. I'll even let you beat each other up. I won't complain, oh my little darlings. . . ." She chased after them as they ran away squealing.

After an hour or so of great fun, Mom said she had to go make dinner, and things immediately fell apart. Alice screamed, "You never play with us!" Dave told his sister to shut up and shoved her. She shrieked. Mom made a humorous scream of her own. "Aah! Now I have to jump into the fish tank and sing." Everyone laughed, and this time they let her leave without a fuss, and they went off to play happily together, for the first time in weeks.

During the play, whenever she felt she was wasting her time or was too tired for this nonsense, Mom reminded herself that she was doing the tremendously important work of building her relationship with each child and their closeness with each other. Later that evening, after the children were in bed, she called her brother and ranted awhile about how obnoxious they were being, then laughed long and hard over how embarrassed she would have been if anyone had seen her on the floor acting so goofy. Finally she cried a little about how much she loves them, and how scared she is that they won't be close to each other when they grow up. Her brother appreciated her for being so honest about her struggles, and he admitted that he had been having trouble with one of his children. She offered to listen, even though she was worn out, as a way of repaying her brother for listening to her. His problem was that his wife tells him that he favors their older son, but he doesn't think so. He thinks the younger one is just more difficult to handle. They talked awhile longer, and after listening to each other, these grown-up siblings were able to remember some funny stories from their own sibling rivalries. They hung up feeling relieved and recharged.

CHAPTER 15

RECHARGE YOUR OWN BATTERIES

Nothing makes us as lonely as our secrets.

—PAUL TOURNIER

A friend called me the other day and asked for some advice about her children. I made some suggestions, and she said, mildly offended, "That's what you told me to do the last time I talked to you!"

"Well, did you try it?"

"No, I didn't, but—"

"Wait a minute," I interrupted her. "I'm not going to use up my limited brainpower trying to think of some new idea if you haven't bothered to try my last one!"

We laughed, and she promised to try it, but I wasn't so sure she would.

Though most parents are eager for good advice, I've noticed that many of us have a hard time putting into practice what we learn, or even what we already know. In other words, I understand that many parents, even if they love the idea of Playful Parenting, will still find it difficult. I wish it were enough to simply say, "Try it!" But there seems to be a missing ingredient. We need something above and beyond more information about children and parenting. I hope this chapter will supply that missing ingredient.

—HAVING OUR OWN TURN—

Before we can really use any parenting advice, I think we need to re-charge ourselves, refill our own empty cups, listen to each other, and come out of our own towers of isolation and powerlessness. In other words, take those same ideas I have been returning to again and again in the description of Playful Parenting, and apply them to ourselves.

The first step to recharging our own batteries is to acknowledge the emotions we feel when we start to play—feelings like boredom, frustra-tion, resentment, anger, annoyance, anxiety, fatigue, distraction, and a sense of being overwhelmed. Here are what parents have told me about playing with their children: They already get way more attention than I ever got as a child. . . . I keep slipping back into the old routines, the old power struggles. . . . No one ever played like that with me. . . . I'm too ex-hausted after working and taking care of the children to play. . . . I try to play, but I get really sleepy. . . . This game is so boring. . . . How can I play with all the work piling up on my desk. . . . I get so angry when he starts acting like a brat.

Not surprisingly, these feelings make us want to give up, or lash out, or take a nap, *anything* instead of continuing to play. When we are swamped by our own feelings, it's hard to have fun and hard to pay close attention to children and see what they need. Playing with children challenges our adult tendency to keep our feelings well buried. Like our children, in order to play we have to release those unshed tears, relax those tense muscles, and unload our fears and worries. It's *our* turn. It's time for us to take a turn be-ing listened to—a turn having our own cup filled—so that we can offer re-fills to our children and play with them the way they want to play.

—GETTING OUR OWN CUPS FILLED—

I have described Playful Parenting as a way of filling children's needs for attachment, affection, love, security, confidence, and closeness. When their cup is emptied, we provide the refills. But who gives us the refills that *we* need? When parenting is a joy, our cup is refilled just by spending time together with our children. But parenting is also hard work. The time we spend with our children (or even thinking about them) can leave our cup empty.

The basic method of getting our own cup filled is pretty simple: Find someone who will listen to you. It might be a spouse, another parent, a friend, or a therapist. Choose someone who will listen respectfully and interestedly, but who won't tell you what to do. Someone who will keep listening even if you start to cry or laugh or shake with fear and rage. We may need to train our listeners to listen without interrupting, and to listen without telling us what we should do and how we should feel. If it isn't a paid listener, we also need to take a turn listening to them.

Most of us have not been listened to enough. Right when we want someone to listen to us, they have the nerve to want us to listen to them! Therapists, meanwhile, charge a lot of money to listen. The result is that many people think listening time is a scarce commodity. But here's a little secret: *There is plenty of good listening available if people take turns.* A turn might be five minutes each on the phone, or a couple of hours of deep heart-to-heart talking. Talking (and all the emotions we release when we honestly share our thoughts and feelings) is the adult equivalent of play. It's how we show what's really going on inside of us, and how we get back to ourselves.

We can especially use someone to listen to us after we make an extra effort to be a Playful Parent. We have exposed our vulnerabilities by trying hard to connect, by encouraging children's confidence in the face of their frustration, or by wrestling to the limits of our endurance. Now it's our turn, and we need to tell someone about it. We also need to reveal those painful secrets about being a parent, the ones we keep even from our closest friends. Most parents are shocked to learn that they are not the only ones who ever have fantasies of clobbering a kid who was driving them crazy, or who get painfully bored during playtimes, or who resent how much attention they give out every day (while getting very little back).

The quote at the beginning of this chapter captures the importance of sharing these secrets. By telling someone else, especially someone who is sympathetic and understanding, we relieve the burden. I think part of why parents seem so tired all the time is that we carry around a hidden pile of worries, embarrassments, secret feelings of being a bad parent, helplessness, and other painful emotions. Sometimes we even keep our deepest joys secret, for fear that other adults will make fun of us for caring so deeply about our children, for being so heartbreakingly in love with them.

Many parents, especially mothers, talk to each other informally. You may, however, have a desire for a deeper kind of listening and talking than you can get from acquaintances, or even from friends and family. I won't give a whole course on listening here, but I will touch on the key points.[1] Good listening means taking turns, respecting confidentiality, and allowing the other person to say *anything at all* without fear of being judged or rejected. Don't interrupt, and don't say, "Me, too," then launch into your own story.

When people talk honestly and openly, they often cry or get scared or have a grown-up version of a temper tantrum. The good listener will just let those emotions flow, without trying to get the person to shove them back inside. So don't say, "Cheer up, have a drink, forget about it; there's nothing to be upset about." After being listened to well, people feel lighter, more confident, more enthusiastic. Remember also that listening to others helps us just as much as when someone is listening to us.

Even two parents who are both running on empty can refill their own cups by taking turns listening to each other. Maybe at first one listener will interrupt every five seconds, or will tune out and think about the grocery list. But every little bit helps, and after a few minutes of this second-rate listening, we are usually able to listen to each other better. So get together with another parent or a group of parents and talk. Here is a list of questions to get you started:

- What do you remember from when you were the ages your children are now?
- Do those memories help you understand where things get hard now as a parent?
- What are your hopes and dreams for your children? Are these realistic? Have you left room for your child to figure out his or her own hopes and dreams?
- We all know from TV and magazines what parenting is *supposed* to be like, but what is parenting really like for you?
- What is great about being a parent? What is great about you as a parent? What are some of your shining moments as a parent?

- What's hard about being a parent? What are you too
  embarrassed about or ashamed of ever to tell anyone?

The answers to these questions, especially the ones that are hard to think about and hard to share with anyone, are very important. Keeping these things buried inside of us just makes it more likely that we will make the same mistakes over and over again. For example, many parents have never admitted that they sometimes feel like hitting their children, or wish they could walk out the door and never come back, or that they like one of their children better than another, or that they have an embarrassing wish inside to be taken care of themselves instead of having to care for children. Our lives and our parenting will go much better—and more playfully—if we can admit these secrets to someone who will listen with compassion instead of horror.

We may even find that we aren't the only ones who feel that way. For example, if you feel as if you're the only one of your friends who ever loses it with your children, it's probably just that you haven't shared these painful moments with one another. My friend Helen wanted me to teach a class on alternatives to blowing up at your kids. She was sure that none of her "perfect parent" friends would be interested, but once she got over her fear of asking them about it, she filled a whole class in no time. The typical response was, "Are you kidding? I thought *you* were the one who always had it all together!"

If you have a caring and thoughtful listener, you might be surprised by how moving and emotional it can be to answer these questions. Even asking them of yourself and answering them silently—with some compassion and understanding for your own struggles—can be a powerful experience. I think you'll notice that afterward you approach playing and parenting with more energy and enthusiasm. Some people feel more comfortable talking to a professional therapist than to a friend about these things. That helps with the sharing part, but if you tend to be very critical of yourself as a parent, it will help for you to hear how other people struggle as well.

—HELPING OUT OTHER PARENTS—

I mentioned parents being highly critical of themselves, but we can also be critical of other people's parenting. Let's look at some common scenes.

We are standing in line at the bank or the coffee shop and a young child is behind us. Things fall apart. The child has a huge temper tantrum about "nothing." The child is fidgeting a little, and the parent yells and threatens. The child pinches the baby brother in the stroller, and the parent whacks the kid, who starts screaming. The child kicks you in the shin, and the parent then smiles sweetly. What do you do? If you are like me, your first impulse is to turn away and shake your head at what bad parents some people are. Perhaps you will glare at the parent, teaching them a lesson by your disapproval. Perhaps you've been glared at yourself—I know I have.

Here's a radical alternative: Offer help to the parent. Reach out. Think about what a hard day they must have had, or what a hard life. Think about the times you have been in the same boat, even if maybe you handled things better. What kind of friendly hand would you have wanted then, instead of a dirty look or a public scolding or a cold shoulder? Forget about your disapproval and lend a hand to a fellow parent in distress. If you're like me, you probably have fantasies of rescuing the child from these awful parents, or at least taking the child and giving them some proper discipline. Those fantasies don't help children much, I'm afraid. What really helps children is making a connection with the struggling parent.

My friend A.J. was at a beach, and he saw a father trying to force his four-year-old son to go into the water. The boy didn't want to, and the father was getting more and more angry. A.J. was sure that something bad was going to happen, either a beating for the kid or a burst blood vessel for the dad. He said, very calmly, "I don't think he wants to go in." The man turned to him angrily and said, "What did you say?" A.J. said, "I might be wrong, but I don't think he wants to go in. My name is A.J.," he added, and put out his hand. The father shook A.J.'s hand and said, "You know, I think you're right," and looked at his son, as if for the first time. He started to laugh. They became great friends.

After I heard A.J.'s story, I started acting differently at the store. Now, when I see parents and children having an awful time of it, I don't turn away in disgust. I go over and say, "Wow, looks like you've had a long day." Or, "You've got your hands full with those kids; let me help you carry your bags out." "Wow, he's really going at it." Sometimes I just go stand nearby, with a warm smile, to counteract everyone turning the other way or giving dirty looks. Usually, if we are just the tiniest bit kind and understanding, things go much better. The child may even stop her tantrum long enough to notice who this odd person is, and that helps the situation, too. While I am making a connection with the parent, I usually give the child a wink or a smile, to let him know that I know he's had a rough day, too.

Does this approach sound familiar? It should. It is exactly the same as Playful Parenting, except this time we offer our attention and respect and help to parents and families, not just to children. Look for what's needed and provide it. No one needs more criticism or disapproval, even if they may need to get a better grip on parenting or discipline. Stay engaged with people, instead of turning away, even if you don't approve of what they are doing. Things will immediately go smoother. That's not what most of us—me included—want to do when we see "bad parents" or "bad kids." We want to punish them, or leave them alone in their miserable isolation. But, of course, that doesn't help anyone.

I have a friend who is more forceful, but still respectful, in her approach to parents when she sees them hitting their children or yelling at them. She saw a father screaming at a little girl for dripping ice cream from her cone onto her dress. She stepped over and said, very calmly, "You can't talk to her that way." "Why the hell not?" "Because you're scaring her. Look at her." He looked, and maybe even saw the way his daughter was trembling in fear from his yelling. So he asked the woman who she was. "Just a person who likes kids. I like yours." This is tricky business, of course. We don't want the parent to go home and beat the child worse for embarrassing him in public. And we don't want another parent to turn an aggressive impulse toward us. But if we feel strongly about how children are treated, we need to take a stand.

I had a friend whose son was blind. When the boy was little, around two or three, shopping with him was a nightmare. He would reach out, knock things off the shelves, and laugh. He would whine for candy in the checkout line like any other child. The worst part was when my friend tried to discipline him. No matter how gentle he was, people gave him dirty looks for being mean to that poor blind child. Not one person ever came up to him and said, "That looks awfully challenging, would you like a hand?" Sure, we are all busy, but I don't think that's why we avoid helping other parents. I think we have an unspoken agreement: I won't mess with your isolation, and you don't mess with mine. Stepping out of our tower of isolation and helping other people out of theirs is just too messy.

It's no surprise that we end up short on support from other adults. To make up for it, we may make the mistake of expecting our children to provide it for us. I think that's why we end up more and more frustrated when we try to scold or lecture them. Since they aren't the best listeners, particularly when we are telling them what we can't stand about their behavior, they tune out. Then we get furious, which often escalates into our dishing out more severe punishments. Try taking a break to talk things over with another parent first, then go back to your child. You'll feel better, and the interaction will definitely go better. We may wish our children would hang on our every word, but, in fact, we get better listening from other adults.

For example, I will never forget an exchange I had with my daughter when she was just beginning to talk. As with most children in that situation, she was easily frustrated by not being able to say everything that she could think. I can't remember what we were fighting about, but I was getting as close as I ever came to losing it completely. I kept trying to leave the room, to give myself a time-out, and she kept screaming at me not to leave. If I stayed, she screamed at me anyway. Finally I told her I was going to call my friend Tina, and she could scream all she wanted. Tina and I would often call each other when parenting got tough. Emma stopped screaming, took me by the hand, walked me over to the phone, and said, "Go call Tina." She knew what we needed: for me to have someone listen to me vent for a few minutes. When I came back from the phone call, which by the way I spent laughing about Emma's comment instead of complaining about her obnoxious behavior, we reconnected and went back to fun playing.

The biggest resistance parents have to this crucial part of Playful Parenting is lack of time. "I already don't have enough time in the day, and now you're saying I should play more, and then when I'm done playing, I should meet with other parents and talk about it?" Yes! It turns out that getting support actually adds time to your life. It's like an Amish barn-raising: you can do things a lot more efficiently and effectively as a community instead of having each family build its own barn. If I had not left Emma's room to call Tina, I might *still* be in there fighting with her. Taking five minutes out to call a friend actually gave us more time.

Bringing more playfulness into your life adds time as well. If things are chaotic in your home in the mornings, the last thing you want to do is devote ten minutes to a fun game about getting dressed and ready. But, if you do, you will save much more than ten minutes in aggravation time, nagging time, and being constantly late. When I first became a teacher, an older professor gave me some invaluable advice: "When you want to get a student out of your office, don't try to rush them out," he said. "They'll just resist, and you'll be pushing them for an hour. Act as if you have all the time in the world, warmly welcome them, and they'll be gone in five minutes."

It often feels as though playing will not only eat up our precious time, but will deplete our cups, which are already running mighty low. Actually, fun play refills cups, ours as well as our children's. The play itself is rejuvenating, but the real refill comes from the connection that grows out of the play. We may have to push ourselves at first, especially to play whatever children want to play, but the payoff is worth it.

—WHEN ADULTS ARE LOCKED IN THE TOWERS OF ISOLATION AND POWERLESSNESS—

Have you ever noticed the kind of language parents use to describe children when things are not going smoothly? The child is "having a meltdown," "bouncing off the walls," "falling apart," or "out of control." Meanwhile, we describe ourselves as being "at the end of our rope." We are about to blow up, explode, or lose it. We give up, surrender, or wash our hands of the whole mess. I have tried in the earlier chapters of this book to offer a different approach that can help us keep our sense of humor and be more effective parents. One important element of this new approach is the metaphor of the towers of isolation and powerlessness. In the words of this language, when children are having a hard time, or giving us a hard time, they are locked in those towers, and our role is to help them out.

Too bad we spend so much time in towers of our *own*—that makes it hard to encourage children to come out of theirs. We are exhausted and irritable after our workdays, so we set up an electrified fence around our tower, making it hard for children to be close to us. I know that I feel terrible when I look back at how many times I have said, "I'm too tired to play; my back hurts; not now, leave me alone; stop bugging me; keep it quiet, I have a headache." We turn our backs on our children out of fatigue or because we don't know how to help them. We fuss at them for being kids, for being curious, for being full of energy when we're not, for needing love and attention.

Fortunately, while disconnections are inevitable, reconnections are possible. Unfortunately, I have seen parents and children miss chance after chance to reconnect. I think we each want the other one to take the initiative to apologize and ask for forgiveness. But if we wait for them, it might never happen. I think it's up to us, the adults, the parents, to take the initiative. Make eye contact. Cuddle. Always make up after a fight. Offer forgiveness without being asked. Apologize when you've been wrong. When things are rough between you, spend more time together instead of less. As a way to resolve a conflict, offer a hug instead of the usual punishment. Tell everyone in the family something you appreciate about him or her.

Often children will try to take the initiative to reconnect, and adults will completely misunderstand. Your daughter won't go to bed, for example, but perhaps she isn't just trying to make your life difficult. Maybe there is unfinished emotional business between you, and she wants some late-night time to work it out. Or your son keeps bugging you while you're making lunch. You're already annoyed, so you send him away. But these children are just doing their best to find a way back to connection, because disconnection is painful for them. In other words, they are trying to step out of their tower of isolation, but we are too locked away in ours to notice. Through the foggy windows of our tower, we don't see their attempt to reconnect, just their obnoxious behavior.

Forget about what you see on the surface; underneath is a basic human drive to *connect*.

Children turn away from connection when they are feeling bad about themselves, and we do the same thing. Or instead of turning away, we may be too clingy and grabby with our children, wanting them to love us enough to make up for other people—like spouses and bosses—who have been mean to us. We also turn away from our children when they express thoughts, feelings, and behaviors we don't like. We punish or ignore them when they enthusiastically explore their dolls' private parts, or make everything long and skinny into a toy gun, or spend all day in front of the computer screen, or spend hours primping and dressing their Barbies or themselves. They need us at these times as much as when they are doing things we think are fun and healthy. Maybe more.

Sometimes adult difficulty with closeness is less complicated. We're just plain bored and tired. Legos don't hold our interest very long. We'd like to play something new instead of the same game again and again and again and again. We want to talk with other adults for a change, or take a rest from our stressed-out lives. We don't want to retreat permanently to the tower of isolation, but we would like a break from all this child-oriented play. By all means, get your own cup refilled. You can't refuel children if your own cup is empty. But our job as parents requires us to push those feelings aside sometimes and play anyway. With enthusiasm, if we can muster it. At best, play is just as much fun for us as for our children. But when it isn't, when our batteries are dead, we just have to kick-start our engines and get back in the race. We do it at work all the time, so why not do it for our children?

Speaking of work, the transition from work to home, or from housework to play, requires a major shifting of gears. I call this the reentry problem. It is easy for adults and children to get off on the wrong foot, since everyone is full of leftover feelings from their time apart. Everyone also has different expectations about the reunion. The parent may be looking forward to some peace and quiet, while the children have been waiting patiently all day for some wild wrestling. Playing is hard enough for most adults at any time. If we have to shake off our work mode and instantly jump into play mode, it can seem impossible.

The way children handle reunions does not make reentry any easier. Though many children greet their parent joyfully after a separation, that isn't always the case. Alicia Lieberman describes this very well: "Some children may burst into tears on first seeing the parent as a way of relieving built-up tension. Others may 'pick a fight' by becoming provocative or defiant. Ambivalence may be expressed by simultaneously clambering up on the parent and pushing away from her or giving little kicks against her. . . . Some toddlers continue to play as if nothing had happened, totally ignoring the parent's greeting. . . . Feeling unneeded and unappreciated, the parent may withdraw emotionally in return."[2] It's no wonder parents, especially fathers, feel superfluous and expendable, and often end up spending more and more time away from the family. Other parents try to use alcohol, TV, or working even more at home as a way to blunt the pain of reentry. But that's not at all what children want or need. They expect us to put down our work worries at the door and make an effort to connect with them, even if they start out ignoring or even avoiding us. Hold them if they cry; set a firm but loving limit if you need to; go after them playfully if they hide or pretend you haven't come home. Transform reentry tension into warm family connection.

When we combine children's feelings about being apart from us with our own difficulties reentering the family scene after a stressful day, you can easily see why nerves are often frayed. Play may be the last thing on our mind, but, in fact, playtime—especially wrestling and pillow fights and clowning around—is the best way to manage reentry. Wrestling around on the floor with an eight-year-old, or cuddling up and sharing secret feelings with a twelve-year-old, however, can just seem too raw, too intimate, for us. We are particularly closed off after a long day in the office, where we're trained to keep our guard up. It's no wonder that many parents' idea of Playful Parenting is to buy more toys for their children.

One last reason we turn away from children's play is that the intense emotions they display make us so uncomfortable. But in order for children to develop emotionally, they need to be able to express themselves fully. So we have to actively *encourage* these emotional expressions, not just allow them. That's hard for most of us, because we avoid strong feelings like the plague, especially men.

A college student named Mel came to see me for difficulties he was having in relation to a horrible history of childhood sexual abuse. Like most men, he hardly ever cried, and, in fact, he described feeling numb and empty inside whenever I asked him about feelings. Then one day, he came into my office brimming with excitement. "I had the greatest week," he said. "The greatest thing happened!" "What?" "I stayed up all night shaking and crying and sweating and thinking I was going to die." "And that was great?" "Yes, don't you see? I finally feel something. I'm a real human being, with feelings! I kept those feelings away so long. Sure, they were scary and terrible, but not nearly as awful as I've always been afraid they'd be." That was the beginning of a remarkable recovery for Mel, and I have told his story to many men in therapy to reassure them about the "danger" that talking will stir up overwhelming feelings. I also like to tell this story to parents who are in such a frenzy to get babies and young children to *stop* crying.

—BECOMING A GREAT PLAYMATE—

As parents, we can't *just* be our child's playmate and friend. We also have to think about safety, about limits and guidance, and about getting dinner on the table. But still, we do need to play, and we can become better and better at it. That means learning how to have more fun and learning how to use play to assist in our children's healthy development. It's pretty easy to learn, but it does take some effort. First, and often the hardest part, is choosing to play instead of avoiding it. We also need to choose play that goes beyond our comfortable routines.

For many parents, the obvious place to start is to spend more time together with your children, especially time spent with the TV off. Expect rejection of your company initially. They may not be used to your wanting to play; and they may not trust that you are really interested in playing the way they want to. Don't plan major outings; just hang out together. Think about having a playful moment at least once a day. If you aren't sure where to start, keep it simple. Make funny faces and fall down a lot. Be silly. Do a play-by-play commentary. Thumb-wrestle. Shout, "And now we dance!" and get up and do a little dance. This helps recharge us, as well as helping their play get going. If you already spend all day every day with your children, then take a break to recharge yourself. Get more child care, go out regularly, and spend time with other adults so that you don't burn out. Even five minutes on the phone each morning with another stay-at-home parent can be a great recharger.

When we make an effort to be more playful, we may run into a spot where children want to do something we find horribly boring. When that happens, we usually quit playing, or space out, or take over the game. That just widens the gulf between us and our children. We think their favorite game is boring; they think we are fuddy-duddies who don't know how to play. We need to do two things. First, find a way to insert a little more connection into the play. Boredom is a sure sign that you and your child are not really connected. Have a hug, or shake hands, or wrestle, or tell each child what you love about him or her. Then go back to playing. I bet you'll be less bored. Second, even if you are bored, play anyway. We make children go to school even though they are often bored there. The least we can do is go along with some games that we find less than thrilling. One day, tired of hearing from children that they were "so bored," I made up a game called the *yawn-a-thon*. Everybody pretends to yawn, and because yawns are so suggestible, soon everyone is really yawning. This brings giggles, plus the yawns themselves relieve tension and boredom. Soon everybody is ready to play again.

Some parents don't feel boredom or fatigue when they play, but anger and irritability. Take a break from the play to cool off, and then take the time to reconnect before getting back to play. In fantasy play, be a character who gets to be angry or nasty. That's a good way to release some of that irritability without aiming it at your child. Still, make sure to sit down later and talk with another adult about those feelings. Usually the playing was just the last straw for an old pile of buried emotions.

I have seen many parents end playtimes abruptly because the child introduces a theme that makes the adult uncomfortable. But they introduce those themes because they need to play them out if they are going to be able to understand their emotions and the world. That's especially true for fantasy play, which often features those emotions that are so unsettling to us: love, sex, death, loss, rescue, danger, hate. If we break off play in order to protect our own comfort level, we give children the message that their feelings are unacceptable, their play ideas are terrible, and they might as well stay locked in their towers of isolation and powerlessness. They need us to keep playing, even if we don't really like chopping the heads off of action figures, or kicking the doll down the cellar stairs, or arranging yet another wedding between the Little Mermaid and the Prince.

As adults we are expected to keep our fantasy life private. We rarely share these daydreams with even our most intimate friends or lovers. Children, on the other hand, can be very open about their fantasies. They aren't embarrassed to introduce characters into their fantasy play who kill or lie or steal or die agonizing deaths. So a five-year-old's suggestion to a parent that "I'll be Cinderella and you be the wicked stepmother—and pretend to be *really mean* to me" can send an adult into a panic of confused emotions. Go ahead, though; be mean, or scared, or play whatever role your child assigns you, and have fun with it.

One of the basic rules for becoming a great player is to be physically close. I know this makes many people nervous. Before I started working with children and parents, I spent most of my time as a therapist for adults who had been sexually abused as children. That work has made me very cautious about recommending close physical contact between parents and children. On the one hand, children need this contact. In fact, infants die without it, and older children develop severe emotional problems without it. But it has to be safe, respectful contact that does not exploit or abuse the child. We have not done nearly enough to protect children from physical and sexual abuse. In fact, some adults don't know how to have physical contact that isn't either aggressive or sexual. But in our fear, we have deprived children of the human warmth that they need.

Over and over I hear from caring teachers that they are afraid to pat a child on the back or give a friendly squeeze to a shoulder. Indeed, this fear of perceived abuse can certainly be taken to extremes. I was in a long line in the men's room at the movies once, a line that overflowed out the door. A mother outside shouted in to her young son, who was standing in line ahead of me, "If anyone touches you, scream!" Not exactly a way to foster his confidence or independence, but I could understand her fear.

We must not touch children in ways that harm them, but we can't be Playful Parents without emotional *and* physical closeness.

Another source of parental discomfort is our embarrassment. Our children might want to take all their clothes off at the park, or dye their hair blue (depending on their age!). They may tease us or make us sing goofy songs or play follow the leader in public. But if you're just embarrassed, don't let it stop you from playing and having fun. Later on, when they are teenagers, *they* will be the ones embarrassed to be seen with you, so you end up getting even after all!

The next step to Playful Parenthood is to break out of our old play habits. Some of us are too competitive, whether our child wants to compete or not. Others are too timid, not giving enough resistance when children want to wrestle or play hard. Playing with blocks or Legos, I will sometimes catch myself ignoring the children I am supposed to be playing with, and building something bigger and better than what they are building. Some parents need practice being more involved in play; others need practice encouraging children's independence.

In short, we need to be responsive to children's needs. Fathers are especially known for something called swooping in. Mothers of infants complain about this all the time. Dad comes home, excited to see the baby, and swoops her up. She has been playing happily and quietly, and now she either starts screaming or gets too jazzed up to sit still for dinner. Dad is frustrated; Mom is frustrated; Baby is dizzy. That kind of rough-and-tumble play can be wonderful for children, but only when it is done *with* them, rather than *to* them. Try swooping in a little slower, maintaining eye contact, and following the baby's cues about how fast and high to throw her in the air. Otherwise, we aren't playing at her pace, but insisting on our own pace.

Variations on this scene happen with older children, too, like when Uncle Louie takes the kids out for ice cream right before bedtime. And the opposite happens as well. The children are enjoying some wild play, until Mom steps in anxiously or angrily to stop it. That time, she is the one who is not tuned in to their pace, and tries to impose her own preferred style of play onto the children (and the father).

Children differ in their sensitivity to touch, sound, smell, taste, movement, distraction, and so on. Some like speed, some hate it; some scream, others whisper; some can play seventeen different games in five minutes, others can focus on one game for days; some need our undivided attention, others just want to be in the same room as us while we're working. These differences have a big impact on how children like to play. We need to recognize these preferences, and match our approach to them. Instead, we often just play according to our own preferences without thinking about it. As the famous saying goes: "Put on your jacket; I'm cold!"

Another example is when we want our children to talk to us, because talking is our way of communicating. But talking is not how *they* express themselves; play is. So if we refuse to play their way, and then insist on their talking to us our way, we are not going to get much communication from them. If we do play, especially if we play on their terms, then they will surprise us by showing us their thoughts and feelings. If we wait patiently and don't push, they may even tell us in words.

> Don't ask your poor children those automatic questions—"Did you wash your hands, dear?" . . . (almost the only conversation that most parents have to offer). Note the look of dreadful . . . boredom that comes into their otherwise quite happy faces. . . . Years ago when my child was four years old, I suddenly learned not to do this. . . . No, I would *myself* tell *her* something interesting and arresting: "I saw Pat Greaves next door running and bawling because he was being chased by a strange yellow cat." My child's eyes would sparkle with interest, and there we were, in the liveliest conversation, and behold! she was soon telling me the most interesting extraordinary things, her own ideas.[3]

In some families, one parent is in charge of fun and games while the other one is responsible and serious. Try switching once in a while, for everyone's sake. Make sure Mom gets to wrestle with the children, not just do caretaking chores. If Dad plays only catch, let him take a turn on the floor dressing up the dolls. If you haven't spent an hour in play with your child, you are missing out on something very fun and creative.

Above all, have fun, and keep reaching for a connection with your children. They do not need us to be perfect—but they do notice when we *try*.

—BUILDING A PLAYFUL PARENTING COMMUNITY—

Building a community of support may be as simple as having a few parents with whom you can talk on the phone or who will drop over for a cup of tea. The conversations may be informal, or they may be structured sessions where each person takes a turn to answer the questions I listed at the beginning of the chapter (page 278), or just to talk about their life as a parent. For those parents who are overwhelmed and need more support than that, offer to take their children for a while so they can get a break. If a parent you know is really struggling, get together two or three friends to go over to her house, like an emotional-support SWAT team. One person plays with the children, one listens to the parent, one cleans the house. Obviously, we have to overcome our resistance to butting into one another's business, which often is just a disguise for wanting to stay isolated.

Even if you feel overwhelmed by your own parenting duties, it is helpful to spend time with other people's children. It's a great way to practice Playful Parenting, because we aren't as emotionally invested. A student in my parenting class, Ralph, told me the story of a recent rock-climbing outing with several families. The leader's daughter, a three-year-old just getting over a cold, was very clingy with her mom. She would not share the harness, which other children needed, and she would not let her mother handle the ropes. The mother was at a loss. Ralph's first reaction was, "What horrible whining." But then he remembered some of the Playful Parenting ideas from our class. He retranslated the girl's whining and clinging in terms of an empty cup that needed to be filled. He went over to her, and in a cheerful voice said, "Oh, Madeleine, I have missed you so much, I was hoping we could have some special time together today. I could tell you a story, or we could play tictactoe—whatever you want." Madeleine was delighted. She let go of her mother, took off the harness, sat in Ralph's lap, and they had a great time together. Two boys watched them awhile; then, when Madeleine climbed off to play on her own, they both climbed onto Ralph's lap. He said later, "Knowing what to do was so much easier with somebody else's child."

I am a big believer in support groups, especially for parents, because we tend to be so isolated from one another. And *especially* for fathers, who usually don't get much of that informal playground support from other fathers. I started a fathers' group when my daughter was a baby, and we met for three years as our babies grew up. Even though I never felt as if I could afford the time as a new parent to go to the group, the recharging and refilling I got there more than made up for my time away. Maybe it's just me, but I actually think men today *are* talking more. The other day I heard two men in the video store talking earnestly about parenting. Naturally, I hovered nearby to eavesdrop a little. It turns out they were talking about how frustrating it is to be a parent of highly energetic boys, and they were swapping tips for how to avoid spanking and other harsh punishments. They were talking about not wanting to raise their sons the way they were raised, but they weren't sure how to do it differently. As I peeked around the shelves and saw those two men standing under the Action/Adventure section, I thought, Things have come a long way in just a few years.

Patty Wipfler and her colleagues have developed some great activities for family support, such as playdays and family workshops.[4] A playday is a few hours when some children, their parents, and other adults get together to play. Generally there are at least two adults per child. That allows some of the adults to go off and take turns listening to each other, while the rest play with the children. The adults make a special effort to be playful and enthusiastic, and to follow the children's lead, so the play can get pretty raucous. In a family workshop, that same basic format goes on for a whole weekend. Part of that time, children have special one-on-one time with a parent or another adult to do whatever they want, as I described in chapter nine. Another innovation is the idea of adult play groups, where adults can get together to reclaim playfulness as a valuable part of life. At these events, it usually takes the adults a while to loosen up and actually play. There is also time for talking about the joys and difficulties of parenting, and for expressing the frustrations, fears, and anger that parents don't want to express directly to children.

When my daughter was three and was obsessed with playing with her doll Ariel, the Little Mermaid, I went to one of these adult playdays. It was good timing, because I was sick of that helpless heroine being saved by the strong hero. If I ever tried to insert any spontaneity, creativity, or feminist theory into the game, I was blasted with, "You're playing wrong! I'm never going to play with you again." I just barely restrained myself from saying "Fine, I hate that game anyway." I wanted to play with her, but I wasn't able to play with my usual enthusiasm and cheer when that was all she wanted to play. My compromise was to be bored and dull when we did play. Not surprisingly, that made her even more insistent on my playing it "just right," which made me more tired and cranky, and so on.

At the playday, as a way of getting help with this problem, I had two other adults ask me to play that game. I got to have a huge half-pretend temper tantrum myself: "*No! No!* I hate that game," I screamed. While they begged and pleaded, I got to storm and stomp around, saying the mean nasty things I had not wanted to say out loud in front of my daughter. I ended up laughing my head off. After nearly twenty minutes of letting off steam this way, with great gales of laughter in between, I realized, with a shock, that I had been telling her over and over that her most cherished possession was boring, stupid, and sexist. Not a great way to build confidence or nourish connection.

Getting all that out of my system, I was able to go home and be enthusiastic about the game. My enthusiasm—which surprised the heck out of Emma—allowed her to be more creative and spontaneous, which made the game more fun for both of us. Soon she was playing all kinds of games, not just that same one over and over. In the months following, whenever she did want to play that game, I tried to remember my enthusiasm. When I could, the game went well, and our connection went well.

—

While writing this book, I came across a quote by Maria Montessori, the great educator: "In the life of the child, play is perhaps something of little importance which he undertakes for the lack of something better to do."[5]

She was right about a lot of things, but I have to disagree with her about play. I can't think of anything more important than play, for us or for them. In fact, I am more inclined to agree with Kurt Vonnegut, who said, "We are here on Earth to fart around. Don't let anybody tell you any different!"[6]

I hope you and your children have fun through Playful Parenting.

NOTES

Chapter 1: The Value of Being a Playful Parent

1. Cosby Rogers and Janet Sawyers, *Play in the Lives of Children* (Washington, D.C.: NAEYC, 1988).
2. Virginia Axline, *Play Therapy* (New York: Ballantine, 1969).
3. Greta Fein and Nancy Wiltz, "Play as Children See It," in *Play from Birth to Twelve and Beyond*, ed. Doris P. Fromberg and Doris Bergen (New York: Garland Publishing, 1998), p. 43.
4. Frans de Waal, *Peacemaking Among Primates* (Cambridge: Harvard University Press, 1989).
5. Greta Fein and Nancy Wiltz, "Play as Children See It."
6. Many hospitals have developed play programs to help children cope with life-threatening or chronic illnesses or to prepare them for scary procedures. See, for example, Elizabeth Kampe, "Children in Health Care: When the Prescription Is Play," in *Children's Play and Learning*, ed. Edgar Klugman and Sara Smilansky (New York: Teachers College Press, 1990).

Chapter 2: Join Children in Their World

1. Brian Sutton-Smith and Shirley Sutton-Smith, *How to Play with Your Child* (New York: Hawthorne Press, 1974).
2. Leston Havens, *Approaches to the Mind* (Boston: Little, Brown, 1973).
3. The at-home-dad network is a great resource for fathers (www.athomedad.com).
4. Arlie Hochschild, *The Second Shift* (New York: Avon Books, 1997).
5. Joe Frost and Irma Woods, "Perspective on Play in Playgrounds," in *Play from Birth to Twelve and Beyond*, ed. Doris P. Fromberg and Doris Bergen (New York: Garland Publishing, 1998), p. 237.

6. J. G. Bernhard, *Primates in the Classroom* (Amherst: University of Massachu-setts Press, 1988).

7. *The Singing Creek Where the Willows Grow: The Mystical Nature Diary of Opal Whiteley,* ed. Benjamin Huff (New York: Penguin, 1986).

Chapter 3: Establish a Connection

1. Brian Sutton-Smith and Shirley Sutton-Smith, *How to Play with Your Child* (New York: Hawthorne Press, 1974).

2. For a more complete picture of attachment theory, see John Bowlby, *A Secure Base* (New York: Basic Books, 1990), or Alicia Lieberman, *The Emotional Life of the Toddler* (New York: Free Press, 1993).

3. Stanley Greenspan, *The Growth of the Mind* (Reading, Mass.: Addison-Wesley, 1997).

4. Stanley Greenspan with Robin Simons, *The Child with Special Needs* (Reading, Mass.: Perseus Books, 1998).

5. For an excellent description of the difference between a casual connection and a deep connection, see Martha Welch, *Holding Time* (New York: Simon and Schuster, 1998).

Chapter 4: Encourage Their Confidence

1. Bill Harley, *Lunchroom Tales,* Round River Records, 1996.

2. Cosby Rogers and Janet Sawyers, *Play in the Lives of Children* (Washington, D.C.: NAEYC, 1988), p. 81.

3. Ibid., pp. 4–5.

4. Brian Sutton-Smith and Shirley Sutton-Smith, *How to Play with Your Child* (New York: Hawthorne Press, 1974).

5. Barbara Brooks and Paula Siegel, *The Scared Child: Helping Kids Overcome Traumatic Events* (New York: Wiley, 1996), pp. 28, 75.

6. Alicia Lieberman, *The Emotional Life of the Toddler* (New York: Free Press, 1993), p. 136.

Chapter 5: Follow the Giggles

1. Cosby Rogers and Janet Sawyers, *Play in the Lives of Children* (Washington, D.C.: NAEYC, 1988), p. 81.

2. Ibid., p. 119.

Chapter 6: Learn to Roughhouse

1. Shirley C. Strum, *Almost Human: A Journey into the World of Baboons* (New York: Random House, 1987).

2. Ibid.

3. *A Voice for the Child: The Inspirational Words of Janusz Korczak,* ed. Sandra Joseph (London: HarperCollins, 1999), p. 69.

4. Elena Bodrova and Deborah Leong, "Adult Influences on Play," in *Play from Birth to Twelve and Beyond,* ed. Doris P. Fromberg and Doris Bergen (New

York: Garland Publishing, 1998), p. 278. Italics added. This article is based on the work of Lev Vygotsky, the great Russian psychologist.

Chapter 7: Suspend Reality: Reverse the Roles

1. Barbara Brooks and Paula Siegel, *The Scared Child: Helping Kids Overcome Traumatic Events* (New York: Wiley, 1996), p. 29.
2. Thomas Maeder, *Children of Psychiatrists and Other Psychotherapists* (New York: Harper & Row, 1989).
3. Stanley Greenspan with Robin Simons, *The Child with Special Needs* (Reading, Mass.: Perseus Books, 1998), p. 192.
4. David Elkind, "Academic Pressures—Too Much Too Soon: The Demise of Play," in *Children's Play and Learning*, ed. Edgar Klugman and Sara Smilansky (New York: Teachers College Press, 1990), p. 11.

Chapter 8: Empower Girls and Connect with Boys

1. S. Condry, J. Condry, and L. Pogatshnik, "Sex Differences: A Study of the Ear of the Beholder," *Sex Roles* 9 (1983), 697–704. N. Bell and W. Carver, "A Reevaluation of Gender Label Effects: Expectant Mothers' Responses to Infants," *Child Development* 51 (1980), 925–27. R. Culp, A. Cook, and P. Housley, "A Comparison of Observed and Reported Adult-Infant Interactions: Effects of Perceived Sex," *Sex Roles* 9 (1983), 475–79.
2. J. Condry and S. Condry, "Sex Differences: A Study of the Eye of the Beholder," *Child Development* 47 (1976), 812–19.
3. Myra and David Sadker, *Failing at Fairness: How Our Schools Cheat Girls* (New York: Simon and Schuster, 1994).
4. Deborah Blum, *Sex on the Brain: The Biological Differences Between Men and Women* (New York: Viking, 1994).
5. Beverly Fagot and Leslie Leve, "Gender Identity and Play," in *Play from Birth to Twelve and Beyond*, ed. Doris P. Fromberg and Doris Bergen (New York: Garland Publishing, 1998), p. 190.
6. Mary Pipher, *Reviving Ophelia* (New York: Ballantine, 1994). For a girl's magazine that is a refreshing antidote to this problem, see *New Moon*, and its companion parenting newsletter, *New Moon Network*.
7. Stanley Greenspan, *The Growth of the Mind* (Reading, Mass.: Addison-Wesley, 1997), p. 62.
8. Jean Phinney, et al., "Preschool Children's Response to Peer Crying," ERIC Abstract #ED267927.
9. Myra Sadker and David Sadker, *Failing at Fairness: How Our Schools Cheat Girls* (New York: Simon and Schuster, 1994), p. 206.
10. Nancy Carlsson-Paige and Diane Levin, *Who's Calling the Shots? How to Respond Effectively to Children's Fascination with War Play and War Toys* (Philadelphia: New Society Publishers, 1990).

11. Quoted by Tim Beneke in *Proving Manhood: Reflections on Men and Sexism* (Berkeley: University of California Press, 1997), p. 38.

Chapter 9: Follow Your Child's Lead

1. *A Voice for the Child: The Inspirational Words of Janusz Korczak,* ed. Sandra Joseph (Northampton, England: Thorsons, 1999), p. 54.
2. Patty Wipfler, *Listening Effectively to Children* (Seattle: Rational Island Press, 1999).
3. Emmy Rainwalker, "An Unusual Lesson in Listening," *Our Children Ourselves,* no. 23 (Summer/Fall 1998).

Chapter 10: Take Charge (When Necessary)

1. Patty Wipfler et al., *Family Work* (Seattle: Rational Island Press, 1999), p. 41.
2. Stanley Greenspan with Robin Simons, *The Child with Special Needs* (Reading, Mass.: Perseus Books, 1998), p. 106.
3. Pamela Haines, "Reaching from Heart to Heart," *Our Children Ourselves,* no. 19 (Summer/Fall 1996).
4. Martha Welch, *Holding Time* (New York: Simon and Schuster, 1998). See also her Web site at www.marthawelch.com.
5. Patty Wipfler, *Listening Effectively to Children* (Seattle: Rational Island Press, 1999). See also the Web site of her organization, Parents Leadership Institute, at parentleaders.com.
6. Stanley Greenspan with Robin Simons, *The Child with Special Needs* (Reading, Mass.: Perseus Books, 1998).
7. Vivian Paley has written two wonderful books on this topic: *You Can't Say You Can't Play* (Cambridge: Harvard University Press, 1992), and *The Kindness of Children* (Cambridge: Harvard University Press, 1999).
8. Patch Adams with Maureen Mylander, *Gesundheit* (Rochester, Vt.: Healing Arts Press, 1993), pp. 8–9.
9. See Alfie Kohn, *Punished by Rewards: The Trouble with Gold Stars, Incentive Plans, A's, Praise, and Other Bribes* (Boston: Houghton Mifflin, 1993).

Chapter 11: Learn to Love the Games You Hate

1. Frans de Waal, *Peacemaking Among Primates* (Cambridge: Harvard University Press, 1989), p. 195.
2. Anthony Pellegrini, "Rough-and-Tumble Play from Childhood through Adolescense," in *Play from Birth to Twelve and Beyond,* ed. Doris P. Fromberg and Doris Bergen (New York: Garland Publishing, 1998).
3. See *Best Friends, Worst Enemies,* by Michael Thompson, Catherine O'Neill Grace, and Lawrence J. Cohen, published by Ballantine Books in fall 2001, for a full discussion of this concept of social cruelty and its relationship to childhood friendships, group dynamics, and popularity.

4. This is a card game in which three or more people get all the cards and take turns putting the cards down. For example, one person puts down two aces, the next one puts down a two, the next says he has three threes, and so forth. If you don't have the right cards as you proceed up the deck numerically, you fake it, and others can try to call your bluff.

Chapter 12: Accept Strong Feelings (Theirs and Yours)

1. Paul Stasiewicz and Stephen Lisman, "Effects of Infant Cries on Alcohol Consumption in College Males," *Child Abuse and Neglect: The International Journal* 13 (1989), 463–70.
2. Alicia Lieberman, *The Emotional Life of the Toddler* (New York: Free Press, 1993), pp. 38–39.
3. Ibid.
4. Stanley Greenspan with Robin Simons, *The Child with Special Needs* (Reading, Mass.: Perseus Books, 1998), p. 151.
5. Patty Wipfler, *Listening Effectively to Children* (Seattle: Rational Island Press, 1999), p. 81.
6. Garry Landreth and Linda Homeyer, "Play as the Language of Children's Feelings," in *Play from Birth to Twelve and Beyond*, ed. Doris P. Fromberg and Doris Bergen (New York: Garland Publishing, 1998), pp. 193–97.

Chapter 13: Rethink the Way We Discipline

1. *A Voice for the Child: The Inspirational Words of Janusz Korczak,* ed. Sandra Joseph (Northampton, England: Thorsons, 1999).
2. Edward Hallowell, *When You Worry About the Child You Love* (New York: Simon and Schuster, 1996), pp. 149–52. See also Murray A. Strauss, *Beating the Devil Out of Them: Corporal Punishment in American Families* (Lexington, Mass.: Lexington Books, 1994).
3. See Dan Kindlon and Michael Thompson, *Raising Cain* (New York: Ballantine, 1999).
4. Idries Shah, *Knowing How to Know* (London: Octagon Press, 1998), p. 11.
5. See, for example, Carole Stock Kranowitz, *The Out-of-Sync Child: Recognizing and Coping with Sensory Integration Dysfunction* (New York: Skylight Press, 1998).
6. *A Voice for the Child: The Inspirational Words of Janusz Korczak,* ed. Sandra Joseph (Northampton, England: Thorsons, 1999).
7. Patty Wipfler, *Setting Limits with Children* (Palo Alto, Calif.: Parents Leadership Institute, 1995).

Chapter 14: Play Your Way Through Sibling Rivalry

1. From Joan Bel Geddes, *Childhood and Children* (Phoenix, Ariz.: Oryx Press, 1997),

2. Jeffrey Trawick-Smith, "School-Based Play and Social Interactions," in *Play from Birth to Twelve and Beyond*, ed. Doris P. Fromberg and Doris Bergen (New York: Garland Publishing, 1998).

3. Patricia Ramsey, "Diversity and Play," in *Play from Birth to Twelve and Beyond*, ed. Doris P. Fromberg and Doris Bergen (New York: Garland Publishing, 1998), p. 29.

4. Peg Flandreau West, *The Basic Essentials* (Madison, Wis.: Protective Behaviors, Inc., 1989).

Chapter 15: Recharge Your Own Batteries

1. The best source I know for more information about listening skills is from an organization called Re-evaluation Counseling. See especially their Web site at ircc.org, or *Fundamentals of Co-Counseling Manual* (Seattle: Rational Island Publishers, 1982).

2. Alicia Lieberman, *The Emotional Life of the Toddler* (New York: Free Press, 1993), pp. 17–18.

3. Brenda Ueland, "Parents Should Be More Fun," in *Strength to Your Sword Arm* (Duluth, Minn.: Holy Cross Press, 1993), pp. 92–93.

4. Patty Wipfler et al., *Family Work* (Seattle: Rational Island Publishers, 1999).

5. Quoted by Patricia Monighan-Nourot, "The Legacy of Play in America in Early Childhood Education," in *Children's Play and Learning*, ed. Edgar Klugman and Sara Smilansky (New York: Teachers College Press, 1990), p. 71.

6. Kurt Vonnegut, *Timequake* (London: Jonathan Cape, 1997).

INDEX

© Eileen Ryan

ABOUT THE AUTHOR

Lawrence J. Cohen, Ph.D., is a psychologist specializing in children's play, play therapy, and parenting. He is the coauthor, with Michael Thompson and Catherine O'Neill Grace, of *Best Friends, Worst Enemies*, a book about children's friendships and peer relations, and of *Mom, They're Teasing Me*. He is also a columnist for *The Boston Globe*. Dr. Cohen leads Playful Parenting workshops for parents, teachers, and child-care professionals. He lives in Brookline, Massachusetts, with his wife, Anne, and their daughter, Emma. Visit the author on-line at www.playful parenting.com.